D1031920

Surveying and Restoring
—Classic Boats—

OTHER TITLES OF INTEREST

Hand, Reef and Steer
Tom Cunliffe
The essential handling and maintenance techniques for traditional boats are covered. This practical book is lavishly illustrated with beautiful color photos and fine drawings.

The Sailing Dictionary
Joachim Schult, translated by Barbara Webb
This Second edition, extensively revised and updated by Jeremy Howard-Williams to include modern navigation electronics, grand prix racing, new classes and many other new developments, will ensure that this classic work remains an essential reference for all with an interest in sailing.

The Boating Bible – An Essential Handbook for Every Sailor
Jim Murrant
This handbook contains all the essential information sailors need in one easy-to-use volume. Thorough descriptions are given for all the topics covered.

Effective Skippering – A Comprehensive Guide to Yacht Mastery
John Myatt
Packed with practical tips and sensible ideas, the book covers a variety of topics from the right boat to sails and the wind, safety, weather, maintenance, crew organization, laying up, sailing with children, and much more. The manual all yacht owners should possess.

Fitting Out – Preparing for Sea
J.D. Sleightholme
This book covers every aspect of preparing a wooden or fiberglass boat for sea. From the bare essentials needed to make a safe delivery passage to a total fit-out, it's all here.

Osmosis and the Care and Repair of Glassfibre Yachts
Tony Staton-Bevan
How to deal with the prevention and cure of osmosis, how to detect potential trouble spots and how to repair the damage.

By Way of the Wind
Jim Moore
A fascinating tale of a memorable circumnavigation by Jim and Molly Moore who, without any experience decided to build their boat and sail it around the world. "The best sailboat cruising book to come out in a long time." *Washington Post.*

The Sea Never Changes – My Singlehanded Trimaran Race Around the World
Oliver de Kersauson
A detailed account of one of the most gripping circumnavigations in the quest for speed under sail. With all of today's high-tech equipment, the challenge remains the same.

Surveying and Restoring Classic Boats

J C WINTERS

ILLUSTRATIONS AND PHOTOGRAPHS
BY THE AUTHOR

SHERIDAN HOUSE

Published by Sheridan House Inc.
145 Palisade Street
Dobbs Ferry, NY 10522

Library of Congress Cataloging-in-Publication Data

Winters, J. C.
Surveying and restoring classic boats/J. C. Winters: Illustrations and photographs by the author.
p. cm.
Includes index.
ISBN 0-924486-42-2: $35.00
1. Boats and boating—Inspection. I. Title.
VM321.W56 1993
623.8'202—dc20 92-28984
CIP

Printed in Great Britain

ISBN 0-924486-42-2

CONTENTS

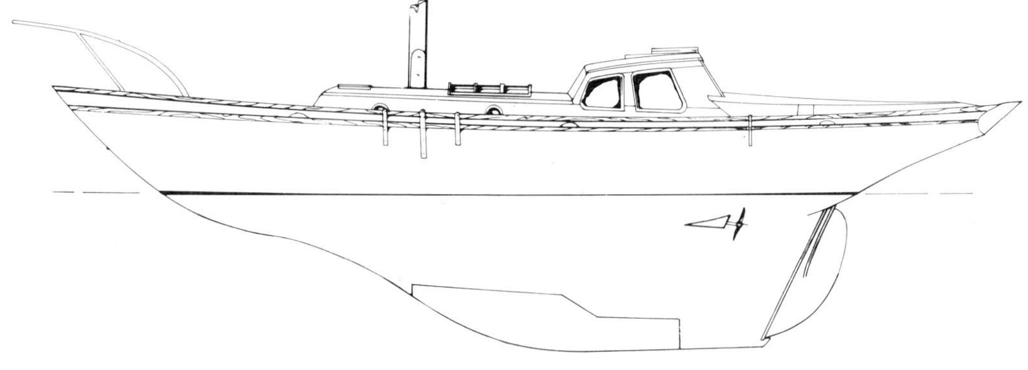

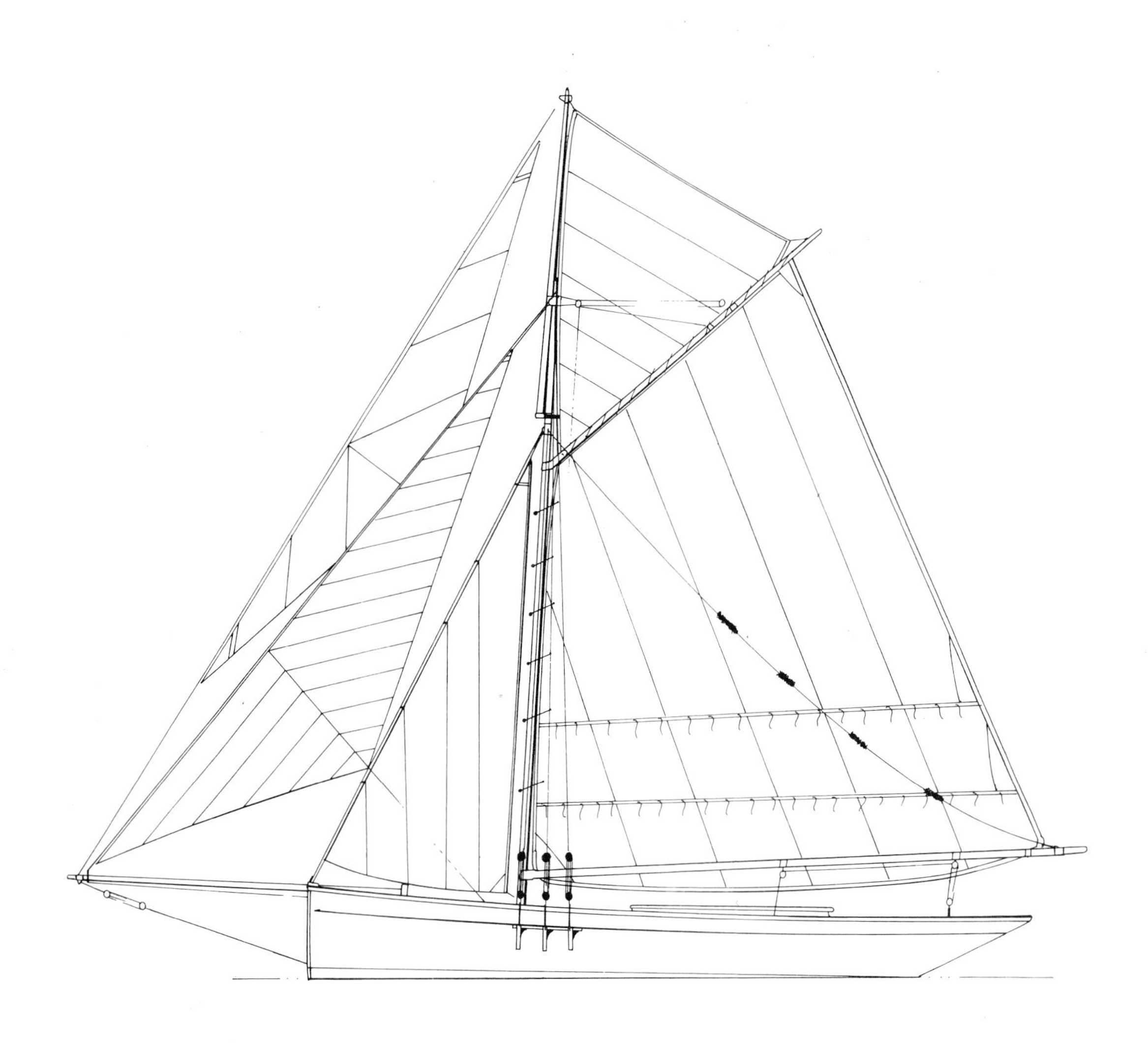

Above: An Essex smack with its powerful rig.
Opposite: Classic timber carved hull, typical of the off-shore cruiser-racer of the 1960s.

Introduction

The last few years have seen a considerable increase in what could disparagingly be referred to as the maritime 'nostalgia industry'. But is this really the sole reason for the gentle back eddy against the mainstream of today's mass-produced glassfibre craft? It may be unfair to be so scathing about these efficient and cost-effective boats, but the almost universal use of glassfibre construction has led to an unprecedented degree of clinical uniformity – and no amount of colour-coded trim stripes nor adhesive logos can effectively disguise this. Each vessel is distinguishable from its immediate neighbours only by its overall length and preferred method of propulsion.

Designed for the demands of today, both power and sailing craft exploit high technology and the latest manufacturing techniques. Moulded to approved standards, they are capable of performance which would, not so long ago, have been considered astonishing; they also afford such creature comforts as are usually associated with a country cottage (or, as the cynic might point out, a caravan). Nevertheless, they fail to arouse any deeper feelings in those who love yachts for their own sake. That subtle combination of elegance and sense of purpose seems sadly lacking. True, worthy exceptions do exist, where the boatbuilders concerned have refused to sacrifice harmony of line for the considerations of the mass market. Such yachts may well be the classics of the future, but they are the exceptions rather than the rule.

The undercurrent of disaffection towards the bulky, high-volume yacht, with flat sheerline and snubbed ends, the product of the assembly line rather than the boatyard, is steadily increasing. Enthusiasts eagerly seek out 'classic' yachts, many of which, until quite recently, would have been thought of as utterly without value – heads would have been shaken sadly should anyone have been sufficiently misguided to enquire about the possibility of purchase. Now, though, many near-derelicts, abandoned for half a generation or more to decay in mud berths, yards and forgotten fields, change hands for quite astonishing amounts of money. Obviously, a number of these will be beyond repair, and the great majority will be in urgent need of comprehensive restoration – or even total reconstruction. Initially, though, an accurate assessment of the degree of depradation by time and tide is not always easy.

Perceived as a fascinating part of maritime history, many vintage yachts and small craft could indeed be considered priceless. Beyond a shadow of a doubt, it would not be possible today to duplicate their original construction on anything approaching a commercial basis. In relatively isolated rural areas a boatyard employing only two men and a couple of lads would have constructed four 35 foot yachts a year and would have been regarded as doing very nicely, thank you! Four new vessels per annum in years gone by would have been approximately the equivalent of mass production today. Sailing in the first half of this century was not quite the élitist pastime it is sometimes imagined to be, and the majority of small and medium-sized yachts were competitively priced rather than merely being the expensive playthings of the affluent.

Even without specific historical interest, a perfectly restored classic yacht (especially one of timber construction) can, theoretically, command a very high market price – although clearly it is the more desirable for still being suitable for its original purpose. Financial considerations are, for the most part, of secondary concern, though; you only have to wander around any marina and take in the bleak and wintry acreage of white glassfibre, tinted acrylic anodised aluminium and stainless steel to understand perfectly the powerful attraction of traditional yachts. The muted tones of umber and ochre, the curving bows, the finely drawn counters and swooping sheerlines of a previous generation of yachts are far easier on the eye. Scrubbed teak and glowing brightwork have an allure all the more pronounced in an age when the minimal maintenance associated with fibreglass is presented as synonymous with complete boating enjoyment. But when does a yacht, even a vintage yacht, qualify as a 'classic'?

The very term 'classic' has become one of the most abused terms in current vernacular, since it has now acquired the connotation of a marketing catchphrase. In all probability, no two people would agree on an exact definition – and both of them might well disagree with mine! It is certainly arguable that all timber yachts of a certain age are classics, but not all classics are constructed of timber. Iron, steel and glassfibre – even aluminium and ferro-cement – have all been employed, singly or in composite form, to produce very fine vessels.

Perhaps the fairest description of classic would be that of a boat where designer and shipwright have merged their skills (and possibly a certain amount of inspired guesswork) in order to bring into being a vessel that is totally unique: a creation that can never be exactly duplicated. Few production craft possess this individuality, despite the other sterling qualities they possess (and there is no doubt that, for all their attraction, not all classic yachts are fast, manœuvrable or easily handled by a family crew).

While some boats are undoubtedly true classics solely by virtue of excellence, some achieve classic status after a notable voyage or outstanding racing success – or perhaps by having had a famous owner. But there are also vessels that have had classicism thrust upon them – by advertising agencies who either create or capitalise upon consumer demands.

Although vintage yachts, cruisers, working and day boats enhance today's nautical scene, the purchase of one is not to be undertaken lightly. There are risks, not least of which is the estrangement of your formerly affable bank manager!

It is a sad fact – and one commonly overlooked in the euphoria of negotiations – that all too many restoration projects are abandoned before completion. This is sometimes brought about by unforeseen events, but more frequently it is the result of two features: failure to assess correctly the vessel's condition, and failure to allow for such unexpected expenses as transport, craneage and rocketing charges for storage as small boatyards are bought out by large leisure conglomerates.

The potential for structural defects, let alone problems with spars, engine or domestic systems, is alarming even with a 20 foot or 30 foot cruising yacht. Many of these defects can be in inaccessible areas and are often discovered by luck more than judgement. Certainly experience helps greatly, but experience itself does not come cheaply.

As a surveyor, I do of course advocate that all those contemplating the purchase of any vessel, classic or otherwise, should insist upon a structural survey prior to completing negotiations. But calling on the services of a professional to inspect a succession of near-terminal cases can certainly prove damaging to your wallet. In my experience, no surveyor has been known to waive the fee simply because the only advice that can be given in all conscience is that vessel is beyond economic restoration. Needless to say, such discouraging advice is not always well received, and may even be ignored – usually, though not inevitably, with unfortunate consequences.

Given some knowledge of construction (and those totally lacking such knowledge would be ill-advised even to consider a large-scale restoration), it is usually quite within the ability of most people to undertake their own thorough examination of a boat before employing a surveyor. Eventually, for the purposes of insurance or finance, a formal written report will be needed – and it is certainly useful ammunition when negotiating the purchase price. It is also worth while to have inspections carried out during the course of any work; both the advice and supervision of a surveyor will outweigh the expense when it comes to a resale valuation. That said, the preliminary inspection by the purchaser, armed with the checklist contained within these pages, can eliminate both disappointment and unnecessary expenditure, especially where the vessel has to be craned and slipped for examination.

The purpose of this book is certainly not to create redundancies of marine surveyors (or, for that matter, boatbuilders and shipwrights), but is rather to point out the pitfalls that beset any restoration project. No single volume can deal with every probability or every permutation of difficulties and defects, but by drawing upon the experiences of others the odds on a successful outcome should be increased.

Admittedly there are borderline cases; in these only the enthusiast can truly judge the skill at his command and thereby also know exactly how much expertise will have to be bought and paid for! But beware of throwing caution and commonsense to the wind and allowing the dream to obscure the day-to-day reality of protracted and often tedious physical toil, the results of which are not immediately rewarding.

I would have found this book useful many years ago when I was beguiled by a 35 foot Victorian cutter. I spent three years rebuilding her, an experience for which I paid dearly, but in retrospect one that I would not have missed. It was the first of several restorations I was to make, some of which were more successful and enjoyable than others. Only two proved to be profitable – and two were most certainly not financially rewarding! It is perhaps ironic that I made the largest capital gain from a yacht upon which I never laid so much as a screwdriver, and which sank peacefully in a mud berth one November night. By chance, she was spotted, and taken pity on, by a gentleman with more optimism and enthusiasm (not to mention a seemingly limitless supply of funds) than I could muster. Today, she is still sailing, immaculate as the day she left the builder's yard nearly a century ago.

One last word of warning, though – restoring classic boats can become an end in itself, and this can negate the purpose of all the effort and expenditure. Attempt to organise matters so that you have the pleasure of actually sailing your classic, perhaps on her home waters, as she was intended to be sailed, *before* you start searching for the next one to restore!

CHAPTER 1

Design

Classic may not mean perfect

Even the most commercially minded yacht broker will admit, in an unguarded moment, that what he sells are not merely utility products made of timber and resin glass; he is also selling dreams. Dreams of ventures to distant shores, to reef-encircled islands and palm-fringed anchorages (presumably those where taxation and exorbitant harbour charges have not yet been introduced). Such romantic longings are perpetuated by the images of advertising, but even without this influence there is an element of the wistful daydreamer in most of us. Certainly the purchaser of any neglected vintage boat has to be a visionary of the very highest order – and such visionaries often pursue their dreams with total single-mindedness, completely undeterred by a damning report of a surveyor.

This is simply because the decision to acquire a vessel for restoration (often at a grossly inflated price) tends to be governed by the heart rather than the head. And the heart is caused to beat faster by the multitude of magazine articles recounting encouraging anecdotes in which amateurs, all blissfully unacquainted with any tools other than paintbrush and putty knife, nevertheless manage to recreate a boat of indescribable loveliness – this from a heap of bleached and rotting timbers unearthed in a farmyard! These accounts insidiously create a mood of unwarranted optimism – such articles also help to sell magazines!

But don't believe everything you read. Such accounts cheerfully make light of all the months of work, the discouragement of friends and financial advisers, and omit to mention the frustration of an unsatisfactory outcome.

It is true that even with minimal skills and a ruthless determination it is possible to restore vessels that appear to be past all hope of revival, but there may be a large element of luck involved. However, any necessity to rely too much on luck rather than judgement can be reduced by a working knowledge of hull structure – and, equally important (but all too often overlooked), hull design. The two are inextricably linked, but so far as yachts are concerned it is more generally hull design that influences hull structure. It also dictates the vessel's purpose and her sailing area to a large extent, and therefore should be of prime consideration to her owner. And as a potential owner and would-be restorer, the matter that should take precedence over all others is that of your expectations of the restored craft.

Your expectations may seem obvious: that the craft should ultimately appear in most respects as she was when she first left the builders' yard. But is this enough? Is she actually to be used on the waters for which she was originally commissioned? Or is the restoration to be an end in itself, satisfying a desire to save an interesting artefact from destruction? For many, the pleasure of working with tools and traditional materials is fulfilment enough.

But if a static museum exhibit is *not* what you envisage, it is essential to acquire a vessel suitable for your needs and intended sailing waters; there is little point in buying

a 26 foot boat with half a lead mine in the keel if you only have access to a half-tide mooring, nor is there much sense in battling with a heavily rigged pilot cutter if you sail with a young family as crew.

On the basis of size and draft many vessels for purchase will be eliminated from the outset, and an understanding of design will further pare down the choice. But it will also add greatly to the interest when traipsing endlessly around yards and creeks, trying to locate a likely craft. There may be a financial incentive too; it is worth bearing in mind that the offspring of some designers and boatyards, while appearing to the untrained eye to be much like other craft of a similar type can command a premium price.

Identification of an elderly vessel is not necessarily straightforward. Time and various owners inflict many indignities upon boats: counters are nailed on and sawn off, and unwieldy superstructures, wheelhouses and doghouses (sometimes raised topsides) are added, so that the original shape of the hull can be hard to discern. By the same token, keels may have been tinkered with, lengthened or shortened or removed altogether, and even the original propulsion system may have undergone a sea change – sail to power being the commonest, but the reverse occurring also.

Hull design: the legacy of working craft

But apart from instilling a useful knack of seeing what lies beneath the additions and subtractions that may have taken place with the passage of time, the comprehension of design, of the influences upon a hull and upon its performance, makes fascinating study in itself.

Any buoyant object will move through the water, but it does so in an uncontrolled manner, subject to random influences of wind or current. A boat, on the other hand, is called upon to move in a predetermined direction, usually at the maximum economic speed of which it is capable, and to remain manageable in a wide range of wind and wave conditions.

No matter how large or small the vessel (and not even planing sportboats are exempt), the design inevitably entails compromise, a trade-off between the effect of water resistance on the underbody, the ability to carry cargo, (whether that cargo be china clay or a complement of crew along with their provisions and gear) and seaworthiness. This last is an elusive quality which can best be described as realising the maximum possible speed from the given length of the waterline with minimum expenditure of power, ease of handling and a motion which, even in severe weather, will not leave the crew prostrate with seasickness.

The experience accumulated over centuries with fishing and coasting craft has been the single greatest influence on boat design. But however widely diversified the working boats of Britain's coastline – and of those elsewhere – are, all owe their characteristics not only to the specialised natures of their individual trades, but also to the rigour of local conditions, both onshore and offshore.

On the south and east coasts of Britain, as well as in Shetland and Orkney, there arose a great tradition of inshore boats of around 18 to 25 foot in length. They were markedly similar in appearance to the Viking longships, the majority being double ended and with lap strake planking. Lightly built, for they had to be hauled up the beach by manpower alone, these small craft nevertheless had to be extremely tough in order to survive heavy breaking seas during the launch and recovery.

By contrast, the deep-sea trawlers operated by a comparatively large crew brought in huge and profitable catches and could afford to make use of deep-water

A Dutch working boier circa 1898. The pronounced curvature at bows and stern imposes considerable strain on the planks – which may be grown, sawn or steamed – and the fastenings. It is not easy to obtain suitable oak today, and a compromise is to replace timbers by laminating suitable substitutes, such as iroko.

harbours whose shoreside facilities were vital for the landing and processing of the fish. These vessels stayed at sea for long periods. Indeed they had to, for even in the last century pollution of the shoreline was affecting fish stocks. So it was necessity that brought about increased hull length (80 feet on deck was by no means uncommon) and the deeper draught that provided weatherly qualities and improved carrying capacity.

The Thames barge with shallow hull, plumb ends, little if any sheer, and flat underwater sections (windward ability being dependent upon leeboards), although endangered by the fierce seas and pronounced swells sweeping the Atlantic or northern North Sea, would slide easily along in the more sheltered waters off the Essex and Suffolk coast. Here, a gale will give rise to a short but vicious chop; this is unpleasant, but is not usually life threatening. The shoal draught permitted the barges to sidle into the shallowest of rivers in order to load or discharge cargo and, if need be, take shelter. Indeed, it was claimed they could sail on a damp dishcloth! Less complimentary was the oft-heard remark that 'Spritties' were built by the mile and cut off by the yard.

The Dutch coastal and inshore trading vessels shared some of the peculiarities of these barges, in that they too were shallow hulled and relied on leeboards for lateral resistance; somewhere along the line, though, this type divided into a number of subspecies, usually classified as to whether they were round or flat in section below the waterline. Although some favoured the spritsail rig of their British cousins, most were rigged with a loose-footed main to a long boom and set to a short and light 'curly' gaff.

The end of the nineteenth century saw the last surge of the great days of commercial sail. Awe-inspiring as square-rigged ships of those days were, they were also very efficient and reliable freight carriers. Many of the steel and composite 'four-posters' approached 300 feet in length and achieved average speeds of around 14 knots. At the start and finish of their voyages they were dependent on the costly mechanical assistance of tugs. Huge fleets of small boats made it their business to act as tenders, inshore pilots (the deep-water pilot boats were specialised, powerful and accustomed to remaining on station even during the appalling winters in the western approaches), buoy jumpers and general go-betweens.

A deep-laden ship, forced to lay off by adverse winds or neap tides, would be besieged by Hovellers, Hoys, Quay Punts and Gold Dusters depending on the ship's geographical location. These small open or half-decked vessels were sailed with a determination that would put many of today's competitive yachtsmen to shame! After all, their livelihoods, and sometimes their lives as well, depended upon their skills and the abilities of their craft. Speed was a most desirable asset, since the first to reach their quarry was generally the first in line for the highly profitable services to be rendered.

All the years of traditional wisdom and practical experience could not, though, eradicate all the little idiosyncrasies of some types of working boats. The cobles of Northumberland and Yorkshire, beautiful little ships with distinctive serpentine sheer, raking bow and transom, were designed to be beached (and towed) stern first and were built with an unusually deep forefoot to grip the water; this grip occasionally proved altogether too firm, and when running dead before a fresh breeze, would trip the boat, slewing the stern into a precipitate and often disastrous broach. The rockered keel with barely immersed quarters also made the coble, designed for both oar and sail, awkward to row, and three men were usually required: two to starboard amidships and one at the port quarters.

The bluff-bowed luggers working from the steep shingle beaches at Hastings and Rye accepted the occasional sea over the stern when landing with a degree of stoicism that must be unparalleled. Although the partial swampings were caused by lack of buoyancy in the after sections, instead of the matter being rectified at the design stage, the crew carried one member reputedly designated as the 'hatchet man'. His express function under such conditions was to hack through a couple of strakes and allow any water shipped to escape in order that the lightened craft could be expeditiously hauled ashore before the next wave caused it to founder completely! Eventually this rather undesirable in-bred trait was eradicated from the craft by simply extending the after decking over the transom to form the distinctive lute stern.

However, larger vessels were not necessarily free of defects; the uneasy balance between large mainsail and small working headsail could render smacks almost uncontrollable because of weather helm, and in reefing weather topmasts and bowsprits had to be housed as the main was progressively reefed. Unfortunately it required very strong winds to move such craft at their maximum speed, by which time the low freeboard necessary for the hauling of nets and gear could reduce life on board to a squalid and soaking hell.

Workboat into yacht: the evolution

The evolution of workboat into yacht was gradual, with the first pleasure craft generally being scaled-down naval vessels,

Replacing strakes on an East Coast smack. The heavy sawn frames of the hull are clearly visible in the photo – also clearly visible is the fact that necessary remedial work has not been carried out on these prior to the planking repairs.

lavishly decorated with carved gingerbread work (and a defiant little cannon for sending imperious signals). Charles II, whose love of the sea and seamanship is well documented, enjoyed a succession of such gaudy craft – and a good deal of success when racing for wagers on the Thames.

Even in the days of ancient Greece and Rome, there are mentions of vessels used for relaxation rather than purely commercial purposes – only to be expected, perhaps, given the warmth of their climate. It is rather more surprising that the inhabitants of Northern Europe took so avidly to the water, since it would be expected that the weather would dampen enthusiasm. It seems quite enough to wrest a living from the sea, let alone splashing about upon its surface for pleasure! Still, human nature being as it is, man attempts to extract enjoyment even from workaday occupations, although this not infrequently turns everything into a contest.

Also, the human species is gregarious and delights in social gatherings and clubs. The credit for establishing the first recorded yacht club goes to the Water Club of Cork Harbour in Ireland in 1720. Actual embarkation upon the water does not seem to have been one of the priorities: these appear to have centred more around what might be termed the epicurean side of things. However, there was a grand parade of sail, ordered according to rank, once a year.

A line of royal patrons, together with royal yachts of considerable splendour, gave the sailing scene a certain cachet; and competition flourished as more clubs came into existence – not only in Britain, but all over the world. One of the most famous is the Royal Yacht Squadron at Cowes founded in

1812, but less exalted institutions provided nautical sport for nearly all strata of society. Most waterside villages too held yearly regattas where local craft settled old scores, with a contest between the giants of the J class – which toured the coastal resorts during the season – providing an added attraction for the gathered crowds.

As racing became more keenly contested (with money as well as elaborate trophies changing hands) it created its own bureaucracy. The many and complicated rating rules, which laid down the sizes of classes, eventually mutated and produced fine individual vessels such as *Queen Mab* and *Satanita*, as well as King George V's *Britannia* (which was scuttled at his death in surely one of the worst acts of maritime vandalism ever witnessed), and many a luckless freak as well.

As is the case today, rating rules in the past produced a breed of innovative designers who were adept at spotting loopholes in the rating system and exploiting them. In the latter half of the nineteenth century, British yachts tended to be long and lean, with length and leanness exaggerated in some cases into the notorious 'plank on edge' type. This type was rendered somewhat less fashionable by the dramatic manner in which one of their number – the *Oona* – sank, taking with her the crew and designer. She had a beam of 5 feet 6 inches on a waterline length of 34 feet (a beam for that length would normally be in the region of 8 feet). The American designs, which favoured lighter, beamier, shallow-draught yachts, often with a centreplate or drop keel, were sometimes considered to be a healthier type. However, they were also prone to exceed the bounds of both commonsense and sound knowledge, as witnessed by *Mohawk*. She was so heavily sparred and set so much sail (neither of which were adequately compensated for by ballast or even form stability) that she capsized and sank – admittedly somewhat to everyone's surprise – while lying at anchor!

The constant alteration to both measurement and handicap systems were halted after the sobering introduction of the Dixon Kemp rules, which relied on at least some acceptance of the basic precepts of naval architecture and which prevailed for thirty years or so. They were superseded at the turn of the century by the International Rules – thought these themselves were fairly complicated.

Sensibly, it was insisted upon that yachts be constructed to a strictly defined specification which curtailed the likelihood of self-destruction through overlight scantlings or a hull built of dissimilar metals which would, often unsuspected, be devoured by corrosion within the space of a few seasons. Quite a few yachts, built to these rules, are still in existence, with some restored ones sailing nearly a century after launching.

Although the technology available at the turn of the century may have restricted the conversion of concepts into actuality, the variety of boats and associated innovations – mostly concerned with the increase of speed – prove that, so far as actual design is concerned, there is nothing new under the sun (or, more correctly, below the waterline!).

Catamarans and sneakies, scows and schooners, lifting keels, sliding keels, multiple keels, winged keels: all were thought of long ago. Yachts came in all sizes and most shapes: from full-rigged ships 200 feet in length, to keel boats and half deckers one-tenth of that size, to wherry yachts and barge yachts, to simple cruising craft. Motor yachts were slowly becoming respectable, but were disguised as sailing vessels with clipper bows and counter sterns. Smaller sailing craft, converted ships' boats and fishing craft proliferated, many of them 'hotted up' for competition. The 'hottest' of these was the 20 foot Norfolk punt; it was narrow, canoe sterned and (in its natural state) heavily armed, wildfowlers' trans-

Motor fishing vessels (MFVs) offer plenty of scope for conversion but are usually only offered for sale at the end of a long working life. This Scottish Zulu (the distinctive heavily raked stern post cannot be seen in the photo) appears to be a reasonable case for treatment, although the state of the fastenings seems to be poor and movement is discernible in the planking at the stem and midships inspite of the heavy reinforcing wales.

portation. Mercifully, as anyone who has seen a punt gun (which blasted duck by the flock rather than individually) can testify, the guns were removed when racing!

Appreciation of the lines of any yacht or small craft is bound to be subjective, but there are numerous subtle permutations. All of these variations have a profound effect upon a vessel's behaviour, but this is not alway obvious.

A basic understanding of at least some of the attributes, desirable or otherwise, inherent in any given hull form can be gained from the lines plans; and once the terms of reference are fixed in mind, the performance of any given vessel, within normal parameters, can be quite accurately estimated.

Line and function

In what are euphemistically referred to as 'the good old days' it is rumoured that hull shape was determined by whittling away at a lump of limewood until a satisfying shape materialised; this was then somehow magically transformed into a full-sized ship. As with most legends, there is an element of truth here, although the reality was not quite so haphazard. It was not unusual for a hull half-model to be carved, and there was a prevailing sentiment that if ''er looked right, well, 'er'd sail right', a view that experience has proved to be not without

The lines drawings of a classic ocean racer of the early 1960s (*below*) and of a small displacement motor cruiser of the type generally constructed in the mid-to late 1930s but still being produced or reproduced in glassfibre (*opposite*).

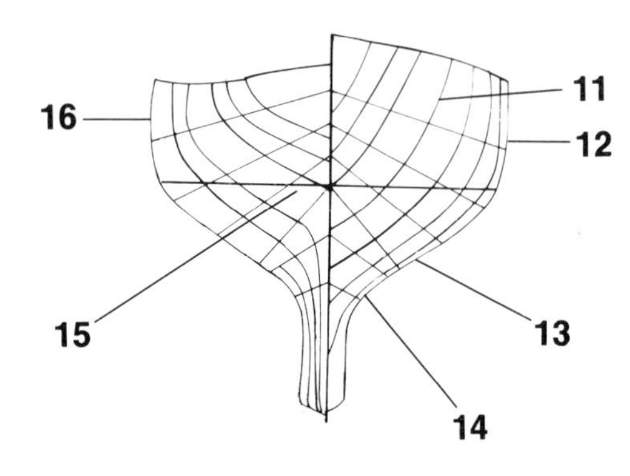

Elevation/Anatomy

1 Sheerline. In this case gently concave, the so-called conventional sheer. Variants include broken sheer (or built-up topsides) as in the case of the accompanying lines of the motor cruiser, and 'hogged' or reverse sheer common on smaller offshore racing yachts in the 1950s and 1960s because it maximises space below and reduces weight (however slightly) in the ends of the craft. General opinion is that it looks horrible, but unless carried to extremes, I don't find it unsightly.

2 The **stem**. Raked and curving in the case of this sailing vessel, straight and uncompromising in the motor yacht. The long overhangs at bow and stern tend to damp out pitching and, in the case of an ocean racer of this classic type, were also measurement effective.

3 Datum or **designed waterline**. This should be identical to the load waterline but in practice rarely is. With a displacement vessel the length on the waterline is the decisive factor in calculating maximum speed.

4 The **forefoot**. Lack of depth here can make it difficult to prevent a yacht from paying off after tacking; too much can cause the hull to gripe and is considered to be a contributory cause of pitchpoling (capsizing bows over stern).

5 Buttock line. A section drawn through the hull longitudinally and vertically, indicating the section and rocker (the upward curvature of entry and run).

6 Keel. The external backbone of the hull (the keelson and hog are internal); keel length is a factor influencing directional stability; keel depth

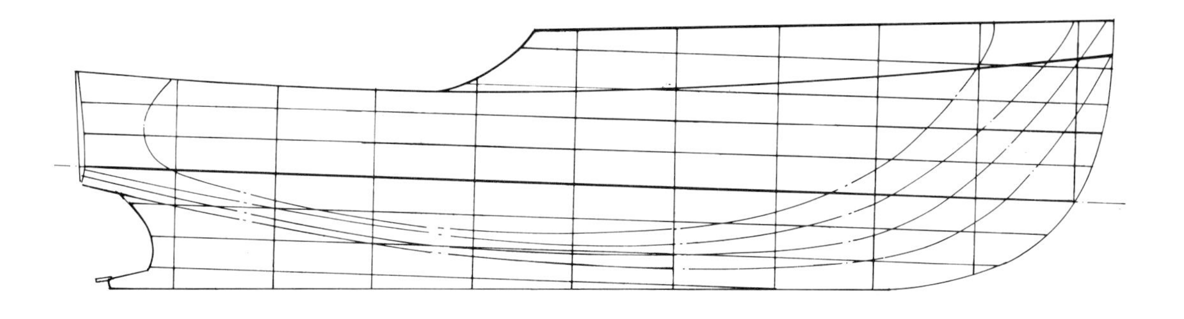

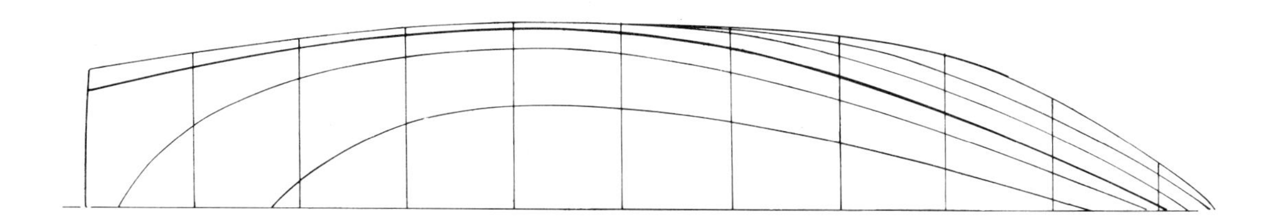

(or indeed the depth of the underbody) plays a part in eliminating leeway.
7 The **run aft**. Generally the flatter the faster.
8 Counter.

Plan
9 The **waterlines**. Sections drawn through the hull longitudinally and parallel with the flotation line.
10 Entry. The point at which the fore part enters the water: the longer and finer, the better the performance to windward – and the less buoyancy there will be to help damp out any pitching moment.

Sections
Compare the wineglass sections of a sailing vessel with that of the motor cruiser.
11 Flare in the topsides. This increases buoyancy and tends to fling water clear of the hull in a seaway. It also increases space on deck and adds weight above the waterline.
12 Diagonal. Used in lofting and fairing. (Also shows heeled shape.)

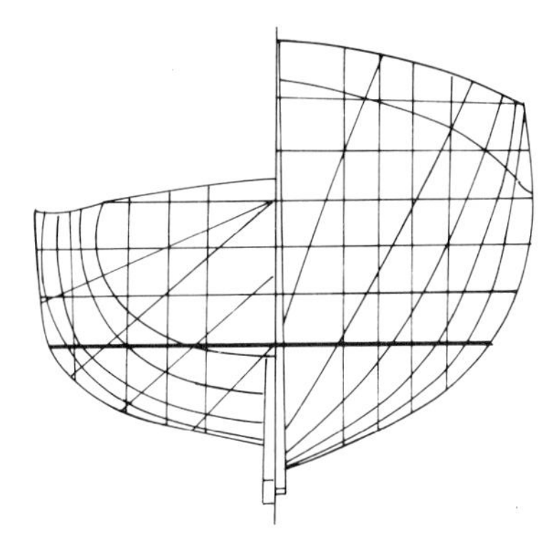

13 Deadrise. The angle formed between keel and waterline beam of the underbody. The greater the deadrise the less initial stability – and space below will be restricted too.
14 Garboard seam. This is next to the keel.
15 Tuck. A very pronounced curvature, usually in the garboard and at the stern.
16 Tumblehome. Here the beam above the waterline is greater than at deck level. This produces an improved shape when heeled, keeps the deck edge clear of the water so reducing drag, but also means less deck space.

foundation. What tends to be overlooked is that accurate plans were still required for construction, even though these might well be carefully lifted from the carving rather than drafted on paper.

An accurate system of measurement is essential when lofting a hull, since that hull consists entirely of compound curves with planking tapered at bow and stern, and chamfered to produce a fair surface at the turn of the bilge.

These complicated curvatures are nowadays generally demonstrated in a series of drawings, each of which deals with one particular plane. Although for the purpose of this chapter it is the hull form of sailing craft that is discussed, motor vessels are subject to identical laws – the major distinction being that, in the latter case, the heeled shape of the hull is arguably of less importance. Otherwise, similar laws apply to all vessels: leeway affects (or rather deflects) the course made good, as a result of top hamper and lateral resistance as well as mast and sails, and hull speed is directly dependent upon waterline length (since this also governs the wave-making property of any underwater shape and therefore, to a great extent, its resistance). Only planing hulls are free from this constraint because they literally override it!

The lines plans that indicate all functions consist of slices through the hull taken vertically, horizontally, crossways and diagonally, combining to produce a three-dimensional picture. This is read in a similar way to a contour map: the closer the lines, the sharper the curve taken by a particular area.

Depending upon the type of boat, certain aspects of the design may be given a greater or lesser emphasis. If, however, one characteristic is overstressed, performance in one respect may be enhanced, but this will almost certainly be at the expense of another. Again, it all comes down to the balancing of speed, weatherliness and ability to provide acceptable accommodation for a specified overall length. This is a devil's compromise that needs considerable expertise – especially if the overall appearance of the boat is also important. Add to the designer's brief the further stricture of competitive pricing, and an arithmetical headache is inevitable – a headache unlikely to be soothed by the knowledge that producing the most boat for the least money is unlikely to result in a masterpiece!

So far as a cruising boat is concerned, speed is not usually regarded as an essential virtue – nor even an especially desirable one. This, however, is a misguided attitude: as long as a degree of performance does not impair ease of handling or sea-keeping ability (and there is no need for it to do so), it should be highly rated on a list of priorities. A slow and unhandy boat is not by any means a safe one. There may well be circumstances when power to buck a foul tide or maintain an offing from a dangerous headland will mean the difference between reaching a safe haven or enduring a frightening time at sea in worsening weather.

One glance at a set of lines plans immediately gives a clear perception of the shape of the hull. However, the reason for favouring a particular form may not be self-evident – at least, not without some knowledge. But this knowledge is in part merely keen observation, so do not be put off by the esoteric terminology.

Sections and stability

Those slices taken through the hull transversely, at a number of equally spaced stations, are known as the sections: from these can be deduced the beam, the degree of form stability and wetted surface, along with the lateral resistance (largely dictated by the depth of the hull). Also, of course, they will show the space available for accommodation.

A section that is semi-circular offers the least wetted surface and, unfortunately, the

least stability (and volume). Its use therefore tends to be limited to those yachts aimed solely at high performance: these can cheerfully accept the penalty of a heavy rolling motion downwind and of the high ballast ratio necessary to carry the optimum sail in heavy airs. Until recently that ballast would have consisted of an external keel; today it might further be augmented by water tanks. Crew weight too is increasingly utilised as an effective – even vital – part of the ballast ratio, even though it could hardly be construed as a seamanlike practice over long distances. (Indeed, it might be considered an irony that today, in an age where safety at sea is of such concern and survival equipment in an offshore racer so precisely specified by the IOR, modern racing yachts – and even a few cruising ones – are designed with the centre of gravity above the waterline, a trait that is hardly conducive to ultimate stability and indeed knockdowns are reported with ever increasing frequency.)

For a given displacement, a vessel with squarer sections will have less hull depth immersed than one whose sections approach the semicircular. This means that a smaller craft, in order to achieve headroom below decks, may be forced to have topsides so high as to be unacceptable both from the point of excess windage and aesthetic appeal.

Lines cutting the hull in a fore and aft plane, parallel with the flotation line, are known as waterlines, and from them can be seen the effect of wave action upon the upright hull. The finer the load waterline forward (the entry), the less effort will be needed to slice through waves; on the other hand, while doing so it will liberally douse the watch on deck. By contrast, a hull with fuller fore sections may pound itself to a standstill if pinched to windward in any sort of seaway. It was common practice in smacks, and other displacement work boats, to favour a rather bluff entry and long, fairly narrow, run aft – the 'Cod's Head and Mackerel's Tail'. This was often superior when sailing upright in light airs, but could result in a poor balance once heeled, since the bows would lift to the sea and the quarters become more deeply immersed; this permitted a pronounced and self-perpetuating pitching moment. Carried to the extreme, however, especially on a beamy boat, an over-fine bow and full stern will, when heeled, bring the larger part of the rudder clear of the water and cause loss of control at exactly the wrong moment.

Clearly, the section of the topsides plays an important role and influences behaviour in any but the most moderate sea conditions. The inherent buoyancy of a gentle flare (that is, an outward curvature, with the beam at deck level greater than that at the waterline) can soften the effect of slamming on to waves and tends to fling spray clear of the decks. However, these welcome attributes are paid for by a slight decrease in the efficiency of the heeled shape. Tumblehome (with greatest beam at a point about two-thirds upwards from the waterline, and topsides narrowing from this point into the deck edge) is, hydrodynamically speaking, very clean when heeled, since such drag-inducing appurtenances amidships – such as rubbing bands, capping rails, chainplates and lower rigging – remain clear of the water. It is also a common feature in the aft sections of motor vessels where deck space is not at a premium, but a slight saving in weight may be regarded as advantageous. Carried to excess, as it noticeably is on some modern yachts with high freeboard, it is unattractive – but so are most forms if taken to extremes!

Profile and lateral resistance

The buttock lines, vertical sections fore and aft through the hull, not only indicate the amount of deadrise in the sections (the angle from keel to turn of bilge), but also the entire profile of the vessel. It is to a large extent the profile that determines the lateral

resistance which counteracts leeway, as vertical depth is more critical than horizontal length. This length, however, is of prime importance so far as directional stability is concerned – the longer the keel, the easier it is to maintain a given course.

Here, once again, the need for compromise can be readily discerned: a boat that steers happily in a straight line may not so easily be deviated from it! Bearing this in mind, it is easy to understand the development of the narrow, deep-ballast fin keel with separate rudder – and to appreciate the deeply held controversy between the advantages of the traditional long-keeled sailing yacht and its modern frisky counterpart.

Apart from the matter of actual strength of construction (it is of course less easy to attach the short root of a fin keel securely and permanently to a light hull, as the abrupt detachment of several keels from 'hi-tech' ocean racers has dramatically shown), a deep and narrow fin-keeled type is very difficult to slip, except with a crane or travel hoist. It is also a delicate operation to dry out alongside a quay with any degree of safety, and the crew, if staying aboard, will need to move very carefully. Beaching for a scrub may run the risk of wringing the bolts or studs – never mind the possibility of an unscheduled grounding in a chop – and the hull will need careful shoring, or preferably a custom-built cradle when laid up.

The depth of forefoot has a pronounced effect on the ability to keep sailing to windward as it provides a 'grip' on the water; if there is too shallow an area here, the hull will tend to be blown constantly to leeward and may become completely uncontrollable. There may also be an unnerving habit, to which many light displacement yachts are prone, of tacking quickly through the wind but then continuing to bear away in spite of any efforts to bring them back up. In close quarters this can be distinctly embarrassing: trying to claw off that proverbial lee shore may imperil the vessel and her crew.

But if the calculations are wrong, and you design too deep and fine a forefoot, what may happen at worst? The answer is that it will bury too deeply when running with a following sea, the stern will rise on the crest and effectively attempt to overtake the bows, and the vessel will pitchpole – capsize bows over stern.

In the profile, the proportion of bow and stern overhangs are also immediately visible. It is the elegance of a long swooping bow, finely balanced sheerline, and attenuated counter stern that is the very hallmark of a classic racing yacht. But beautiful to the beholder as these lines may be, the plain fact is that development was largely brought about by the measurement rules that only took into account the length on the waterline and never anticipated wasteful extensions at either end! These extensions, of course, came into their own the moment the yacht heeled, increasing the waterline length and, with a reserve of buoyancy, helping to damp out pitching. The economics of modern boatbuilding (and recent IOR rules) have abbreviated overhangs to the point where a quarter of the waterline length would be considered wasteful. In older yachts curtailment of overhangs has often been brought about by rot and stress in areas inaccessible to man!

Although the foregoing text greatly oversimplifies the subject of design, it should provide a starting point from which to make comparative studies between boats of apparently similar type and dimension. I say 'apparently' advisedly, because when reading advertised dimensions and tonnages it is as well to remember that there is more than one way of arriving at the tonnage measurement of any boat. These measurements are listed opposite. There is always the case of the incredible 'elastic' yacht, well known for growing 5 feet in overall length when being measured for a sales brochure, but shrinking 8 feet for harbour dues or the moment the crew try to fit into their bunks!

Thames measurement

This is the method of obtaining the tonnage of unregistered vessels, originally for the payment of light dues. It is calculated by this formula:

The length from the forepart of the stem to the afterside of the sternpost i.e. outside of perpendiculars (LOA or LOD excluding bowsprits and bumkins).

LOA – beam × beam × beam ÷ 188.

Thus, for a vessel LOA 30 ft with a beam of 10 ft:

$$\frac{(30 - 10 = 20) \times 10 \times 10}{188} = \frac{2000}{188}$$

= 10.64 Thames Measurement.

CHAPTER 2

Finding and funding

Your earnest intention may be to negotiate a purchase with a dispassionate eye and a hard line in bargaining, but you may also have a dream of an abandoned boat wasting away in a corner of a country boatyard – and with all the tantalising possibilities that has for someone (like yourself, of course!) possessed of that extra bit of perception... Force the dream out of your mind, at least in the early stages of the search. If, after sizing up several possibilities, a vessel has not completely lost its allure, it *may* be worth another look – but to purchase purely on the basis of a dream can be the path to insolvency.

This once fine Victorian yacht might be worth the high cost of mounting a salvage operation if of historical interest; the frames are basically intact and the sheer remains remarkably undistorted. However, in the case of such an abandoned vessel where no owner can be traced, it will be necessary to undergo formal and possibly protracted negotiations with Her Majesty's Receiver of Wrecks.

There is no one sure way to locate a good buy, though conversations in country pubs as well as sheer good fortune often play a part. The most usual practice is to pore through the classified advertisements of both brokers and private vendors in the boating periodicals. However, you need to be aware of the bias of the particular magazine: power or sail, inland waterways or offshore voyaging. Non-specialist advertising journals and newspapers are also worth investigating; here genuine bargains do occasionally crop up, for the seller may not realise the potential of the vessel he is offering. A boat may have been reluctantly taken in exchange for a bad debt; it may be an inheritance; or it may even have been included in a property deal. However, the reverse can also occur, in that any loose formation of rotting timber and ironwork vaguely resembling a boat may be claimed to be a classic, and therefore, it is assumed, of immense value. Such misguided assumptions are commonplace and can be the cause of much pointless expenditure of time and money.

But it must also be remembered that no yacht broker, however well informed, can fully guarantee the age of the craft on his books. Cold-blooded misrepresentation is quite rare, but over the years builders' plates on vessels may have been removed and not replaced. The well-patinated brass plaque mounted in the cockpit may not always be contemporaneous with the boat.

An eye well attuned to tiny details can sometimes pick out the stylistic idosyncrasies of certain designers, but these cannot in themselves be relied upon to establish identity beyond all doubt – not unless there is the additional proof of British (or foreign) registry. A registered boat should have the official number and tonnage carved into the main beam. (These can be prone to re-siting; I recently found the carving in the sill of the lavatory compartment doorway.)

Negotiate a price

Haggling may turn out to be a protracted affair, and one that often develops into a game of double bluff – with the vendor, claiming to have lots of interested would-be purchasers. Whether or not you believe this will need to rest on your gut feeling. It should be remembered, though, that no matter how pleasant and courteous a broker may be, he or she is acting primarily in the interests of the client rather than your own. A broker works on commission, and the amount of that commission depends entirely on how much a purchaser can be persuaded to pay. It is not, by the way, unusual for a broker to have bought in the boat being sold 'on behalf of a client', but in practice this is of little importance; the only indication may be in the rapidity with which an offer is accepted or declined!

Once a decision has been reached in principle, you have to decide if you are going to trust your own judgement or employ a surveyor to act on your behalf. It is unwise to purchase a vesel on the basis of a pre-existing survey that has been made out to any person other than yourself (or co-owners in the case of a partnership), because there will be no comeback in the event of undiscovered or latent defects. Common-sense suggests the use of an independent surveyor, who will not necessarily be the same one suggested by the broker or private vendor.

It is at this stage of the procedure that money usually begins to change hands. Any reputable surveyor will insist on the vessel being hauled out – or at least dried out on hard standing – in order to inspect the underbody, skin fittings, propeller, rudder, etc (as, naturally, you would yourself), and the cost of the haul-out and scrub-off (if needed) is borne by the intending purchaser. Of course, less formal arrangements are often made between the interested parties, but trying to inspect the underwater hull with the boat ashore, possibly lying on one side on a beach somewhere, is not very conducive to a thorough examination, particularly when the tide is making fast!

Time deals lightly with lovely little cruising designs such as this Blackwater sloop – more than 30 years young! These small classics are quite affordable and much in demand.

The general practice prior to a survey is for the buyer to make a deposit of 10 per cent of the agreed purchase price, subject to a satisfactory surveyor's report. At this stage ill-feeling can sometimes occur. There may be numerous things wrong with the vessel which, individually, are not over-serious but, when considered as a whole, suggest that proceeding further with the sale may be a waste of time. Of course, no one wants to lose a sale, but whereas a private vendor may back down with good grace and return the deposit, a broker may insist on the completion of the deal unless a structural defect has been discovered. And the definition of such a structural defect may well be open to argument. Such a situation can result in deadlock, with only two alternatives for the buyer: to back out and lose the deposit, or to accept the vessel on the condition that each and every one of the surveyor's recommendations is implemented in full at the vendor's expense.

It is only fair to say that, in the majority of cases, the seller may be unaware of the ailments to which his boat is subject – and of course a broker, acting as agent for his client, is also only doing his best by that client. Still, it is best to avoid any possibility of argument, so spend as much time as possible sizing up the vessel accurately before any commitment whatsoever is made. After all, there can be quite a sizeable sum of money at stake.

The auction option

If you are prepared to put complete faith in your own judgement, there are some very good bargains to be had at auctions. Small craft are sometimes virtually given away at country deadstock sales, since there is little if any prior notice of the boat's inclusion and few people at the sale have the means of removing it once purchased.

There is nothing unduly daunting about bidding at auction. Contrary to popular belief, the auctioneer is not going to mistake an unthinking head shake or sneeze as a signal (unless previously arranged beforehand, that is!). Indeed, it can sometimes be quite hard to catch his eye.

Most craft will be subject to a reserve price; you may be able to discover this from the auctioneer's assistant, although this information does not necessarily give a guide to the actual sums bid. It is normal practice at auctions to 'bounce bids off the wall', with an agent of the auctioneers (appearing to be a member of the public) forcing up the bidding in order to reach the reserve.

Assuming the basic condition of the boat to be fair, the major disadvantage of buying at an auction is that you have to arrange transport – and fast (although the auctioneers can nearly always put you in touch with a delivery firm). But at the fall of the hammer the lot is legally your responsibility, so it is your misfortune if any damage or vandalism occurs subsequently.

All goods purchased at an auction are expected to be paid for in full at the close of the sale in hard cash, banker's draft or by building society cheque. This means having an adequate supply of funds, and this in itself may be a problem.

Hard facts of finance

It is lack of adequate funding that so often dooms a restoration project right from the very outset. There is no difficulty, with one or two caveats, in approaching an advertiser or a broker, settling on a price and paying up – *if* you actually have cash in hand. Even if you do not have sufficient money in your wallet, then surely acquiring it (as soon as a suitable boat is located) will be a simple matter of borrowing it from a bank or other financial institution? In reality, where a boat is concerned, there is a tendency for banks to convince themselves that if you have to borrow money to buy it, there is no way you can afford the actual upkeep! Having said this, a small personal loan (given a reasonably clear credit record) is not impossible to raise. Wildly fluctuating interest rates, though, should not be forgotten. Allegedly friendly banks can be somewhat less friendly should you find difficulty in meeting repayments.

Security for a loan often reduces the rate of interest charged, but for most people the security put up would be their home – and would you really be prepared to lose it (because you could) if things went wrong? The vessel itself can be used as security, but only if it is in sound condition; a surveyor's report will be required to convince any lender of this.

Can finance for the boat be raised if it is classed as a business proposition? This is not impossible, but all figures will have to be meticulously calculated and this can prove more complex than might be first imagined. If you have chartering in mind, it is not difficult to produce acceptable figures, making due allowance for such items as initial cost, restoration and refitting, advertising, storage, launching, maintenance, etc. Although basic in outline, these might just be enough to persuade a bank that you are on to a good thing – particularly if you are dealing with a bank unaccustomed to the harsh realities of the charter business.

On the face of it, a classic boat, preferably one that is quite photogenic (or at least well known) and is capable of accommodating perhaps six guests and two crew, would seem to be the maritime equivalent of a 'nice little earner'. With reasonable luck it ought to bring in during the high season in Britain at least £1,200 per week gross. And such yachts are in demand, especially if they are of interest in their own locality: spritsail barges in the Essex rivers and wherry yachts on the Norfolk Broads.

Once safely ashore, this Edwardian yacht has been allowed to dry over a period of time before work gets underway. A vessel of this size – around 60 feet overall – is a daunting project for an individual and really needs the efforts of a syndicate with adequate funding and a clear idea of what the completed restored craft is to be used for. The cost of rebuilding the hull will be far outweighed by the cost of fitting out and the masting and rigging.

But do you want to be committed for five months of the year as skipper (or as galley slave, for that matter)? And if you pay a professional crew, this will virtually halve the takings. If bareboat chartering, could you endure the havoc the hirers might wreak on your lovely craft, not to mention others in the immediate vicinity? It can be quite a wrench to be forced into hiring out a boat for which you have a deep-rooted affection.

Allow for the unexpected

Sentiment aside, there are other pecuniary aspects to operating a boat as a business – whether as a static diving or school base for day charters, or more protracted cruising. The possibility of illness or redundancy prior to completion of the restoration should be a consideration, but provision can (and should) be made for these from the very outset.

But other 'hidden extras' can also eat voraciously into working capital: insurance, both during building and upon commissioning, and advertising (and this encompasses such costly ephemera as brochures, mailshots and promotional literature sent to magazines – and not just yachting magazines, either).

More alarming by far is the rise in mooring and storage fees around the coastline; boating has become a growth industry with large multinational conglomerates buying

The hull of this little barge yacht is in a pretty dire state; vandalism as well as the ravages of time have wrought their worst but on the face of it, a rebuild – and it would be a rebuild rather than a restoration – is still feasible. It might be easier to start all over again from a set of plans and new wood but on the other hand there is some fine teak in the coachroof and cockpit.

up small local boatyards and 'upgrading' them into marinas. Such marinas often levy very high charges and sometimes their attitude is: 'If the punters don't like it, well tough – they can just go somewhere else.' The problem for the unfortunate sailor is that there is not always anywhere else to go!

Finding a suitable site for a mooring and base of operations is a besetting worry for a larger boat, especially one with over 6 feet of draught. Even if the mooring is satisfactory it may prove awkward to lay up alongside when provisioning or when embarking clients. (A charter party rarely consists of those who actually enjoy wading through mud or saltings!)

By keeping your eyes and ears open, it is sometimes possible to chance upon a mooring plot for sale; this is more usually on a leasehold basis, although freeholds do crop up from time to time. Such a purchase is very cost-effective (and more attractive to a bank than lending money to buy its intended occupant!) and will undoubtedly increase in value – which, quite frankly, might be more than the boat does.

A brief cautionary note: ill-feeling will result if you operate any sort of business from a boatyard without specific prior agreement. Remember also that the management will probably require an agreed amount of commission. This, in fact, is only fair as your clients will be making use of car parking and other facilities at the start and finish of a holiday.

In some forgotten corner of a boatyard lies an attractive motorsailer – or the carcass of one. On the face of it, there seems little amiss that a coat or two of paint will not cure – but closer investigation clearly shows the midship and planks to starboard have pulled away and now gape. Still, not beyond the bounds of someone with patience and elementary woodworking skill; the project could even show a slight profit.

Search and rescue

Whatever your reasons for wanting a classic boat, it has so far been assumed that the craft in question is more or less in one piece and reasonably accessible for inspection. Regrettably, though, some of the finest vessels are not lying in well-known boatyards, carefully shored and neatly tarpaulined, and awaiting the day when they will be recalled to life.

Many vessels have been abandoned, and virtually reduced to wrecks. This is sometimes the outcome of a loss of interest, occasionally because the scrap value of certain parts exceeded the cost of restoration, and often the result of fire damage or unchecked vandalism. Sadly, too, many boats were decommissioned at the outbreak of the Second World War, and were simply left to rot. Some can be seen in the 'debtors' corner' of yards (where, in many cases, their sad fate is to be bulldozed flat, concreted over and become part of yet another car park). Many rest forgotten in mud berths, decaying in the slime.

Twenty years ago, there was hardly a tidal rill or winding river in Britain without its sad complement of hulks. A quarter of a mile stretch of salt marsh near Burnham-on-Crouch was the graveyard of no fewer than twenty-three carcases: among them a clipper-bowed steam yacht, a fine 40 foot ketch, a Thames barge, two bawleys and a pretty little Harrison Butler (not to mention the ubiquitous half-dozen landing craft). At that time, several of the boats could have been salvaged, and even ten years later one or two were not beyond restoration. They were not considered then to be worth the effort. Last year I walked that stretch of salting once again: the steam yacht was old bones, one bawley showed a recognisable portion of stem above the mud, the barge displayed her transom. Only the ketch retained any semblance of the fine vessel she once was, though she was now draped in seaweed and rusting chains. The companion, surprisingly undamaged, descended sadly into a saloon filled with muddy ooze.

A great number of larger boats bereft of their lead keels – which had a value considerably above that of the actual hull – were demoted to the ignominious status of houseboats. Hardboard was tacked on, window boxes, porches and even double-glazed conservatories were precariously attached, and all those who cared for boats shuddered at the sight. Ironically, despite all the eyesores that resulted, this conversion process led to the preservation of the hulls of such vessels – being watertight was obviously a major consideration to those living on board! In recent years it is regrettable that certain councils – intent on 'improving the environment' – have abolished houseboats from waterfront areas, often using the drastic measure of towing them out to sea and scuttling them.

If it can be ascertained that tenure of the berth for the duration of the restoration and refitting is secure, certain of these abandoned craft are worthy of closer inspection. Where a designated residential mooring is involved though, the combined cost of ship and plot will probably be so high as to rule out the purchase; indeed, a three-cabin houseboat may compare pricewise with a three-bedroom cottage.

The abandoned derelict – worth the gamble?

Any vessel that has been left lying derelict in a mud berth (as opposed to merely overwintering in one) is, even when presented as a gift, to be regarded with the greatest circumspection. If it is a gift, ensure that this fact is recorded and a receipt obtained so the giver cannot ask for the hull back should it be found, after hauling out, to be in better condition than was anticipated!

True, it will be a gamble, and not one stacked in your favour should the area be noted for ship-worms. One variety of teredo worm is capable of survival in northern waters and evidence of its activity can be extremely hard to detect on an old and battle-scarred hull. This is because the creature tunnels lengthwise with the grain of the timber, leaving only one entry and one exit hole. The ravages of the gribble worm should be easier to see, since the pest merely tunnels in and out. It repeats this action many times and can reduce timber almost to the consistency of a honeycomb. Evidence suggests that this undesirable crustacean is growing rarer, probably as a result of the increased efficacy of modern antifoulings and the dearth of its food supply, since reinforced concrete has largely replaced timber pilings in wharves and harbours (and wooden boats are less commonplace too). Certain locations are still rumoured to be infested and extra caution should be exercised if the boat is – or has been – berthed in one of these areas. Even boring that took place many years ago will have allowed water permeation, with the increased likelihood of rot in the affected areas.

Bear in mind that any craft abandoned for a long period is going to be in very poor condition, and so the cost and effort involved in freeing her and extracting accumulated silt from the inside is going to be substantial. Moreover, the work will be undertaken with no guarantee of a successful outcome. An old wooden vessel is a very delicate structure, and even with the greatest care it may not survive in one piece. Equally possible, indeed probable, is the fact that the hull is not intact anyway, but

Preparing to tow a derelict Folkboat alongside. In this case, there was no worry as to the watertight integrity of the towed vessel (although the deck fittings gave rise to some consternation). If there is any doubt as to whether the victim will remain afloat, a third vessel with lifting strops should be on stand by – and a number of safe landing sites should be sought out prior to embarkation, just in case!

there is no way of knowing this for sure at the start of the salvage operation.

Some years ago I watched a Dutch botter being painstakingly excavated from a berth only for the working party to discover, after many hours of back-breaking labour, that the major part of the stern was missing. There is, too, that little matter of the lead keel, lead being quite a pricey commodity. Will it have been looted by scrap dealers? If the keel is of iron, with steel keel bolts, will it still be attached? And even if it appears to be, will it still remain attached after the vessel has been lifted?

The absence of a keel is something of a setback, although the pattern and mould making (or even the casting) of a lead keel does not present insuperable problems for a determined amateur. The casting of an iron keel is less practicable, although a considerable sum can be saved by the home construction of the timber pattern. The exact dimensions of said keel, though, may not be readily apparent and, if no plans or drawings are in existence, the size and weight will have to be calculated. To be honest, rule of thumb will give an idea of the ballast ratio – usually in the region of 50 per cent for a racing yacht and 35 to 40 per cent for a cruising vessel. The deadweight of the hull without ballast will have to be estimated and a fair idea can be arrived at arithmetically by working out the area of planking and scantlings, the weight of the timber per cubic foot, and deducing it from there.

Although the use of a planimeter is often recommended to give an extra idea of the surface areas of the hull, such an instrument is expensive to buy and almost impossible to borrow – in practice, graph paper and a scale drawing will, unless there is a need for absolute precision (rare), give a very good idea. Apart from the construction and alterations that may have been made in an older vessel, there are so many other variables, such as weight of spars, engines (of types that may never have been envisaged at the design stage), and of crew and stores, that fine calculations, except on a racing boat or one of light displacement, are to a large extent superfluous.

Be wary – wrecks can endanger your health!

Clambering around abandoned derelicts is not without its dangers: it is easy to slip and there is the ever-present risk of a deck, sole or companion ladder giving way. More perilous by far is gaining access to the vessel if she is not alongside and reached by a fixed ladder or firm gangplank. It is not uncommon for a boat gradually to slip down the incline of the mud towards deeper water until she is 50 yards or so offshore. Boarding will then entail a slither through mud of varying viscosity! There have been several fatalities as a result of the unwary falling into a deep but invisible hole where a vessel has previously lain. Unable to extricate themselves from the semi-liquid mud, they slowly died of hypothermia. Basic precautions should be observed – the first of which is DON'T EXPLORE ALONE. The wearing of thigh boots is inadvisable as they can be almost impossible to remove in deep mud; even a short boot, once topped, may be a danger. If possible, take along a quantity of wide planks and place them on top of rubber tyres; the latter tend to stabilise the boards as they subside slowly into the mud. Always let someone know where you are, and don't set out in failing light or on a rising tide.

By the same token, if you are buying the occupant of a mud berth which (allegedly) floats at high water, there are still precautions to be observed. It is only commonsense to go on board, ensuring that you have a dinghy alongside in case an escape route is urgently needed, and remain there for a couple of hours at the top of the tide. I have known a vessel quietly scuttle herself during the twenty minutes in which I was engaged in note-taking. The water rose silently until the sole boards beneath my feet lifted to the wavelets and I had the uneasy feeling that all was not well. As peacefully as she filled, the boat settled back into her berth without fuss, the tide ebbed from her, and left her ready to repeat the performance on the next high tide. In the circumstances, it was hardly possible to write a glowing survey report, although the would-be purchaser still decided to buy the vessel. It can still be seen ten years on – but only at low water!

Extracting a vessel that is deeply embedded in mud is an exacting job: one that demands a mixture of manual effort, accurate timing, and an element of luck. Digging a trench to free the hull is only the beginning: a suction dredge or pump to remove semi-liquid mud may also be needed. The final lift may require additional buoyancy – either in the form of attendant launches alongside, oil drums or flotation bags. Any lifting aids must be attached to webbing encircling the hull and air bags should on no account be sited internally under thwarts, decks or coachroof, where the positive force exerted could rip the hull structure apart.

In addition to the clearing out of silt, all other heavy weights should, if feasible, be removed. Internal ballast may not be too difficult to move unless corrosion has welded it into a homogenous lump (don't be tempted to lay into it with a sledge-hammer *in situ* as it will almost certainly damage the hull timbers), and ideally the engine should be lifted. In practice, though, this last task is not going to be easy as a strong platform

will have to be erected unless the structural integrity of the hull is beyond question. Similarly, the base of any sheerlegs, gantry or other lifting gear, must, if sited within the hull, be taken to known strong points – if, indeed, any such exist. Certainly it should not be asssumed that decks or cockpit sole are sound – nor the internal soles, if any remain in one piece. It would be an ignominious start to any salvage operation to have engine and sheers disappear through the bottom of the boat!

While the actual work of freeing the hull for movement is under way – and it could take at least a week, even for a 30 footer – ensure that the tides are coming up to springs. However, make the first attempt at towing at least three days before the highest, in case of delays. Should the hull be anything less than watertight (and it can safely be assumed that this will indeed be the case!), transportation to a temporary berth prior to hauling out provides one more opportunity for things to go wrong en route. Generally, the simplest method is to tow alongside with a heavily fendered launch. If it can be arranged, it is far safer to have boats to port and starboard with heavy-duty webbing slings under the casualty. This should impart sufficient reserve buoyancy for long enough to beach the tow in an emergency. Any attempt to take the weight of a sinking ballasted hull upon its deck fittings is to invite rapid disintegration of both deck and hardware – and a portion of the hull planking into the bargain!

When plotting the salvage operations, contingency plans ought to include at least one carefully inspected emergency 'landing site', where the hull can remain for a tide should the mission be aborted – as well it might be, if the ingress of water proves faster than that of forward progress.

This yacht was laid up during the Second World War and simply left to deteriorate. Even 30 years ago she might have been saved; now nothing remains but a few sad timbers and the mainsheet horse.

Once the hull is released

Some gradual drying out of a saturated hull is beneficial before the commencement of lifting, but as long as all water and as much interior debris as practicable has been removed, you have done all that is humanly possible to ensure success. After this, it is a matter of trusting to luck and the crane operator (and trying to take the sanguine view that, if the vessel falls to bits at this stage, then at least there will not be any future worries!).

Theoretically, sophistications like the construction of a customised cradle around the hull will minimise the possibility of stress damage, but in practice this will be impossible if the underbody is lying in mud; even with a fairly hard surface such as sand or shingle, the boat would first have to be levered upright and then temporarily shored in that position. If this much can be achieved, arguably the structure is tough enough to withstand the haul-out without any need for a cradle.

What is absolutely vital though, and the importance of this cannot be overstressed, is that spreaders or spragging pieces of adequate width must be used in the crane slings as the compression force upon the broadest section of the hull (which is not always the strongest) is enormous. I have known several previously sound boats injured in this way (including one of my own). Such damage is not necessarily apparent at the time, so there is unlikely to be any redress. An elderly or unsound vessel is generally, in any case, craned strictly at the owner's risk. Most crane drivers are highly skilled (although the operator of a mobile crane may not be as familiar with boats as the employee of a boatyard), but try to be present during the lift. If you are really worried at any point, be prepared to say so. Better to be a nuisance than be faced with

Not exactly the recommended way of supporting a clinker hull but one which is, nevertheless, all too common. Eventually the ground will settle and the prop will lift the strake; there are indications of this having happened here.

damage that could have been avoided by speaking up. It is, after all, *your* money that is at stake.

If employing a mobile crane, ensure that you have not underestimated the deadweight of the vessel: unless the class or type is specifically known to you, add at least 40 per cent to the original guess. Hiring yet another crane with greater lifting capacity will add considerably to your expenses.

Once the vessel is on dry land and shored, it can be hosed down, But take great care: a high-pressure system should not be employed as the water jet is powerful enough to rip caulking from seams and may also wash away corroded fastenings, thus causing planks to spring. Time spent in cleaning off, with repeated gentle washing and allowing the timber to dry properly, will help to prevent immediate splitting or cracking of timbers. Remember that the change of elements is traumatic for a wooden hull.

After the wash down, you can see what you have actually lumbered yourself with – for better or for worse! An in-depth inspection can then take place, and either provide reassurance that all the effort so far expended has been worth while – or show up the worst fears!

In the case of a derelict stored for years on dry land, there will not be such a period of suspense before the examination. You will, however, still have to bear in mind the difficulties of physically moving a relatively delicate structure if the decision is taken to go to an alternative work site. An over-dry hull with brittle ribs, shakes in the planks and suspect fastenings requires the same gentle handling that a waterlogged one does. A sturdy cradle can be constructed for travelling and eventual storage, but in many cases frapping the hull with webbing to hold sprung butts and hood ends is just as effective a precaution. (Use webbing rather than rope, at least in way of the slings, as it will not cut into the wood when under pressure.)

Supporting the hull

Since any structural restoration will, in all probability, keep the vessel landbound for at least a season, the support of the hull is critical. It should be realised that more distortion can occur during a protracted lay-up period ashore than in the equivalent period afloat. In particular, both fine-ended, short-keeled sailing vessels and motor yachts with a long external keel call for meticulous attention when blocking up.

A long timber-keeled type should be chocked every 3 feet if the backbone is not to develop undulations along its length; these irregularities, while not initially of dire consequence, will in time cause the planking to move and, eventually, the seams to gape. The bow overhang and long counter common to the majority of fast sailing yachts of earlier years must also be supported to prevent gradual drooping and subsequent wringing of the structure.

It goes without saying that the turn of the bilge must be supported with blocks and fairing wedges at approximately 4 foot intervals (depending on hull type) and that some form of lashing will be needed to ensure that these remain in place no matter how energetic the movements of those

Shoring up errors
Correct supporting of the hull is of prime importance: the sketch below and on the following page show common errors, all which can ultimately lead to serious distortion.

This example shows a relatively lightly constructed yacht of the type built in the 1960s for racing under JOG (Junior Offshore Group) rules. Hull shores have no pads to distribute the weight and, as the ground settles under the keel, they may eventually penetrate the planking. Weight will increasingly be placed upon the lashings through the chain plates, causing the seams to gape and the sheerline to distort. There is no support aft – and that outboard is hardly going to improve matters.

working on board. What must never be contemplated, though, is reeving any line from supporting legs to chainplates (or, for that matter, the vessel supported for more than a week or two up on her own beaching legs if there is provision for these). Any slight settlement of the ground or movement in legs or lines will place a strain on the fittings, and thus the hull planking. This will distort the seams, and maybe even the sheerline.

It may seem hard to believe, but it is not unknown for a keel boat to be laid up without any blocks whatsoever directly underneath the ballast keel. This means that the entire weight of the boat is taken by the bilge area, which was never designed for such a loading. Eventually, the bilge blocks may go right through the hull itself. This is certainly not good practice, even for a glassfibre vessel, and for a timber one it amounts to wanton vandalism. As some boatyards expressly prohibit owners from altering the position of shores, be prepared to fight it out with the foreman: it is a battle you cannot afford to lose.

When investigating a derelict on hard standing, always check the condition of the shores before boarding; and in all other aspects be as wary as if exploring one that is entombed in mud. Apart from the risks of rotten timber, lurking unsuspected under paint and filler, there is a real possibility, if stepping directly on to the internal planking, that it may spring under your weight. A vessel that has caught fire has, apart from easily visible defects in the structure, one additional hazard: heat-fragmented glass from windows. These tiny splinters often cover every flat surface, both on deck and below, are hard to see, cut deeply and

This long-keeled motor yacht shows how inadequate blocking under the keel will cause the ends to droop (a common fault in a vessel designed originally to carry cargo). Blocks should be spaced at three to four foot intervals. The uprights are secured through the bolt-holes of beaching legs which, as with a lashing through chainplates, can also cause stress. The shores are positioned under the lands of the hull; over a period of time this will certainly strain the planking, although it is in fact quite a common practice. The diagram also shows them fastened through the planking; until recently I would not have believed this would ever be done but, when my back was turned, a boatyard actually perpetrated such an indignity on my own Folkboat!

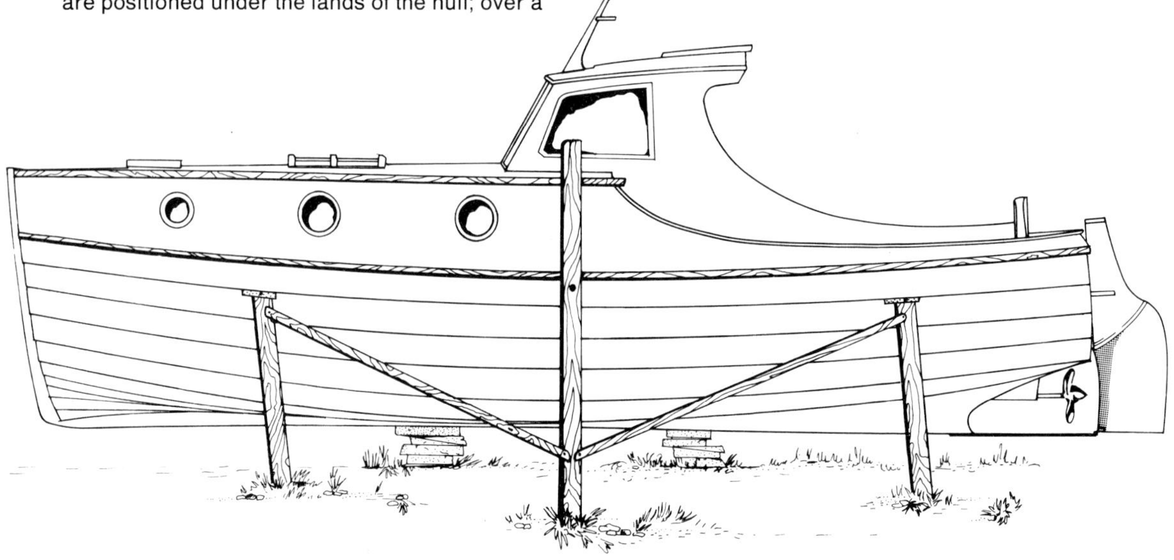

severely, and are prone to causing later infection.

Acquisition of a hopeless case can only be regarded as a game of chance: the higher the stakes, the greater the potential for profit or loss. Before committing yourself to purchase, or even to the expense of hauling out for survey, there is one final and sobering possibility that must be faced: what happens if the project turns sour?

Worst-case scenario

The 'worst-case scenario' is often the last thing in mind amid the euphoria of the search and the heady excitement of bargaining. But things do go wrong – the very boat you lust after may well be someone else's broken dream.

Anything connected with boating is expensive, and one reason for this is the monopoly that boatyards and marinas have of waterside access. It is unwise to assume that, while on their premises, you can do as you wish. In the majority of yards, it is not possible to employ subcontract labour since this is, in effect, doing the yard's employees out of a job. Generally, those designated as your regular crew are allowed to help with minor fitting out, but a wary eye will be kept upon their identity and number. The boating industry is a small and closely knit one, so trying to smuggle in a marine engineer as your brother-in-law does not usually meet with great success. Even if such a professional would consent in the first place, the likelihood is that he would be recognised. A similar restriction will also apply to most other external services, including the employment of a travelling crane service to haul out or lower the mast. (It may not be allowed upon the premises at all if the yard possesses its own hoist; but, if it is, a fee will generally be levied.)

The charge for hauling out, scrubbing off and lowering the mast will often be all inclusive and subject to a minimum charge, to which VAT must be added. If the vessel is to spend time on a slipway, that will be charged for on a daily basis – sometimes even when the yard itself is involved in the remedial work.

When the boat is to be loaded on to a transporter equipped with its own crane, the yard will insist on the employment of its own (as will the boatyard to which it is transported). There *are* premises in Britain that offer facilities for those wishing to undertake their own work with the help of additional imported labour, but they seem to be getting rarer.

Rocketing charges must be anticipated and allowed for. What can be even more threatening is the boatyard changing hands and being taken over by a concern whose sole preoccupation is to make more and more money. It is in fact just your type of boat that is most at risk in the event of a management change: after all, the firm's accountants do not themselves perceive anything especially attractive in an assembly of bulky wooden objects, shrouded by unsightly patched tarpaulins and surrounded by the usual detritus of refitting. Neither do they much appreciate the owners of such craft, who are unlikely to squander their money on the pseudo-nautical fripperies offered at the souvenir shop cum chandlery, or order new diesels or interfaced navtronic systems!

The reality is that most classic boats, along with their owners, are seen as a dead loss, and in many cases their departure for a less fashionable destination is earnestly entreated. Even if notice to quit is not actually given, a boatowner may well be subjected to a programme of forced relocation within the yard, possibly involving several moves (and the yard may well charge for each movement). Rarely will the new location be a more attractive or convenient part of the boatyard. The message will be pretty clear, but with a half-completed boat there is little to be done but sit it out.

All this hassle is hard enough to accept

Over a period of years, the entire weight of this Dragon's hull has come to rest upon one single bilge chock. Inevitably, the planking has been forced inwards, also damaging the internal ribs in the process.

with a viable boat that is responding to treatment. But what happens if the realisation dawns that the whole project is a waste of time since the vessel concerned proves unworthy of restoration? If this seems clear at an early stage – the moment perhaps of leaving the mud berth – then it ought to be possible to reinsert the vessel surreptitiously and bow out – embarrassed, but (with luck) not financially ruined. (Leave it more than a day or two though, and you can bet the mud berth will have been re-let to another occupant!)

But if the boat is already in a commercial yard, there are three basic alternatives. The first is to pay all the bills as they become due and do your best to sell the boat on (at the right price, everything is said to find a buyer). Or you can move it, at further expense, to a cheaper site and once again put the craft on the market. The final alternative is to burn the boat or dismantle it and cart the remains away, after salvaging any fittings. To write your vessel off to experience is a hard decision to take, but there are times when it is the only option.

CHAPTER 3

The practicalities of surveying

What a survey entails

Once the vessel is accessible for inspection, the full survey can get under way. Whether or not a professional is employed at this stage is optional. Quite often – and somewhat to the surveyor's chagrin – those buying classic boats have an intimate understanding of the species and the ills to which it is prone. Thus such would-be purchasers are quite able to decide for themselves, after an initial inspection, whether to proceed further with the business in hand. Matters maritime being as they are, however, when insurance is arranged a surveyor acceptable to the insurance company will have to sign on the dotted line to confirm that the vessel indeed exists – and will, in all probability, continue to do so for a reasonable period of time – and is not so over-valued as to make barratry profitable. On resale, too, the surveyor's stage reports carry weight, even though the purchaser should insist upon his own survey being carried out.

A doctor is to a human being what a surveyor is to a boat: someone who is reluctantly summoned when unwelcome situations arise, conveniently forgotten when a cure has been effected, and quick to be recalled should an ailment recur! When a doctor's patient dies, this is the end of the case. In contrast, surveyors can find that vessels they have written off in cold print return to cause embarrassment as, against all odds, they are restored to life.

Those who care about boats tend to care very deeply, and certainly feelings are severely hurt at the sight of a pessimistic survey report. In contrast, a report insisting that all is well, in each and every respect, will rarely be questioned. As a surveyor, I feel that a calculating amateur eye can in theory find most defects. The trouble is that infatuation with the boat under survey can lead to blurred vision, whereas a professional, being completely dispassionate (although quite a number of surveyors have discovered they are not immune to the lure of a once-beautiful boat), will be more concerned with the negative aspects. True, a disclaimer against liability for latent defects and/or faults not discovered as a result of inaccessibility usually forms part of the report, but overlooking the obvious can have very serious consequences.

Since in the long term it is virtually impossible to escape the scrutiny of the professional, a strong case could be made for calling upon such services from the very first. However, it is not uncommon for two or even three boats to be turned down flat by a surveyor, and this is discouraging, expensive and, in the end, may lead you to wonder if he is correct in any case! Such a feeling is understandable, and may even be justified, since in order to protect himself a surveyor will err on the side of caution. It is therefore in your own best interest to carry out an initial survey yourself, examining the essential specific points; perhaps a pre-survey check would be an apt description. You have at your disposal one asset that many professionals do not: time. Even with the boat on a slip, once the hull has been examined it should be possible to spend as long as you want on decks and interior – even longer than a whole day if necessary.

What does a structural survey involve? As the term suggests, it covers a complete and thorough inspection of the integrity of the hull, decks, superstructure and cockpit, both internally and externally. Naturally, in order to facilitate this, the hull must be clear of the water and blocked up to a height sufficient to allow inspection of the underbody, keel, rudder and all underwater fittings.

In reality, just about every single fitting or system on a seagoing vessel affects the structural integrity, and thus the safety at sea. Therefore it is also necessary to inspect, with the greatest thoroughness, the condition of all hatches, windows and skylights and all other openings through the hull including seacocks, gate valves and skin fittings. Not to be ignored is the state of all through-fastenings (including the keel bolts).

The steering, whether rudder and tiller or wheel with hydraulic, rod or chain/wire and quadrant system, must be checked meticulously, as also must the provision for emergency facility, fitted as a back-up to wheel steering.

In a sailing yacht, masts, spars, sails and all standing and running rigging must be checked. With a motor vessel, the engine space must be inspected, having regard to access, cleanliness of the bilge, fire extinction, and the installation of the propulsion machinery itself.

The engine should be checked for oil leaks, hose connections and clips, and the free movement of controls; it should also, if practicable, be turned over by hand. Since the vessel is on hard standing, the propeller and sternbush should also be inspected. Fuel tanks, piping and connections should be examined, as should the exhaust, shaft and stern greaser.

It is not usual for a structural survey to be much more specific than this regarding the engine; a marine engineer would normally be called in to report in detail upon the actual condition, carry out compression tests, etc.

The electrical system must be checked out, including wiring to a marine fuse panel where applicable, and external connections with watertight plugs and sockets. The siting and type of battery(ies) must be examined, and also the provision for their charging must be ascertained.

A meticulous inspection of the domestic systems is essential; ironically, it is these very life-support systems that can endanger a ship more than anything else. All lavatory installations must be checked and double checked. So must the gas supply: all piping, connections and the siting of the gas locker – if, that is, bottled gas is used. Heating stoves, whether gas, paraffin or solid fuel, must also be looked at and careful attention be paid to flues and ventilation.

Safety equipment is next on the list: such essentials as bilge pumps (also hoses, strum boxes, etc), fire-fighting equipment and, of course, the provision of personal safety gear such as lifebuoys, lifejackets, etc.

Lastly, check the inventory; this could be regarded as a catch-all, but obviously it must comprise equipment of a type compatible with the size, type and intended use of the vessel, and guidelines are strict as to weight of anchor, size and length of chain cable, etc.

When contemplating a boat in need of refitting and refurbishing, there is a strong possibility that many items described cannot be examined because of their absence – a craft on the market after an attempt has been made to restore it may well have been completely gutted. This provides a good opportunity to examine the

On a drying mooring. Those heavy timber bilge keels as well as the deadwood and rudder are all vulnerable to attack from gribble, so if buying a wooden boat which regularly takes the ground, enquire whether that ground is noted for marine borers!

'bare bones', but also use it to work out an accommodation plan and access to the engine space if the position and nature of such things are not self-evident.

Respect the boat – and the vendor's feelings

When examining a boat yourself, you may or may not be accompanied by a worried owner who is intensely preoccupied as to what faults are about to be unearthed (if he is not already aware of these). Surveyors tend to make it pretty clear that they do not enjoy being followed around by anyone – even those who have actually employed them. They claim, not without an element of truth, that it is difficult to concentrate on the job in hand while answering questions. It is also possibly due to the extreme difficulty of maintaining the slightest semblance of dignity while delving into the grubby and claustrophobic innards of most small boats. In pre fax days, when a postal strike made it impossible to mail a written survey, I (with the greatest reluctance) handed over the cassette recording made during the survey (of a narrow-gutted ex-six Metre). True, there were occasional wise comments, though these were outnumbered by curses as unyielding beams, etc coincided with my human anatomy.

If the vendor insists upon being present, do not allow yourself to be deterred from the job in hand for one moment: view all distractions offered with suspicion! If attention is drawn to the magnificence of the newly replaced galley, concern yourself (initially) only with what lies behind it; if requested to enthuse over a newly panelled shipside lining, ask why it has been done as a first priority. Be suspicious of everything: insist on soles being lifted, drawers removed, and gain access to every part – and this holds just as true for a vessel of glassfibre or even steel construction.

One of three things will then take place: the vendor will realise that the game is up and all that he has attempted to hide from prying eyes is about to be discovered (at which point you may be ordered off, never to return); he may simply retreat philosophically into the background and leave you to get on with it; or alternatively, he may set to work and start removing soleboards, companions, etc to assist you!

It goes without saying that a great deal of respect should be shown to any boat – even one that has apparently been abandoned and is perhaps being sold as a bad debt by a yard. The precise borderline between legitimate probing of rot (or suspect glassfibre) and the causing of physical damage may be easier to overstep than to define. Tempting though it may be, it is prudent to avoid pulling away rotten wood in great chunks or wielding hammer and chisel with abandon. (The same goes for puncturing gelcoat blisters on a glassfibre hull!)

When inspecting fastenings for evidence of nail sickness or excessive corrosion, be very careful not to loosen them further, especially those below the waterline. Neither should suspect caulking be gleefully ripped out to see if all of it is as bad as the first impression suggests: it may well be, but such removal will hardly bode well for the hull's continued integrity of structure. The vessel may have stood around for years, but the owner may not realise just how much it has deteriorated. If it is then launched without further checking and you have exacerbated its tendency to sink (albeit as a result of a pre-existing condition), he would be more than justified in feeling aggrieved and seeking redress.

The vessel after inspection must be left exactly in the state in which you found it: nothing must be left disconnected, damaged or removed.

Responsibility for damage

In reality, it can prove very hard to carry out a satisfactory inspection because internal linings and sole boards are screwed into place so firmly that this precludes their removal. If this is the case, and the vendor can be contacted, ask permission to remove any joinery or soles if you have reason to believe they are concealing evidence. If consent is freely given and you are 100 per cent certain that everything can be returned to its original condition afterwards, go ahead (some photographic confirmation of your actions could be helpful in the light of a later argument). Bear in mind that others may look at the boat after you, or have preceded you, so the identity of the person responsible for inflicting injuries might be open to question. Remember that any professional report will contain a caveat regarding defects undiscovered as a result of lack of access. In only a few cruising boats is it possible to see all areas of bilge, deckhead etc; this is not only because of linings and domestic furniture, but also because of fuel/water tanks and, of course, engines. Large areas of the shipside lining are often impossible to remove since mouldings and interior fitments may butt up to them. Sometimes the assistance of the yard's own shipwright is invaluable; such an employee will have to be paid on a full hourly rate, even if the job only takes ten minutes of his time, but he will be indemnified against any damage inadvertently caused. It takes only a slip of the screwdriver on a highly polished panel to ruin the surface and necessitate re-veneering or, at least, re-finishing.

It is accepted that small areas of paint will have to be removed for inspection; once again, though, take off the bare minimum, and be prepared to repaint if asked. With a

Lifting a submerged yacht with air bags.

boat hauled out just for a survey and intended to be relaunched on the next tide, it is common practice for the surveyor to be pointed in the direction of a paintbrush and tin of antifouling. It would be churlish not to take the hint!

Should a serious fault be discovered on a vessel about to be refloated, ensure that someone is aware of it. Planks can and do spring when an old boat is lifted, tingles also can sometimes let go with a sigh of relief – and it doesn't take much to cause a foundering. Seacocks also must be examined carefully to ascertain that they are closed and all windows should be secured. Check all hatches and lockers as well: a burglary occurring shortly after you leave the scene is going to be as difficult to explain away as an unexpected scuttling!

The tools of the trade

The contents of a surveyor's toolbag are, on the whole, eclectic in nature, with personal preferences inclining towards a variety of filed-down, bent or otherwise modified items that have come to prove useful over the years. Certain basic equipment and tools are always required, though, whatever the vessel's construction material or type. The first piece of equipment necessary is a trustworthy ladder: rigid, but light enough to be easily moved around the hull when making a close examination of the topsides. An aluminium loft ladder, extending to some 10 feet in length, is fine for any vessel drawing in the region of 5 feet (allowing for the blocks beneath the keel), but if the boat is larger than this a longer reach is desirable. Short lengths of elastic or rope are handy for keeping locker lids and odds and ends clear when working underneath, and a powerful torch (with spare batteries) is essential. Such tools as are necessary are mainly those of a poking and prodding nature, along with a comprehensive set of good screwdrivers. A brace with screwdriver bit will prove capable of dealing with most embedded screws, though if it slips it can leave a nasty gouge mark.

Chisels, thoughtfully used, are quite effective, and it is advisable to possess at least two of these: one about $\frac{3}{8}''$ in width and the other of about $1\frac{1}{2}''$. When testing for softness in timber, use the blade across the grain and press softly – *any* sharp object will penetrate along the length of even the soundest wood. If rot is found, use the flat of the blade to discover the extent, but resist the ever-present temptation to whittle away unnecessarily. Pliers will also be needed, so take along a fairly large pair and some finer ones – also, a Mole grip if you have one. Scrapers will be useful if sharp; the type used depends on personal preference, but I prefer a triangular shave hook with curved edges (used with greatest circumspection). I trust to a trimming knife blade for finer work such as plank edges, where serious harm can be inflicted on the timber if due care is not exercised. A hammer for tapping ironwork, a gauge for sizing rigging, magnifying glass and tape measure should also form part of the surveying inventory; in addition, I take a palette knife, with a thin and flexible blade that can explore the extent of delamination without adding to any deterioration. A can of penetrating oil also has its uses – especially where the freeing of a seized padlock is needed to gain admittance in the first place!

Notebooks (more than one, as your first one will inevitably fall into a patch of water or oil scum) are essential, as is a cassette recorder if you enjoy the sound of your own voice. That, however, is quite likely to be drowned by the persistent sounds of wind whistling through the standing rigging and frapping halyards, both of which are amplified inside a boat. Take along rags or kitchen paper for cleaning up (both the boat and yourself) as a thorough structural survey is not the cleanest of jobs.

Inevitably, with the archboard missing, planks have sprung on the counter – but lack of support will tend to exacerbate any further movement.

The preliminary inspection: grounds for suspicion

On arrival, no matter how impatient you are to begin, spare some minutes to take a long look at the boat from a distance, preferably from angles where a view of the hull in its entirety is not impeded by other craft in the vicinity. The sheerline reveals a good deal – and not just about wooden boats either: it often makes it plain whether a boat has been built or finished by an amateur. In the case of a timber boat it shows if distortion is present and it is the primary area to investigate for damage inflicted by a collision. A survey calls for a suspicious mind, and one that is intent on the investigation of all clues to any past disasters, as well as poor building practice and inferior materials.

Follow up this first, long hard look by measuring the vessel: dimensions may not be as advertised. Usually, it will be apparent that a vendor's estimate of the overall length and beam errs towards the optimistic, but the opposite may be the case if the vessel is registered and the particulars taken directly from the Certificate of Registry. In this case the length shown will be that as measured from the fore part of the stem to the after side of the head of the stern post, so the length on deck may be greater. While the registered length is deemed to be the legal length, harbourmasters and boatyards persistently measure to the extremities of the hull – including all fittings from pulpit to davits – and charge accordingly. (So do a large number of surveys – myself included – whose fees are calculated on the same basis.)

Not everyone will set about an inspection in quite the same fashion or identical order of procedure. With a timber boat (where as much, if not more, can be learned of the condition from the interior hull) I tend to look, rather quickly, at the externals, note relevant points on the checklist, then settle down to peer at the inside. One reason for this is that the final examination of the engine space and external underbody usually entails an encounter with grease and mud (to say nothing of a snowstorm of scraped flakes from antifouling) and, even when wearing overalls, it is difficult not to track unwanted dirt into the accommodation. This is of little importance in a stripped-out hull, but another thing entirely if the upholstery and trim are still in place.

With ample time at your disposal (and it is not unreasonable to assume, if working single-handed, that the investigation of a 30 foot auxiliary yacht will need five hours or so of undivided attention), it ought to be possible to look at the hull in differing angles of light. A number of defects that remain obscured when light is cast from one angle will be thrown into relief as the sun passes on its course. The slightest shadow can reveal unfairness in apparently smooth topsides and will assist in the detection of minor blistering in a fibreglass hull (this defect might otherwise pass unnoticed).

Using the checklist as a guide, procedures will be much the same for a glassfibre yacht as for a wooden one – with the inevitable frustrations occurring when investigating those irritating areas of bilge or shipside (which, after the initial date of building, whether by design or accident, were never intended to be seen again by the human eye!).

Powers of observation and a grim determination to get at the truth are not, in themselves, a guarantee that all faults will be spotted at the time of the survey. Some knowledge of the construction of the vessel in question is also necessary. Both modern technology and traditional timber boatbuilding methods have variants; some of these are the result of experimentation with new glues or resins and exotic timber or core materials – and not all of these ventures have been a great success.

An introduction will be given in the following chapters to wood and glassfibre technology, and to their drawbacks. Wood construction (whether of time-honoured solid timber or veneer and glassfibre) suffers from an interesting range of peculiar conditions – many of which can be effectively hidden by the unscrupulous. So let the buyer – and surveyor – beware.

CHAPTER 4

Timber

Seasoning and strength

While not every classic boat is of timber construction, at the time of writing most of those vessels regarded as classics are wooden. However, an increasing number of glassfibre vessels (albeit derivative in design) are also accepted, if somewhat grudgingly, as having similar status. But to classify all timber construction as a mere matter of nailing strips of planking on to a framework is to underestimate grossly the ingenuity of builders and designers.

Timber is a very adaptable substance: it can be bent or laminated to form just about every curve imaginable; it is immensely tough, resilient and durable; and it has a good strength to weight ratio. Also, with a very few exceptions such as lignum-vitae, it is buoyant.

These attributes are common to most timbers, though some properties are more pronounced in certain species than in others. The moisture content at time of construction has a considerable bearing too – not only on strength, but also on stability (shrinkage and/or expansion) and resistance to fungal decay. If too much moisture is extracted (as it may be with kiln drying, as opposed to a slower and more natural process by air circulation), the dried timber loses resistance to the breakdown of its cell walls. Allow it to remain damp, though, and the bacteria that cause wet rot thrive and multiply. (Dry rot, on the other hand, is a spore-borne fungus and is relatively rare in boats. It is very occasionally present in vessels that have been laid up for a long period of time and have become 'infected' – perhaps from dry rot in surrounding buildings.)

The structure of wood consists of a series of tubes, each standing on end. These are built up from long cells and provided with non-return valves that syphon up both moisture and nutrients, dispersing them through leaves and branches. A slice cut transversely through a tree closely resembles a slice taken through the boiler of a steam engine.

It is through the tubes in wood that decay-bearing fungus travels. Since water also passes through them – and may, in icy conditions, freeze, expand and split the timber – it is vital that the end grain be sealed by paint, resin or a glued capping.

Because timber can be severely affected by decay, the choice of boards is all important, especially those used in planking or decking. First, the wood must be free from sap, which is the early outside growth on the tree and is rich in the vitamin-bearing moisture so greatly relished by a host of undesirable micro-organisms. Sap wood is not hard to recognise in such trees as the oak, since it is lighter in colour and softer in texture; however, it is not always so obvious in the faster-growing softwood species. The wood should also be free, as far as possible, from double grain; this makes it difficult to machine or plane. Of course, an excess of knots is most undesirable, in that the structure is dramtically weakened in their immediate vicinity.

Although the selection of timber for boatbuilding is generally dictated not only by experience, but also by the availability of supplies, it is interesting to note that an official average standard of strength and properties does in fact exist. It is arrived at by a programme of evaluation conducted by research laboratories and the British Timber Research Board. The tests involve small samples of approximately 2 inches by 2 in cross-section and of defect-free structure, thus they must be regarded as establishing an average only. Six strength tests are carried out: static bending; impact bending; compression parallel to the grain; hardness; shear parallel to the grain; and cleavage. There does appear to be an interrelationship between good performance in the static bending test and the impact test, and a correlation between the hardness factor along with that of compression strength, but it should be duly noted that all evaluation is carried out using dry specimens.

Boatbuilding timbers

The types of wood that can be used in boatbuilding are almost as varied as the boats that can be constructed from them. British tradition praises the 'hearts of oak', but oak (at least, for smaller craft) is not the best available timber for all-round construction. It may, when thick enough, be quite resistant to cannonballs, but its tendency to split in normal use rather outweighs this quality today – at least, so far as the building of a small boat is concerned.

There are, of course, a number of species of oak available, some more suited to the shipwrights' needs than others. American red oak has, as its name implies, a russet tinge, but is of rather unpredictable strength and limited durability – although its bending qualities are good. American white oak, though, is a different proposition entirely, being straight grained and creamy white in colour, similar to European oak. Oak from southern states tends to be tougher and harder than that from more northerly regions because it grows faster. Like the European oak, it is a somewhat acidic timber and one that will tend to cause corrosion in ferrous fittings, so the use of such fittings should be avoided in its proximity (unless they are heavily galvanised or made of the highest-quality stainless steel). European oak is fairly prolific throughout the Continent and known by its country of origin: Austrian, French, Spanish, etc. All belong to the same species, although characteristics are altered by the conditions of growth: that occurring in Central Europe being more even in colour and closer textured than the oak of northern climes.

The drying and seasoning of oak is a slow affair and one that has to be constantly monitored as the cells release the moisture with great reluctance. There is, too, a marked tendency to splitting and distortion if the process is unduly hurried. The shrinkage rate is also quite high: often 1 inch per foot on the tangential surface and half that on the radial face. This timber scores on its bending properties, but, if it is to be steamed into shape, it should not be dried beyond 25 per cent moisture content or the risk of fracture increases. Taking into account the competitiveness of world trade in general, it is not surprising that there is a Japanese variant available. It is a pretty good copy, although it is paler and less durable than its European counterparts. Nevertheless, it possesses straight and clear grain and is perfectly acceptable for interior joinery, to which use it is mainly restricted.

At first glance, ash and elm could be confused, for they are quite similar when sawn along the grain. Also, both could just conceivably be mistaken for oak. But their attributes are very different and thus their usefulness to the boatbuilder.

Ash is a straight-grained and very tough wood when force is applied along its length, hence its used in the manufacture of oars. It claims to be the toughest of our home-grown hardwoods, but its durability is indifferent. It is very difficult to plane as

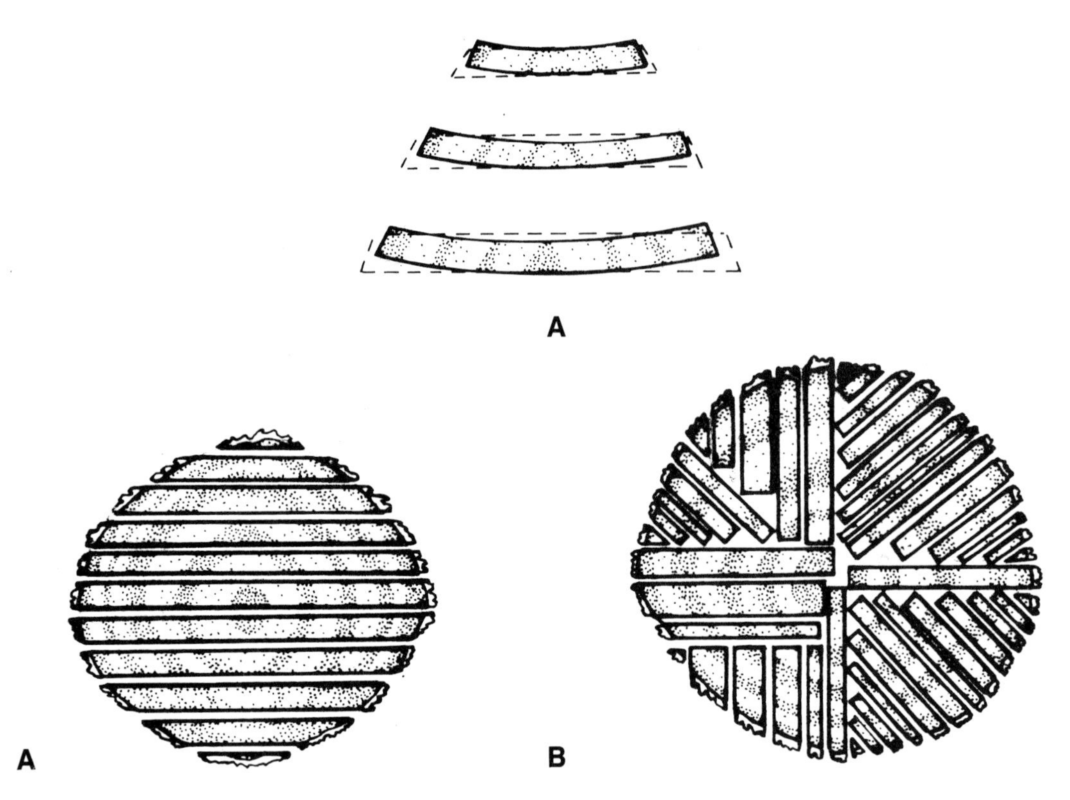

A A plain-sawn plank will shrink and curl as it dries out.

B If at all possible, purchase quarter-sawn timber. From the diagram it can be seen that this method is rather wasteful, but the planks will be far superior. Many yards will quarter-saw to order; a general surcharge seems to be in the region of thirty per cent, but you almost certainly have to buy the entire log or length of log.

areas tend to be double grained, and achieving a smooth-sanded finish calls for a lot of patience. That said, it does bend readily and, so long as it remains accessible for inspection (and, if necessary, remedial action), it can be used for ribs and light frames. Its use is increasingly fashionable as a decorative veneer in modern boats, in spite of its rather lifeless appearance (and its habit of blackening once any defects occur in the varnished finish and allow the penetration of damp).

Elm – more usually employed in Britain for coffins and 'rustic' pub tables – combines many of the least desirable features encountered in timber. However, it can have a most attractive flower to its grain, be highly decorative when burrs are cut for the veneer, and finishes to a delightful honey-gold tone. On the debit side, it splits, rots and obstinately refuses to bend when ordered; thus its use, even when seasoned with loving care, is limited to deadwood, knees, etc – and occasionally planking in small boats. (Here, since it opens and closes according to prevailing extremities of weather with the speed of a Venetian blind, it is highly unreliable.)

A less widely available variety of elm – known as mountain elm or wych-elm – is slightly lighter, more stable and clearer grained. Thus if elm *has* to be used for planking, this is a far superior variety.

Canadian rock elm (usually abbreviated

to CRE on a specification) is, unlike the English country elm, an excellent timber, particularly for the frames of a carvel boat: it is straight grained, fairly knot free, and very tough. However, it is also fairly heavy – and comparatively expensive (if, indeed, it can be tracked down in the first place). Like its English cousin, it requires great care when drying as it is prone to distortion and warping.

Many softwoods have a place in the boat-building world; widely used is the timber from such coniferous trees as Douglas fir, BC (British Columbian) pine, pitchpine, Paraná pine, white pine, spruce and larch. All have a high resin and moisture content and must be thoroughly seasoned. Those grown in plantations tend to be straight grained and knot free for a greater part of their length than those occurring naturally, as the branches form higher up the trunk. The timber is relatively light, works easily along the length, is very flexible and glues readily, but is inclined to split on through-fastening. White pine used to be common in decking and for the planking of small boats as well, and larch was employed to a large extent in the planking of fishing vessels of small to medium size. Pitchpine, although heavy, is clear grained and used for hull planking because it is a tough and durable wood when well seasoned, though it is subject to longitudinal shakes. Spars of cruising yachts and working boats are often made of pitchpine, but only where the consequent weight aloft is not considered to be of paramount importance. For the mast of a racing yacht or dinghy, Sitka spruce would be your first choice. It is tough, straight grained and light – but horrendously expensive when of prime grade.

Cedar is also a softwood, but one that has never found much favour in Britain. Although it is markedly resistant to rot, it has a low impact strength; and finding a clear, knot-free run for planking is not easy. Its low weight has, in spite of these drawbacks, led to the use of both the northern white and the western red cedars in the hull planks of some day boats and small launches. When used in conjunction with epoxy encapsulations systems, its lightness and relative ease of working make it an excellent material for building one-offs – in particular, high-performance sailing craft and multihulls – and its use has recently started to increase.

The finest hardwoods – but should we use them?

Arguably, the most sought-after, highly prized timber for hull planking and decking (and just about every other component part of a vessel if its high cost can be disregarded) is teak – known to the Victorians as the oak of the East. It is a heavy, dense and fibrous wood of great strength, and one that is almost impervious to rot. The trees, which are ring-barked prior to felling in order that they die back slowly (in effect, seasoning the timber 'on the hoof'), grow to enormous size – thus giving long and very clear runs of planking. Working along the length of the grain is simple and the dark golden wood takes an excellent finish, although it does need adequate surface degreasing prior to any application of varnish. Certainly it is not a timber that is readily glued and the use of resorcinol or epoxy will be essential.

Much in demand for laid decks and cockpit seat slats, teak is often left unvarnished and simply scrubbed to maintain the desired appearance (although an excess of zeal will, in the end, erode the wood, leaving fastenings and paying to stand proud). It can, when liberally seasoned with salt spray, prove to be a great irritant to the skin during sunbathing, so never lie on this wood when sunbathing.

Iroko and afrormosia both have many of the qualities of teak, though only the former is used in planking because of its superior stability along the grain. Like teak, both

have a considerable resistance to rot; but they are more liable to split or splinter when worked, and thus need careful handling. Afrormosia, sometimes referred to as Rhodesian teak, is a pleasant mid-brown colour, reminiscent of walnut. It often suffers from double grain but, in spite of this, it is occasionally specified for laid decks – a purpose for which it seems, to put it mildly, rather unsuitable.

Mahogany, one of the loveliest of all hardwoods, may arouse feelings of guilt: should these trees be felled to add to the destruction of the rain forests? Actually, little if any mahogany comes from the areas that have been so appallingly ravaged in the name of market economy. Fortunately, timber is now recognised as a valuable asset to the economies of Third World nations and, under the aegis of non-profit making international development agencies, intensified Agro-forestry programmes are well under way. These ensure vital replanting, realistic pricing – and, in the case of endangered species – conservation.

It is reputed that mahogany became known to the British in 1598 when Sir Walter Raleigh was forced to put into Trinidad to effect urgent running repairs on his vessels. Indigenous timber was felled and the shipwrights were astonished both by the ease with which it could be crafted and by the sheer beauty of the grain and colour. Thereafter, in the best British tradition, no one thought any more about it for three generations! It was a hundred years or so later that its importation on any scale began, but the high price restricted it to cabinet work – and then only for the most affluent members of society.

The finest types of mahogany are Spanish, Cuban and Honduras. These are all the same species, but are much affected by the conditions of growth – with the densest and most closely grained woods coming from trees that have struggled hardest for existence in arid and inhospitable regions. African mahogany, which is far cheaper and easier to obtain, is, if carefully selected, just about acceptable for use in planking and coachroof sides; however, it is short in the grain and can be very brittle. The Spanish – American types, however, are clear, strong and of a mellow purplish-brown colour. As is the case with all dark woods, they fade in sunlight (light woods generally tend to darken).

The higher-quality mahoganies are greatly in demand for boats that are intended to be varnished, elevating the timber to luxury status once more, and for the best veneers (whether these be for interior panels, marine ply for structural use or, of course, for cold moulding).

There are several 'bastard' species that are widely sold for domestic building work; these are greatly inferior and should only be used in a marine environment where neither strength nor the varnished appearance are of great importance.

This list is hardly complete: many other timbers such as native fruitwoods (stable, tough but short in length and useful mainly for grown crooks), beech, chestnut and poplar, and such exotics as satinwood, rosewood and maple, may also be seen. These last, however, are confined to decorative veneers, and only then in the interior joinery of vintage 'custom-built' yachts. Ramin, a white, close-textured hardwood, is occasionally used for inlay and trim (it is uncertain why, since it discolours horribly and holly is superior). Even balsa (which is, oddly enough, categorised as a hardwood) can be employed in boatbuilding, though only as an insulating or encapsulated core material.

Selection of wood: the inseparable criteria

Time, paint and rot may make exact identification of a given species of timber difficult, but, even when it can be ascertained, this is

not to say that replacement with an identical type may be practical or even advisable. If it *is* felt to be essential, though, it may be feasible to purchase excellent (and well-seasoned) second-hand examples from a demolition contractor (or even from the site: it is a matter of being on hand at the right moment). Where teak and mahogany are sought, keep an eye open for refurbishment projects in pubs and banks: both types of premises were fitted with solid counter tops, panelling and heavy doors. If buying oak, ash or other traditional home-grown timbers, carry out at least a cursory inspection to ensure that the good old traditional furniture beetle has not been there before you!

Probably in practice there will not be time available to sort through likely sources of re-usable wood; the alternative is to make use of the resources of a local timber-yard. These vary widely as to the timbers in which they specialise. There should be an opportunity to examine the timber as stored for seasoning and get a good idea of its state of readiness.

Timber, while air drying, is normally stacked as rough sawn planks, each separated from its underlying companion by spacing slips (of wood identical to that comprising the stack) inserted between the boards. It is, unfortunately for those seeking stable boatbuilding timber, most often plain sawn; in other words, the planks are cut vertically through the trunk. This results in a low wastage, but the boards, through the process of drying, shrink and show a marked propensity to curl with the run of the annular rings. To overcome this, the tree can be quarter sawn and, as can be seen from the drawing on page 40, the shrinkage takes place more evenly. The trouble is that there is less usable timber as a result and so the boards themselves are narrower.

The direction of any possible further shrinkage must always be taken into account when building, for an imperceptible amount may well continue over the years – no matter how well the wood was seasoned. This is not only of importance when planking with solid timber, but should not be overlooked if any double-skin construction or cold moulding is envisaged.

Seasoning, stability, strength and sawn section: these four are so closely linked that they should be regarded as inseparable when searching out quality timber for a large-scale restoration project. Finding top-class wood will pay dividends in the long run, but it is not so straightforward a task as it once was. However time-consuming it may prove to be, resist the temptation to settle for second best simply to speed up the start of the construction work.

CHAPTER 5

The timber vessel

Traditional construction: the clinker hull

Timber vessels can conveniently, if rather loosely, be categorised into two types. There are those that popular opinion decrees to be of a proper no-nonsense traditional type: in other words, good substantial planking on frames sawn or steamed to shape. The second type are those built of glued and laminated veneer. The latter are largely post-1945, since glues capable of withstanding a nautical environment were not perfected until the latter days of the war. There was some experimental, and disappointing, use made of glued components in the late 1930s. One example that I saw of this was in a German Windfall class in which the design had specified the inclusion of glued, laminated floors; unfortunately, at the time of survey, these had degenerated into unglued and delaminated ones that had acquired the appearance of an elderly leaf spring as found in a car! Quite a number of boats of the 1950s and 1960s – as well as a small proportion of the few wooden vessels built today – utilised a combination of both methods to good effect. Undoubtedly, the replacement and making good of defective woodwork has been greatly assisted by marine glues and laminating techniques.

The traditional forms of construction can further be subdivided into four main methods: these are *carvel, clinker* (*clencher or lapstrake*), *strip planking* and *diagonal laid*. Vessels may be of either round-bilged section or with a pronounced sharp angle at the turn of the bilge which is known as a chine. This is simpler to loft and build, but regarded as less sea-kindly and less pleasing to the eye – although a rebate to the chine will soften the angle somewhat.

The clinker hull, where the planks or strakes overlap one another and are through-fastened to ribs and one another for the entire run of each plank, is one of the oldest existing forms. It is possibly predated only by such basic native craft as balsa and papyrus rafts, coracles of woven wicker or with skins of hide and, of course, the primitive dug-out canoes.

The clinker hull is familiar to us in the historic guise of the Viking longship and its direct descendants, the Shetland sixareens. Until the beginning of the last century, it was common in a great many working fishing vessels of medium size and was only gradually superseded by the carvel form with far heavier planking and sturdier internal frames. Most of the inshore fishing craft, beached at the end of a working day, were of this type. In fact, they still are – for this hull form, when regularly checked and maintained, can (barring accidents) have a life span well in excess of its owner! Even apart from the Thames wherries and elegant pleasure skiffs where the art of the shipwright is at its peak, clinker building can produce a fine strong workboat hull that has a great functional beauty of line. Possibly something of the image of the working boat remained associated with the clinker boat and lessened its appeal to yachtsmen, for, apart from ubiquitous lifeboat and fishing boat conversions, there were relatively few yachts expressly designed with this type of

A Norwegian-built clinker Folkboat, sadly neglected and awaiting restoration. The external appearance suggests the hull to be sound, although the coachroof and doghouse have been subjected to years of misguided attempts to cobble them together; removal and replacement are inevitable.

construction. After the Second World War, though, the demand for reasonably priced small cruising and racing yachts saw a resurgence: the Folkboat, its cousin, the Stella, such shoal-draught and able cruisers as the Mapleleaf, Finesse and Dauntless, and also the Kestrel, which (like the Folkboat) was actively raced as a class.

There seems to be no manner of construction which is without certain inherent faults. In the case of clinker planking, repairs – even to localised areas – can be difficult, and may (especially in the case of the garboard) require removal of the adjacent plank. The ribs, being on the light side, are liable to split, snap and also to rot around the through-fastened copper nails. If a high proportion of ribs in close proximity to one another suffer damage for any reason and are not speedily made good, there is a risk that the hull may distort. Refastening, whether the nails are riveted with copper roves or clenched over, takes some patience too. In a small boat with ribs closely spaced, but less than an inch across, this will often mean that the ribs have to be dowelled first.

Fastenings are frequently responsible for splits and shakes in hull planking, a process worsened by the tendency for some clinker craft to be built to a limited price specification. Sometimes poor-quality timber was used to cut costs.

Unless a boat has unique appeal, it might be wise to pass the purchase over should more than 30 per cent of ribs be faulty – especially if all these occur close together in a load-bearing area. True, each rib can be doubled by inserting another alongside

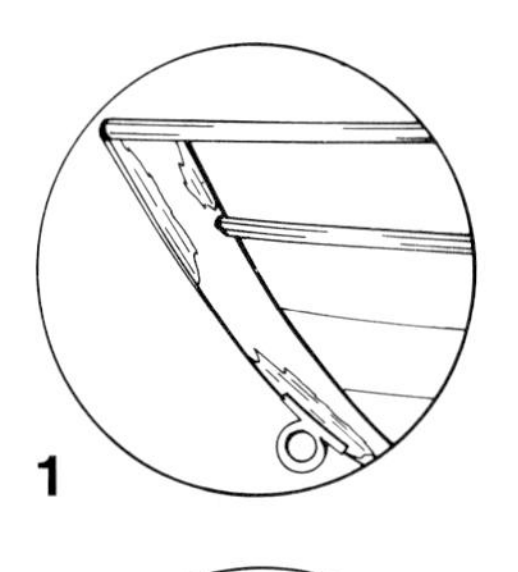

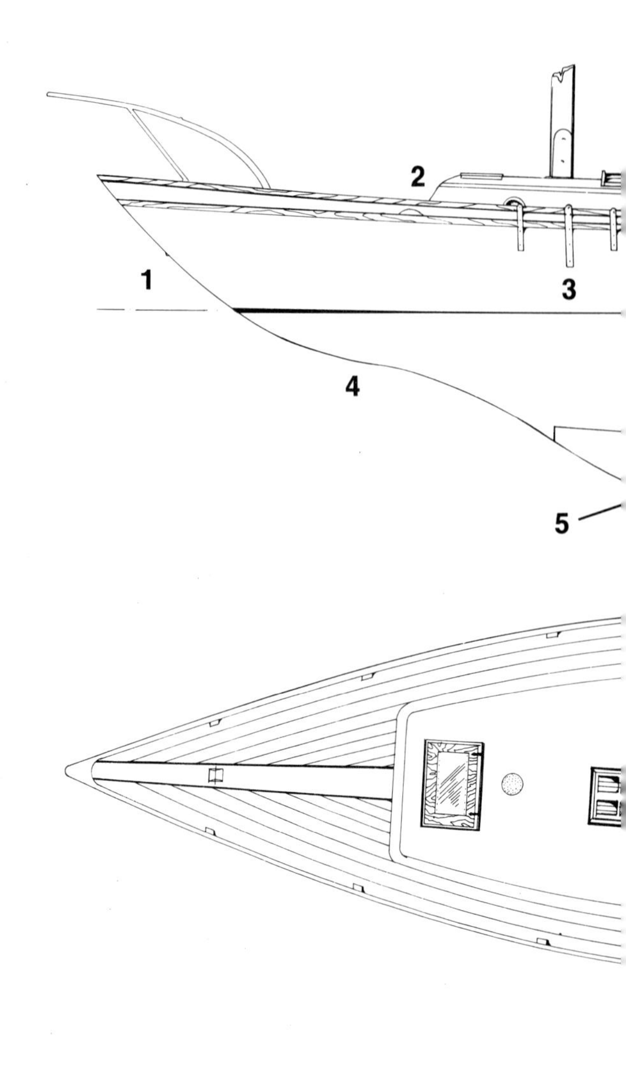

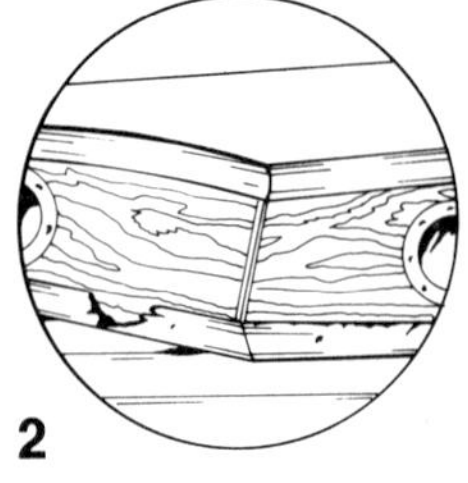

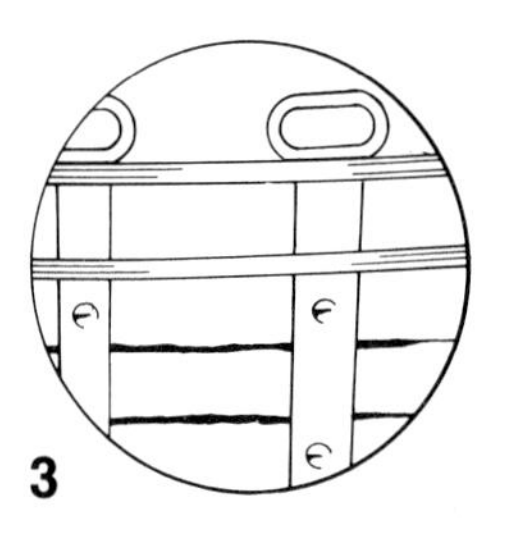

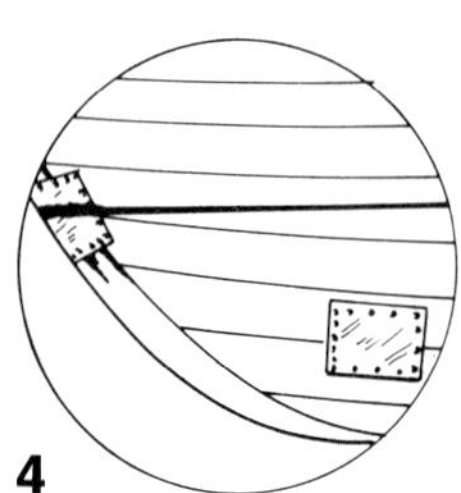

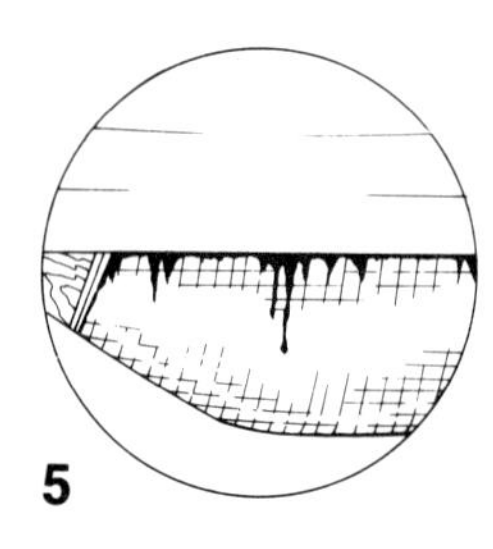

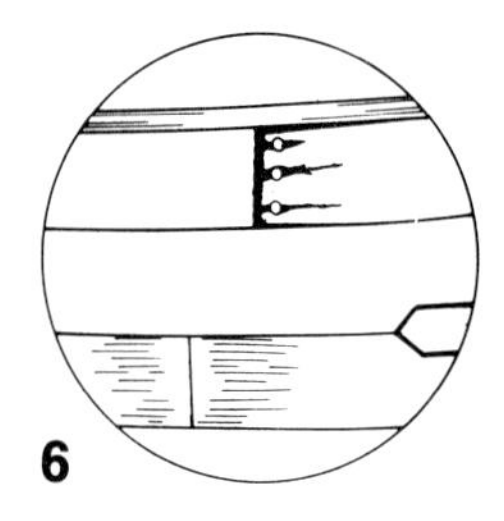

Structural faults on the external hull: timber carvel yacht.
1 Expect to discover rot in the stem where iron fastenings or a bobstay eye pass through the oak.
2 Rotted deck canvas, poorly paid seams or a damaged quadrant moulding around the coachroof's lower edge can allow water penetration which leads to rot.
3 The first evidence that a hull has been strained in the case of a sailing vessel is usually manifest in the seams around the chainplates – also the counter and the sheerline.
4 A tingle may indicate nothing more sinister than an old skin fitting which has been removed, but beware of any which extend over seams or in the stem itself.
5 Sealant which appears to have been forced into the upper edge of the keel from the outside suggests a last ditch attempt at curing the seepage of corroded keel bolts. Shims or packing pieces at the forward end are sometimes indicative of a heavy impact with an underwater object, in which case the bolts of the keel may be bent out of alignment.
6 Points to watch when inspecting the planking: fastenings too closely positioned to the butt end causing the wood to split and the plank to spring outwards; a graving piece over a seam which may distort the plank; and over-enthusiastic use of a

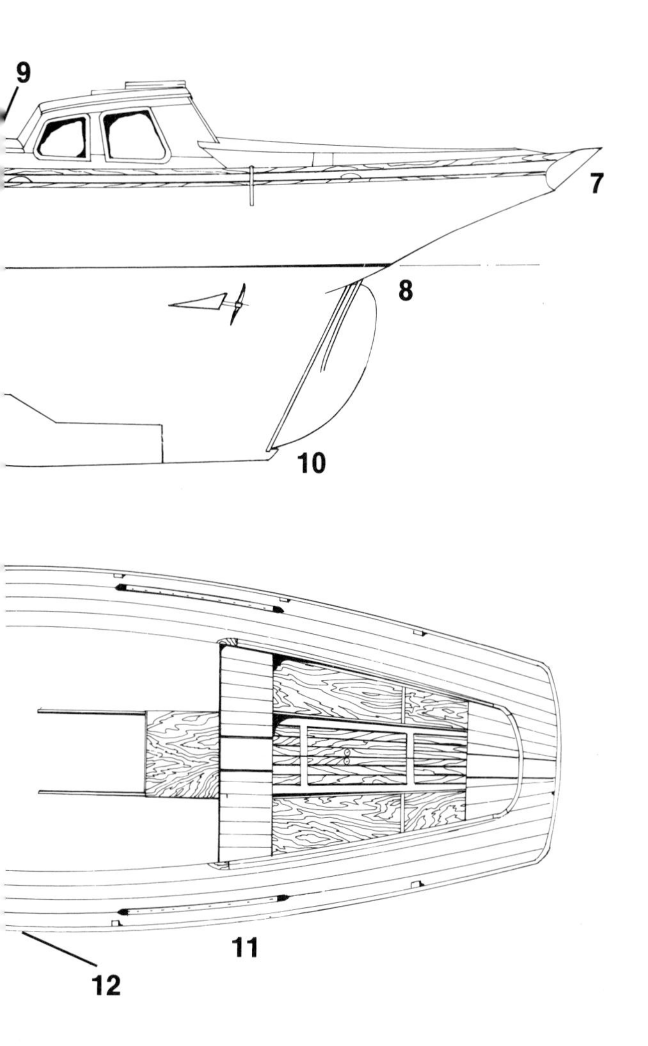

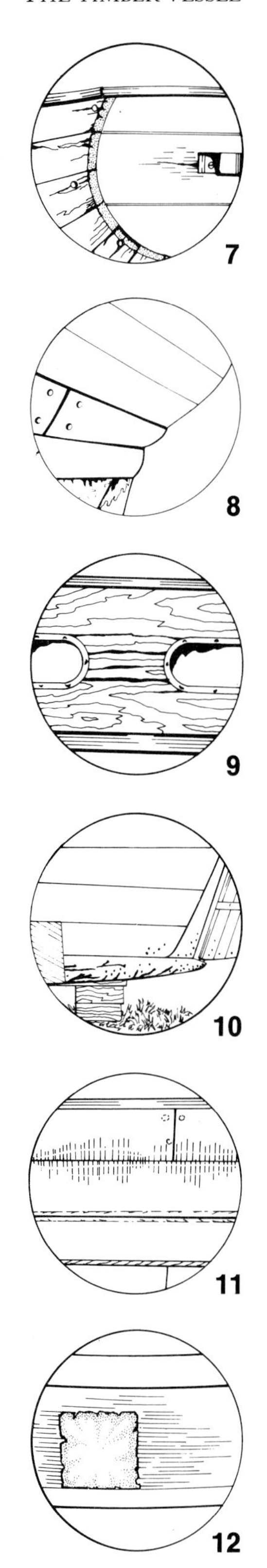

plane to fair in butt ends after re-fastening. Sometimes the butts will be found to have less than half the thickness of the strakes!

7 Splitting and erosion of the hood ends aft.

8 Planking which has curled due to shrinkage. This is very common, and particularly noticeable in areas of curvature such as the garboard strake. Unskilled cutting and chamfering of the planking at the stern exacerbates this condition, which is unsightly rather than a serious structural impairment.

9 Splitting of the coachroof sides between windows. Filling may hide the signs to some extent, particularly under paint (as opposed to varnish). Glueing and splining is the only certain cure – after first removing window frames or portlights.

10 Evidence of the dreaded gribble worm: try to find out if the area is noted for the presence of this beastie, and if so be extra wary when you examine the underbody.

11 Eroded plank edges, usually the result of careless stripping out of old caulking. The only answer may be to spline affected edges.

12 Rot in the covering board around the extended frames which form the bulwark; very common but easily obscured from a surveyor. Pay close attention to the internal frames and suspect capilliary rot.

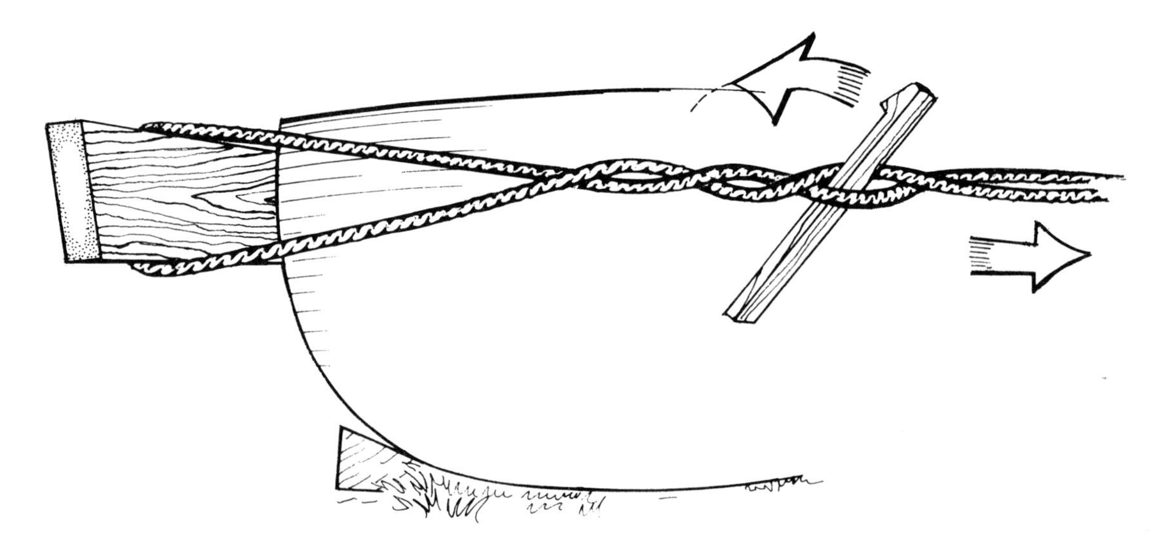

Perhaps the most useful device known to the boatbuilder: the Spanish windlass. This can exert enormous pressure to spring planks or sections of glassfibre. Care should be taken to secure the lever, however, as once under pressure, it can lash back and cause serious injury.

while leaving the defective one in place, but this smacks of a botched job – albeit a common one. It is far better to steam a replacement or to laminate one *in situ*.

Carvel construction

As a rule, the carvel planked hull has heavier scantlings for a given overall length and is reckoned to be more robust (albeit less limber) than a clinker boat of comparable size and type. Even though modern technology produces lighter and tougher hulls, this time-honoured method has little to equal it for the cruising yacht or displacement power boat. All that can really be argued against it is the necessity for the attentive care and meticulous fault investigation that is an ineradicable part of such a complicated specimen of timber engineering.

Involving, as it generally does, the use of differing timbers for frames, floors, beams, knees and planking, it can be seen that the first priority of designer and builder alike is to produce a first-rate product. But the very nature of the carvel hull means that there are literally dozens of inaccessible areas where moisture and then rot can develop unnoticed over the years. The use of timber preservative on new boats and also on new timber employed in restoration is of great benefit, but those vessels built half a century ago mostly relied on creosote or paint – and a dousing with the former does tend to have a deleterious effect on the appearance and adhesion of the latter. Prior to that time, a few bags of cement-mix in the bilges was not looked upon with disfavour: at least it made any rot invisible!

The planking of a carvel vessel fits closely on the interior of the seams, but the outer edges, which are slightly open, are filled with caulking cotton (or oakum: hemp saturated with Stockholm tar in the case of large vessels). Red lead and putty mixed to a soft consistency is generally inserted prior to the fibrous material, with a layer of stopping applied afterwards and smoothed flat. There is an intentional allowance for the expansion and contraction of the seams according to humidity of the environment. When acquiring a boat that has been laid up ashore for any length of time the seams will almost certainly have opened; indeed, this can occur in a matter of days during the summer months, with any dark coloured paint on the hull accelerating any drying-out.

Prior to recommissioning, guesswork will be needed in order to assess the rapidity with which the hull will take up (the time required for the wood to swell and the seams to tighten accordingly). Hardwood, with a lower initial shrinkage rate, will swell at a correspondingly slower rate than most softer timbers.

The greatest care should be taken to ensure seams are not over-caulked, for if cotton and timber expand to an unforeseen degree, some stress will incur to both the seams and planking. Use of a thiokol-based polysulphide composition stopping, which will be extruded from seams as they take up, is very effective as any excess can be simply trimmed away and, once fully cured, the filler can be sanded and painted. This type of paying may be expensive, but it is very effective. Tallow smeared along a suspect seam is occasionally advocated; in theory it prevents leakage as a result of minor defects in caulking or paying, but in practice its very presence may prevent the hull taking up, for water is unable to permeate the fibres of cotton or timber.

Paint that has been inadvertently allowed to penetrate the seam and thereby seal the plank edges will also impair the ability to expand, because moisture will be unable to infiltrate the timber.

Variants of carvel build

Splined seams – that is, where a timber slip is inserted between the planks in place of fibrous caulking – are seen from time to time and are intended to produce a tight, rigid and leak-resistant hull; moreover one unaffected by extremes of temperature. The idea is excellent so long as the timber involved is perfectly stable and the shrinkage of planking and splines is virtually identical. The splines are glued and, as modern resin glues are stronger by far than the wood to which they adhere, it is possible during an extended lay-up in exceptionally dry conditions for the hull planking to shrink and split – not along the glue line, but through the length of its own cellular structure. But, at its best, a splined hull can look as good as one that is moulded; and, since there are no contrasting lines of paying, it is more attractive when varnished.

Seam batten carvel is, as the term would suggest, a system whereby each seam is backed internally by a batten, with the outer edge being glued or caulked. Not often seen today, this method does allow the use of slightly lighter timber for the planking as each batten becomes, in effect, a stringer giving longitudinal rigidity. Sometimes called ribband carvel, it is commoner on chine hulls where it is not necessary to fair the internal section of the batten to the extent required in a round-bilged format.

A seam batten carvel does necessitate a wary eye when a survey is carried out, as sometimes the seams have been reinforced for a very good reason – such as undue ingress of water! If this is the case, an examination could confirm that the stringers are present as a last resort; suspect this if they abruptly stop short on encountering internal joinery only to resume their interrupted course on the other side (there is cause for certainty rather suspicion if they do not extend further). Unless glue alone is the means of securing the battens, the planks are susceptible to an increased risk of splitting because any nails or screws will have to pass dangerously close to their vulnerable edges.

The fastenings of a carvel boat may be of half-a-dozen or more types: plain iron spikes, copper, iron or bronze dumps (blunt headless nails, twisted or notched for extra bite – and very hard to extract), copper nails, barbed ring nails, and screws of almost any chosen metal. Add to these assorted flooring brads, clouts and coach bolts, and it is easy to see the immense

A double-diagonal hull of the type commonly constructed for fast patrol vessels and air-sea rescue craft. The structure is tough and light but depends, to some extent, upon the soundness of the inter-skin lining, which may be linen or paper treated with marine glue or paint. Careful filling and fairing of the seams can restore such a hull to a good state, but more extensive repairs may call for the services of a professional shipwright.

potential for serious corrosion when in contact with salt water; and also, there is the problem of incipient electrolysis that can lead to localised rot in the timbers.

Diagonal planking

Double diagonal planking (often a misnomer since a vessel may commonly have three rather than two skins, and one or more of these may be laid fore and aft) is often associated with the construction of light naval craft of chine hull form. This includes fast rescue launches and small gun-boats, to say nothing of service and patrol vessels, tenders and admirals' barges. Its use is not generally recorded as preceding the First World War; this, though, is incorrect as a number of fast cruising yachts were built in this manner before the turn of the century.

I owned one such vessel for a number of years: a Linton-Hope design, 35 feet over all and with soft, almost semi-circular, sections that suited her well for conditions in the Thames Estuary. She was constructed from two skins of teak, the outer being fore and aft, and the inner one diagonal. Though almost frameless, she was virtually as tight and fair as when she left the builders yard in 1898 and is, as far as I am aware, still sailing, despite the indignities I wrought upon her some thirty years ago!

In all cases, watertight integrity depends to an extent upon the layer of thin canvas or flax that is laid between each skin and sealed with the lavish use of paint; unfortunately, even minor damage to the outer skin, or simply the slight shrinkage of each strip, may allow water to penetrate between skins. This will rot the fabric and then the hull itself. Since glue is not as a rule employed in the construction, the vessels are mostly through-fastened, usually with copper nails and roves; these also erode slightly over the years and allow moisture to permeate.

The diagonal system, especially when used to produce a hard chine hull, offers the merit of straightforward construction, and indeed many designs are available for the amateur to build. The availability of decommissioned, large-engined types sold off by the Ministry of Defence means that many have been converted to motor yachts and at a very reasonable cost. The continuance of a trouble-free life span is dependent, to a large extent, on whether the conversion has resulted in the inaccessibility of areas liable to rot, while at the same time increasing the likelihood of deterioration by the inadequate provision for ventilation in built-in fitments and full linings of the shipside. Admittedly, it is difficult to obtain the appearance of an expensively fitted-out luxury yacht without fairly lavish use of panelling and upholstery, but air must be allowed to circulate in order to prevent the condensation that leads to rot from within. It goes without saying, or should do, that all linings and soles should be easily removable so that inspection of the hull can be carried out at regular intervals.

Strip planking

Strip planking is something of a hybrid form of construction, and one that enjoyed the reputation of being suitable for the amateur. Each plank is both glued and nailed to the next, with the strakes being narrower than would be the case in carvel construction. Instead of being chamfered for a close fit, each plank has one convex edge and one concave one, thus allowing sufficient curvature to follow the sections of a round bilge hull. In reality, without the additional fore and aft tapering essential to the more traditional building method, it is not easy to achieve any degree of fairness in the garboard area and it is often all too obvious, particularly in the case of a conventional deep-keeled sailing craft, that it has been home built. For either a motor vessel or a sailing vessel with a separate ballast keel and no tuck in the garboards, it is a good form of construction as it is quite light, tough and without the heavy internal frames of a carvel hull.

A number of vessels were built commercially using this method, although the advent of glassfibre removed some of its attractions. Many were resin and scrim sheathed at the time of building, and this only adds to the major single disadvantage of strip planking: it is extremely awkward to repair. Unless a portion of affected planking can be replaced with a purpose-laminated section (or possibly one laid up over an in-hull mould), several adjoining planks may have to be cut back – or taken out in their entirety – to reach the repair site. Since these are glued and fastened with nails (often barbed ring nails), the chance of removing any portion intact is small. As the internal scantlings are on the light side, the shape of the hull is to all intents and purposes dependent upon the integrity of the external planking. The removal of a large portion – necessary to facilitate repairs – can cause distortion; the erection of some form of internal and exterior bracing is therefore a wise precaution.

Veneer construction – sheet ply

Since the majority of problems encountered in a timber hull tend to occur either in the immediate vicinity of such essential components as beams, knees, frames and floors and are either the result of, or exacerbated by, the effect of water upon through-fastenings, surely a boat constructed from veneer, whether moulded or in the form of

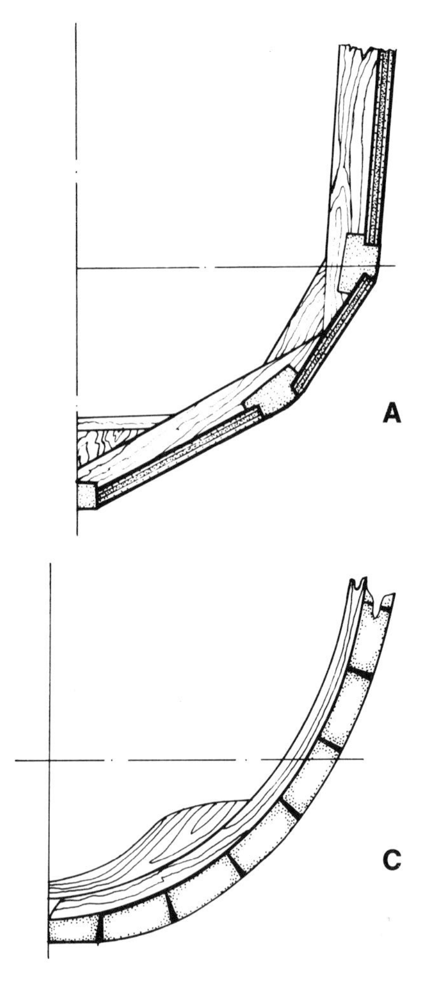

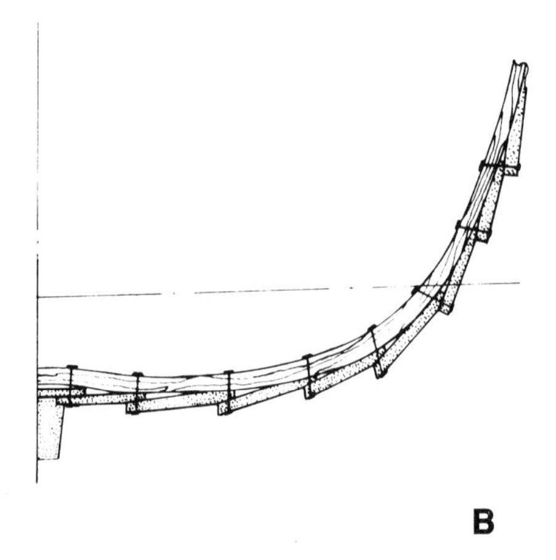

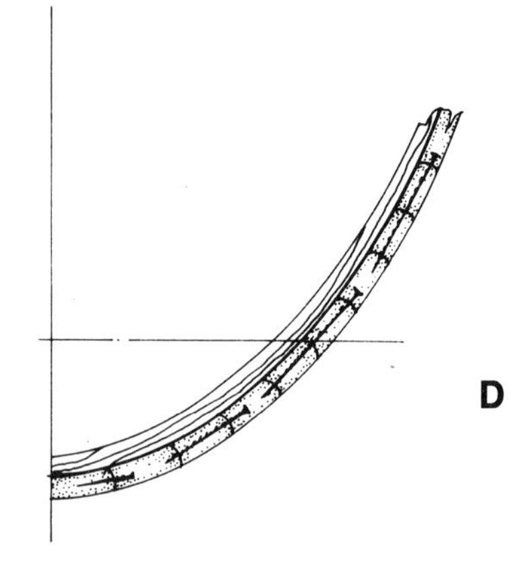

Sections through common types of timber construction.

A Plywood: chine with rebated stringers to 'soften' the sharp angle of the turn of the bilge. Often it is possible to virtually merge the ply sheets at bows and stern and thereby greatly improve the appearance of the hull.
B A clinker or clencher-built hull: fairly light and closely spaced ribs with overlapping planking fastened through each other and to the rib.
C A carvel hull with the planks laid edge to edge and each fastened directly to a frame. The inner edges of the planking should be tight; the slight gap in outer edges sealed by caulking or, occasionally, by glued splines or fillets.
D Strip planking: each plank fastened with barbed ring nails. This method was regarded as suitable for amateur construction and certainly the planks are easier to loft. Repairs, however, are very difficult.

sheet ply, should be completely trouble free? After all, there are considerably fewer internal structural items and the hull and superstructure mostly held together by glue or resin. If only this were the case!

The idea that a classic boat can be of glued veneer construction guarantees raised eyebrows in certain circles and that is putting it mildly. However, to preclude such vessels from being categorised as classics is shortsighted in the extreme. The advance of technology associated with the advent of reliable resin glues produced a quantum leap in boat construction, with small craft becoming available to those with limited funds. Such boats were not restricted to simple family dinghies, either.

The construction of quite an able 'pocket cruiser' was made possible by the innovative design skill of the late Robert Tucker. Perhaps his most famous little boat is the 17 foot 3 inch Silhouette, a pretty sloop built by the thousand. They were updated and/or revamped for glassfibre, but they always retained the original spirit of an uncomplicated resilient and buoyant explorer of creek, river and estuary. (However, because of the short waterline length and the combination of bilge and centreline ballast keels, they were lamentably slow.)

Quite a few such vessels went as far afield as Holland, and a Caprice, which is only fractionally longer, is famous for a round-the-world venture. Tucker's designs have not yet quite achieved classic status, though Maurice Griffiths's Eventide, Golden Hind and Waterwitch closely approach it – perhaps due to their solid appearance and the extended voyages many have made.

There are also vessels such as the Van de Stadt-designed Black Soo, a light displacement sloop with dinghy-type hull and ballasted fin. This is capable of planing in bursts at over 20 knots, creating a new attitude to speed under sail. Some plywood fast motor vessels also claim (whether or not with any degree of justification) to be classics, and are described as such when offered for sale. The would-be purchaser must make his or her own decision on this, but without doubt certain marine-ply vessels can be categorised as classics.

Hot- and cold-moulded veneers

Less doubt is engendered by cold and hot-moulded boats, and those produced by the hot-moulding techniques of Fairey Marine in the late 1950s and 1960s (where the hulls were vacuum formed and baked in an autoclave to ensure absolute and uniform curing of the glue lines) are in great demand. The power craft – Huntress, Huntsman and Swordsman – are good-looking planing vessels that are capable, depending upon the engine type and installation, of speeds belying the date of original construction; the hulls too are almost always in excellent condition for their age.

The sailing cruisers have drawn a dedicated band of enthusiasts, although the inherent attraction of the Atalanta (which is the best known) may not be immediately obvious to the uninitiated. Ingenuity there is in plenty so far as the twin lifting keels, light displacement hull with centre cockpit and blister coachroof are concerned; but aesthetic appeal seems, to the jaundiced eye, rather limited. Undeniably, though, it is an interesting vessel and one that was well ahead of its time. It sailed fast off the wind, was docile to handle, and could be trailed, beached or, for that matter, creep into a creek accessible only to a dinghy or duck punt! Part of the fascination undoubtedly lies within: the snaking complications of the hydraulic pipework and pumps involved in the operation of the lifting keels are reminiscent of the cockpit of a Mosquito fighter bomber of the Second World War (when, indeed, much of the wood technology was pioneered).

But, without doubt, the hot-moulding process has proved its worth. I have inspected many of these vessels, power and sail, and the basic structure is, unless subjected to physical damage or ill-considered improvements, basically sound.

However, the condition of a cold-moulded hull after a few years is a different matter, and there are two main reasons for this. The first is that, as with strip planking, cold moulding was (and still is) deemed to be a means of construction within the scope of any amateur who was averagely competent with tools. The second is that, when undertaken by a commercial yard, the

A localised repair to a delaminated cold-moulded hull showing removal of the affected veneer. The inner veneer skin can, if necessary, be held in place while the glue cures by a length of timber spragged across the interior of the hull.

technique was used a great deal to produce lightweight offshore racing yachts, often of quite extreme design. These, no matter how perfect they looked upon launching, were not necessarily envisaged as having a working life much in excess of twenty years. More care was taken to reduce excess weight than to eliminate the potential for rot. This propensity towards self-destruction has thinned the ranks of such boats, which were mainly products of the early and mid-1960s, before glassfibre was fully exploited. Some are still sailing and capable of being restored to their former structural strength, but many have been doubled, stiffened and patched – thus bearing the scars of a losing battle with stress and decay.

With this type, the hull, built over a mould, generally had steamed slender ribs inserted, closely spaced, after the lamination was completed. This was not altogether satisfactory as the ribs required fastening through the veneer skin itself, thereby losing all the advantages of a seamless hull. Later boats were often able to dispense with ribs as building know-how increased; they relied instead upon interior bulkheads (and the decking) for transverse rigidity.

Repairs can be difficult

As with strip planking and the diagonal hull, cold moulding is difficult to repair; unlike the former two, though, deterioration even when quite severe, is not always apparent. And in no other type of timber boatbuilding is it quite so easy for hull defects to be literally in-built without anyone being aware of it. These latent defects are usually the result of imperfect spreading of the glue between the veneers, fluctuations in temperature, or careless mixing of the two-part resorcinol resins commonly used. While curing, the veneers are held in place with staples that are then removed once they have fulfilled their function. Sometimes one or two are overlooked and water may permeate the structure as these corrode.

By no means are such imperfections restricted to boats built by amateurs – although to levy accusations at a yard of any repute would bring down a deluge of wrath and indignation. The fact is that, even having located an area of rot or delamination, the exact cause or date of onset is almost impossible to prove.

A boat constructed by an amateur may have an increased risk of problems with the glue lines simply because it is not always possible to achieve controlled conditions, but the fact remains that, as with strip-planked hulls, the curvature is simply too pronounced for the wood. The specified thickness and width of veneers may be impossible to bend without splitting, either at the time of building or at a later date. Even a thorough soaking prior to the stapling in position may not eradicate this. After the passage of the couple of days needed for encouragement, the wood may still split when dried and finally positioned. If the staples do not immediately retain the timber in the desired situation, there should be no hesitation: whip the offending veneer away at once and scrape the glue off before it has a chance to dry. Once the curing process has started, the glue is virtually impossible to remove and new glue will not adhere to the old.

There are still fine and beautiful cold-moulded vessels in existence, many of which represent the most advanced thinking of their era. It should not be forgotten, though, that the heyday was about thirty years ago and few craft of any type survive such a time span in a perfect state. It is not an exaggeration to say that, of all desirable types, these cold-moulded craft require careful scrutiny more than most.

Vessels built from plywood sheets, of single or multi-chine hull form, are, by the simple nature of both design and construction, far less inclined to suffer from such deep-seated and hard-to-detect faults (in fact, delamination of the inner skins of a moulded vessel may be impossible to ascertain without a core sample). This at any rate is the theory; in practice, since many of them are home built, they too have their little problems. Many of these problems are undetectable, because of heavy-handed use of glue and sawdust in strategic sites (the most notable being along improperly faired internal stringers).

No matter how soundly built and carefully finished, a plywood hull is often argued to be unattractive and slab sided – though this is not entirely a view I share. Certainly some design constrictions are imposed by the characteristics of the boards (which will not accept more than a very limited amount of compound curvature), but the chines at stem and stern can be almost invisible and a boot-top line will mitigate the angle amidships. The material itself is oustandingly tough and fairly impact resistant; and the hull of, for example, a 30 footer – whether power or sail – can be light enough to plane or strong and heavy enough to shunt ice according to the design parameters.

If there is a single factor to be wary of, it is that of the building specification, or, rather, faithful adherence to it. Both the ply and the glue used must be of appropriate kinds and there is no way of ascertaining whether they are, unless the boat is from a reputable builder. There is, in any case, quite a difference between first-rate marine ply and the cheapest (although both may conform to BS 1088); and, short of demolishing a small area of the boat and examining a section of the wood concerned, it may not be possible to reach a firm conclusion. Admittedly, there are cases where it will be pretty obvious that a boat has been cobbled together from shuttering plywood and household glue, but, however, there will be some instances where insufficient evidence is available for the surveyor to make a definite judgement.

The safest guide is the general standard of interior finish and attention to such important details as quadrant mouldings and capping strips around each exposed piece of end grain ply (delamination starts here) and a fairly even width along the stringers. The presence of stopping (or preferably, its absence) in the joint between stringers and the internal hull planking (also, in the exterior chines and butt joints) helps form an opinion: if not as to the materials themselves, at least to the integrity of the builder. With very few exceptions, skilled craftsmen do not work with second-rate timber or resin.

CHAPTER 6

The external hull: terminal afflictions

Before starting to survey the external hull, it has to be realised that no form of timber construction is totally trouble free and that there are many ailments that can be regarded as exclusive to the traditional yacht. This does not necessarily imply defects or weaknesses in the actual building as such, but no vessel can hope to withstand the passage of time completely unscathed. A period of ten years is quite long enough for wet rot to start manifesting itself, for fastenings to corrode, and for the boat in question to have suffered damage from collisions or stranding.

Certain afflictions cannot be successfully treated. Some, such as dry rot, are not only pretty much beyond help, but also very contagious. Indeed, one boatyard manager recommends burning the vessel concerned to prevent further spreading of the disease.

Hogging

Most terminal defects will be apparent from the initial cursory external examination, but others may require a quick glance into the interior. Immediately obvious in a clinker, carvel or diagonally built boat is the condition known as hogging. Here the internal backbone, or hog, has either been strained and distorted, or possibly even partially broken, because of grounding – usually across a sand bar or bank. The term is frequently uttered in hushed and doom-laden tones, but is often bandied about without real justification. This is because what appears to be a major symptom of hogging – distortion to the sheerline and planking amidships – may be produced by other more mundane causes. True, these symptoms might be sufficiently unsightly to deter a purchaser from further inspection, but there are plenty of cases where the actual structure may not be irrevocably ruined (although the cost of remedial work will still need careful consideration).

First, though, the cause of any distortion does have to be established. This is simple enough on a long-keeled vessel such as a smack or motor cruiser; here, if the hull is truly hogged, the external keel is likely to droop at the ends and pronounced midship hollowing will be visible along the length. The garboard planks will almost certainly have opened excessively and, in all probability, if the case is severe, others amidships will also gape. Butt joints too may have sprung outwards, and also the stem and hood ends at the stern.

Often, unfairness attributed to hogging is caused by a thoughtless lay-up procedure and careless positioning of shores (old habits die hard and the same mistakes are, astonishingly, witnessed over and over again). Some practices, which might not (with any luck) result in harm over a five-month period in the damp winter weather of Britain, will have severe consequences over a longer period.

A 25 foot Glen class yacht, once owned by the author.
Above: The sheer-line had distorted through shoring with lines rove through the cap shroud chainplates. In this photo, both these and the chainplates for the fore lowers have been removed, along with deck hardware, toerails and rubbing strake, prior to sheathing the deck and plank edge with GRP.

Below: Launching – after building up false bulwarks, fitting a new rubbing band to create the illusion of a concave sheer, and caulking and paying gaping seams and varnishing the hull. The drawback with this method, if applied on a one design hull, is that it may de-class the yacht. However, in a case where the class has been disbanded (or other alterations have been made to convert the vessel for cruising, as was the case with this particular boat) the cosmetic improvement more than repays the effort.

The most damaging single action is to reeve a lashing through chainplates or to deck fittings, because, if the ground settles at all (and, as yet, not all boatyards have concreted hard standing), upward strain will be transmitted via the chainplates. This will, in nearly all timber vessels, eventually cause the midships seams in the area to open and the sheerline to pull upwards at that point (with a corresponding dip fore and aft of the hump). This looks unsightly in the extreme and means that, once the immediate cause is removed, the seams must be recaulked (or, in some cases, a complete plank refitted). It does not, though, automatically rule out a successful restoration.

Similar distortion is also commonplace in light, long-ended racing yachts such as the Metre classes; here, while ill-judged laying-up procedures do create most of the damage (the overhangs being most vulnerable to strain unless properly supported), stress will have been imposed by the rig itself. Any undulations at gunwale will be exacerbated because of the flat sheerline often adopted in these craft.

A cosmetic cure

Even allowing that integrity of hull structure can be restored, a wavering profile is not easy to rectify – at least, not where the intention is to maintain faithfully the original lines of the vessel. This criterion precludes the one fairly uncomplicated way of effecting a cosmetic cure (and leaves little alternative but the replacement of the entire top strake of the hull and relaying the deck).

However, where strict adherence to the original design is not of paramount importance, a degree of lateral thinking can be brought to bear upon the problem and an entirely new and fair sheerline be created. It is seldom realistic to hope to follow the exact original line, and the new sheer will need to be of pronounced curvature if the eye is to be fooled into accepting it without reservation. The method of achieving this complete 'new look' could hardly claim to be strictly in accordance with the best shipwrights' practice, but it works remarkably well in just about every case. It must be admitted, though, that it is far easier to carry out on a medium displacement craft; one under 50 feet or so in length.

Although quite straightforward, it is a painstaking job and, since the ultimate appearance of the boat depends upon it, the time entailed should not be stinted. The first essential is the removal of any toerails, fittings at the extreme deck edge, and any fabric deck coverings. Paint should be stripped from any surfaces, although the resin of a GRP-sheathed deck can be left intact. The run along the deck edge has to be free of dirt or grease and ready to accept glue or resin. If a rubbing strake is fitted, this too will have to be removed since its eventual resiting will underline the new sweep of the sheer.

The success or failure of the job depends entirely upon meticulous measurement, backed up by visual assessment, before and during actual construction. This being the case, first cut a cardboard template. Tack this lightly along the top strake and mark the intended upper line of the sheer and the lower one of the repositioned rubbing band with a crayon or thick felt-tip pen, so it can be easily seen at a distance. As soon as an acceptable line is sketched in, stand back and admire the result (or, alternatively, start all over again if the first attempt does not look quite right). Then start the building: a new bulwark will be glued (or, in the case of a glassfibre-sheathed deck, be seated upon a layer of resin) and through-fastened along the length of the margin (and to the underlying shelf if the decks are of plywood). This is easiest if two or three laminations are laid one above the other (as shown in the diagram) since the bow and stern will be deeper than the waist. The uppermost lamination can, in that case, be pre-shaped prior to fixing. So far, all is simple enough: the upper edge is faired and capped (see diagram C).

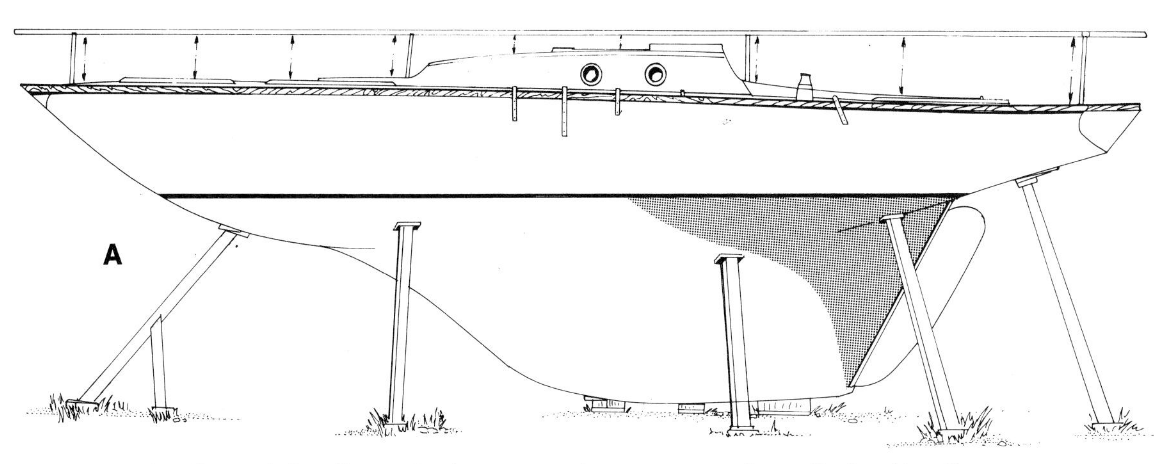

Dealing with a distorted sheerline: a simple cure (or perhaps more accurately a disguise) and one which is very effective on a small yacht or cruiser.

A Strain, either through years of hard sailing or, just as likely, years of being laid up with lines to supports rove through the chainplates or beaching legs, distorts the sheerline and causes the midships seams to gape. In many cases the seams can be caulked or, if really necessary, splined, but the undulating sheerline remains as a testament to past mis-treatment!

The first stage is to strip all covering from the deck edge, remove rubbing strakes and toerails, and then set up a datum from which to decide the new sheerline. A rigid batten set up on deck and a measured constant height from the waterline may be helpful.

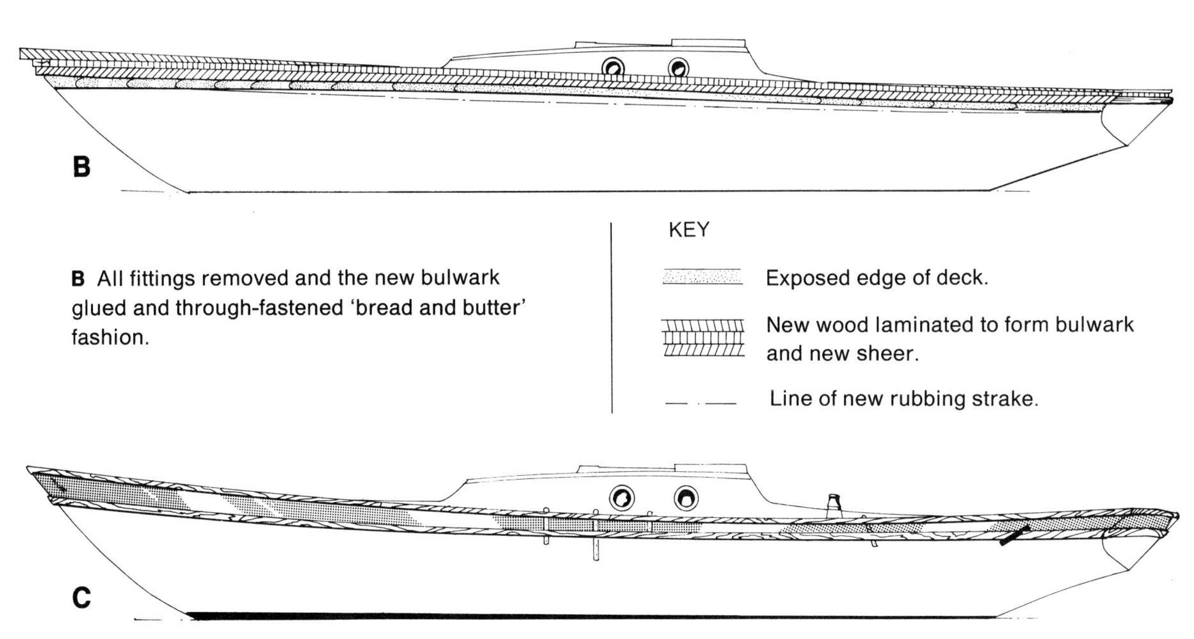

B All fittings removed and the new bulwark glued and through-fastened 'bread and butter' fashion.

KEY

Exposed edge of deck.

New wood laminated to form bulwark and new sheer.

Line of new rubbing strake.

C The end result after filling and fairing the deck edge and sealing with paint or epoxy. With a new capping rail and lowered rubbing strake it should be virtually impossible to detect that this operation has been carried out!

But the real skill consists in fitting the new rubbing strake; this will, amidships, be lower than the original to create the illusion of a continuous bulwark of uniform depth for the vessel's entire length. Any end grain timber of the deck exposed by the removal of the old rubbing strake must be sealed, all holes left by fastenings should be dowelled, and the greatest attention paid to the finish. The end result should be a remarkable improvement. If bulwarks are already in existence, so much the easier; the major task will then be lowering the rubbing strake, although, in a traditional vessel of any size (and a good number of those with bulwarks are), a stringer may have to be positioned inside the hull to accept through-fastenings. In no way does this operation mean that essential remedial work to planking and seams can be overlooked; such a view would, even in the short term, be asking for serious structural trouble.

This technique can also be employed to distract the eye from a superstructure of ungainly height that is impracticable to remove or radically alter. The extent to which this is an improvement is governed by the freeboard, but height is generally more acceptable in the topsides than in the top hamper.

Nevertheless, if hogging has definitely occurred, with severe twisting and wringing of the hull planking, it is better to forget the boat. It is unlikely that a sailing yacht so affected could ever be restored to its optimum performance; with a motor vessel, intended for inland waters only, it is just possible that once the engine has been removed a new backbone could be laminated *in situ* over the damaged one, affected planks made good, and the hull given additional longitudinal strength by the addition of external bilge runners. This is a chancy operation at best, but one that might just be worth while if the vessel is of historic interest.

Underbody sheathing – the last resort?

Sheathing of the hull of a carvel or diagonal-built vessel is also decidedly bad news. Strip-planked yachts were often sheathed either with nylon and resorcinol or glassfibre at the time of building, but that second skin should, prior to close investigation, likewise be regarded with suspicion.

There are two reasons for such a prejudiced viewpoint. First of all, it has to be questioned why the operation was carried out in the first place. In other words, is there rot beneath the sheathing? And secondly, the plain fact is that the sheathing of a timber hull whose seams are subject to movement, however slight, is a recipe for disaster as the sheathing along those seams will, over a period of time, lose adhesion. Water will then permeate and the slow but inevitable course towards deterioration follows.

It has to be faced that sheathing is, at best, the result of a misapplied attempt at labour saving; at worst, it is a last desperate attempt to retain some degree of watertight integrity and hide the reasons for a lack of it.

It is not so much that it is the cause of structural defects, but it does render a detailed inspection of the exterior hull almost impossible – although movement in seams and butts may be discerned through the scrim.

Prior to any remedial work, the sheathing will have to be stripped; this, in itself, is a time-consuming task. Taking this into account along with the suspect condition of the underlying timber, it may be considered that the element of risk is unacceptable and any further examination of the hull would be pointless.

If 'conventional' sheathing of a traditional hull mitigates against an optimistic outcome, ferro-sheathing, a practice that is becoming increasingly widespread, totally precludes such an outcome. If the object of the exercise is the purchase and restoration of a *timber* boat, then obviously ferro-sheathing is not suitable.

Likewise, a well-applied cement carapace will undoubtedly be strong and stands a reasonable chance of being waterproof (and may remain so for a number of years), but there is no escaping the fact that the essential structure is reinforced concrete rather than timber. It is true that the interior, if not also sheathed, can retain all the traditional charm of the original timberwork, but even retention of the original joinery is not necessarily a plus point since, without total encapsulation of both interior and exterior hull, concrete and timber will flex at slightly differing rates.

This gives rise once more to the ever-constant problem associated with timber: rot. Rot in turn allows more water penetration and therefore even more rot. But there is an added hazard where ferro-cement is involved: the fact that the presence of even the smallest quantity of water can lead to corrosion of the steel armature over which the concrete is plastered. The result? A breakdown of the structure (a phenomenon increasingly seen in reinforced concrete structures such as motorway bridges).

It may be that the sheathing is seen as an advantage rather than an overwhelming disaster, and there are certainly some very attractive smacks and bawleys that have been sheathed. However, there remains the sober fact that it is well high impossible to ascertain just how well or badly the work has been executed. One core sample is hardly enough to give an accurate picture, and it would be a rare vendor who would willingly agree to the taking of more than one. (Some will be less than delighted at the prospect of taking the first sample!) Hairline crazes may possibly be discernible on the outer skin, but if the vendor has seen them first it is a safe bet that their presence will have been disguised by paint and filler and only come to light if the hull is stripped off.

Removal – a dubious prognosis

If the sheathing is not regarded as the ultimate deterrent to purchasing, it is worth asking around to ensure that the vessel has been launched and in commission for a couple of seasons; if the boat is going to 'slough its skin', it is most likely to do so upon initial contact with water. More than one ferro-sheathed vessel has needed hasty retrieval on first immersion, and emerged with a hull closely resembling crazy paving.

In the event of this possibility, which is admittedly more likely to be caused by the user rather than the material itself, any idea of simply removing the sheathing in its entirety is almost certainly doomed to failure. I have known attempts to do so, but (as with most adhesive substances) a portion flakes off at once, a little more after great efforts and the remainder defies any physical assault upon it. At this point, an owner could be forgiven for losing all interest. Use of an angle grinder to erode the ferro offers one possibility, but this will be a gritty and back-breaking job, and one that will have to be carried out either in total seclusion from all other craft or within the confines of a tented area provided with a powerful dust extraction system. It goes without saying that protective clothing and masks, and possibly respiratory apparatus, will have to be worn.

There is yet another disadvantage in purchasing a ferro-sheathed vessel: insurance can be difficult, or almost impossible, to obtain; and the premium is likely to be at a special rate. So before you consider buying such a boat, make absolutely certain that adequate cover can be arranged and that, if further improvement and refitting is contemplated, an increased valuation can be agreed upon. It is best to do this via a specialist in marine insurance rather than using a neighbourhood broker who is more accustomed to dealing with motor and house contents cover. This should eliminate any later shocks when details are confirmed and the invoice presented.

It may seem a harsh statement, but such a vessel should be realistically thought of as a lost cause so far as restoration to its original condition is concerned. But if the thought of sailing a near replica of an earlier yacht appeals to you, by all means consider the vessel. (In truth, the boat probably requires hammer testing to ascertain that a major structural constituent is ordinary Portland as opposed to tree wood.)

Such a craft, though, must be accepted as an unknown quantity. There are some boats that have been sheathed carefully with attention to the mix and expert construction of the armature and plastering and such examples should have a reasonable life expectancy (though this has still to be proven by the passage of time). Most, however, are dubious, and a handful are potential maritime disasters – though the latter can usually be spotted without the need of a detailed inspection.

Cement in the bilge

Unacceptable as cement may be when plastered on the exterior of the hull, discovery of a bilge full of the stuff is disheartening. (It is even less heartening if its internal presence can be detected from the outside, as it sometimes can be, in the form of sagging bilges and yawning seams at the turn of the bilge.)

There are two diametrically opposed opinions as to the use of concrete as the ultimate internal stiffening.

On the one hand, it is pointed out, and quite fairly so, that a great number of smacks – and not a few yachts – had cement poured into the bilge at the time of building, generally after treating the interior timbers with bitumen. This effectively sealed planks, frames, fastenings and ballast into a permanent solid amalgam. And it does indeed seem to be resistant to the ravages of time. Recently I saw the sad skeleton of a bawley, probably built in the later years of the last century. All that remained were the bones of bow and stern posts, a couple of frames – and a concrete casting of the bilge space, an odd-shaped lump that could have been exhibited as an abstract sculpture. But it was as hard and sound as the day on which it was poured, having outlasted the boat by about half a century.

It was quite common practice for a certificate to be issued when the bilge was cemented to testify as to the soundness of the hull at the time (and thus making it clear that it was not a last and desperate attempt to cure leaks). Certainly, where a yacht or working boat with heavy scantlings was treated in good time, it does not seem to have had an adverse affect. It certainly prevents the need for cleaning and chipping internal ballast (and also keeps it permanently in the designed place) and water should not be able to reach areas vulnerable to rot, such as the hog and floors. Neither does it seem to affect sea-keeping qualities; after all, Major Tilman's pilot cutter, *Mischief*, sailed for thousands of miles with a belly full of the stuff!

Wet rot, though, always thrives in the presence of both air and water, which in practice means that a wary eye has to be kept for its formation where the frames pass into the upper surface of the concrete. Consider a fence post, for example: this deteriorates most rapidly at the point of entry into the ground. Unless it is possible to be absolutely sure that a boat was treated when new or, at any rate, acceptably sound, there will always be a nagging suspicion that rot is continuing under the lime and sand.

Where cement has been tipped into the narrow bilge of a relatively lightweight cruiser racer, abandon all thought of purchase. It has to be assumed that the cement is there to alleviate underlying problems with the timber structure. Not only will its presence strain the planking, it will render it impossible to remove keel bolts (and the concrete will not prevent deterioration of these). Of course, if the vessel is seen afloat or in a mud berth, the very sight of concrete will suggest that it is acting as a substitute for the ballast keel which may have been removed.

Ridding the bilge of concrete is slightly more feasible than the stripping of sheathing, but it will be a protracted and physically demanding slog using hammer and cold chisel. It is a job with a very uncertain outcome too, although if the external appearance of the vessel has not suffered there is a possibility that all is not lost. On no account, though, attack the concrete with a power hammer, in spite of the irresistible temptation to do so. The repeated shock and vibration could do real harm and could even finish the vessel off completely. Obviously, the removal of cement is not best undertaken with the boat afloat as the moment of truth will likely come in the form of a swift inrush of water. But, with the bilges cushioned in a mud berth, there is a decreased likelihood of straining the scantlings and hull – and little risk of unexpected flooding (though it would be prudent to remove any objects that could be damaged by damp before the first tentative strike of the chisel).

Marine borers

The realisation that marine borers have attacked a hull should have any purchaser backing away at great speed, if only because there is little doubt that where one colony has dined sumptuously, so have others.

Any boat that has been ashore for any length of time, whether in a mud berth or saltings, must be suspected of having been attacked by the gribble worm. There are areas where this crustacean is still purported to survive, although warnings as to its continued activity are often not taken seriously. Where it does exist, though, the depradations inflicted is no laughing matter. Its presence is usually discovered after damage has been done, and by then it is too late to issue a warning.

It attacks areas of a vessel that have been in contact with salt mud, i.e. timber external keels, bilge planks and runners, the deadwood and perhaps – worst of all from the point of view of taking remedial action – the rudder trunking. Any boat that has been left without regular antifouling in mud or wet salt marsh stands a fair chance of being contaminated. Affected areas are usually localised, being often only a few inches square, but usually with dire consequences: holes a few inches deep. Repeated attacks can weaken a structure beyond all hope of repair. Once a hull has been washed free of all mud, the evidence is clear: the wood will have the appearance of a honeycomb and the extent of softness can be confirmed by probing.

Should a vendor be aware that his vessel has been attacked by these borers, a tactical cover-up may have been hastily carried out – with all signs of activity being obscured by filler and paint. This disguise may be sufficient to ensure that affected areas can only be found by chance, so be wary if you know that the craft has spent time in a gribble-friendly habitat. Be doubly meticulous when scraping areas of the underbody, and do not neglect the underside of a keel. Suspect any areas of stopping underneath whose cause, such as a sprung butt or split plank, cannot be explained. And if there is the slightest sign of one attack, remember it is odds on that there will be others. Without doubt, reconsider the purchase.

All the above problems have been noted as though they solely affect timber vessels of traditional type rather than those constructed of glued, moulded veneer or ply. Like all generalisations, there are exceptions.

The main reason for such afflictions as hogging or distortion, indifferent sheathing, an interior full of concrete, or ravage by the

Ships that pass . . . This clinker 22 foot Kestrel class was apparently rammed whilst on her mooring by a renegade coaster but, astonishingly, remained afloat. Damage is in fact quite localised, affecting the strakes, four ribs and the shelf. Nevertheless, the greatest care had to be exercised when bringing the casualty ashore, with the hull supported in a cradle.

gribble worm is, simply, the age of the vessel. It is largely elderly boats that are sheathed, whether it be glassfibre and resin, Cascover or ferro-cement and of course it is mainly boats of a certain age that are carvel, clinker or diagonal built. Inevitably it is vintage craft that have suffered most from neglect and require drastic, and often ill-considered, action. (Also, there are a few more carvel boats than moulded or plywood ones in existence.)

The older a boat, the greater the possibility that it will have suffered damage through collision or grounding or have been over-stressed by improper shoring during lay-ups. (I have seen the short counter of a small cold-moulded vessel slightly distorted by drying out to beaching legs, with a weighty outboard motor cheerfully left dangling on the stern – a procedure that would have produced a major distortion in a carvel hull.) It is not uncommon for light canoe-bodied hulls with short fin keels, also planing power boats of moulded construction, to suffer what amounts to hogging through rot that affects the veneers alongside the hog then spreads to and weakens this backbone itself. This destroys the integrity of the hull as a monocoque structure and allows wringing to occur.

Moulded yachts of conventional long-keeled form are, though, both tough and highly resistant to strain so long as they are constructed to stringent standards.

As to the risk of assault by the gribble worm, once again the antiquity of the craft is very much a factor. Comparatively few veneer yachts have been built and only a small percentage have spent their lives in mud berths. In any case, the borer would be unlikely to penetrate far into the hull because of the unpalatability of the resin glues employed in the construction.

Once these few terminal conditions have been eliminated, the detailed inspection of the external hull can proceed with a fair chance that the time will not be wasted. Hopefully, defects that are uncovered will be the type that can be remedied, though at what cost is another matter – to say nothing of the initial cause.

It is probably simplest to assume that a carvel hull is the subject of the survey since the majority of defects affect all timber types. Diagonal and veneer types have their own specialised ills and these can be dealt with separately.

CHAPTER 7

The structural integrity of the hull

Cosmetic appearance

After a first tentative look around to ensure that the entire boat is present and correct and no vital parts such as chunks of bow and stern are missing (obvious as this may seem, it can never be taken for granted), it is best to consider the external hull methodically and as a complete entity, and examine decks and superstructure later. A second inspection of the hull, in the course of the survey, is to be recommended since queries may be raised that can be resolved by a look at the condition of the interior.

It matters little at which point inspection commences; boats, unlike horses, do not mind being sneaked up on from behind. Indeed, the condition of the quarters and the planking at the transom often reflect the overall state of the hull. It is then a good idea to proceed resolutely around the boat in one direction only. This is because, unlikely as it may seem, you can become disorientated while walking around and thus forget details.

Hopefully, the hull will quickly be deemed to be free of all intractable conditions such as undue distortion or an unacceptable ratio of ferro to timber. This having been checked, the next thing to strike the eye is the cosmetic appearance: how well has the paint been applied, how good is the finish, and what state is the hull in beneath the skin? Although a sound coat of paint free from runs or 'holidays' does suggest a reasonable standard of maintenance, do not judge by paint alone. There are more owners handy with a paint brush and putty knife than blessed with any other skill. Obvious blemishes in yacht enamel, such as blisters, dull spots and 'crackelure' (this is a random pattern of open crazing, rather like the grain in old leather), all are suggestive of a coat of paint slapped on with an uncaring hand. Blisters signify poor surface preparation and possibly underlying damp, flat spots suggest rain or other unfavourable climatic conditions at the time of painting, and a crazed finish implies that one coat has been painted over another with which it is incompatible.

Since a timber hull moves slightly according to weather conditions, and the painted surface – even when slightly elastic in nature as most modern marine coatings are – moves rather less, the degree to which the paint cracks along the seams does give an idea of how recently the paint has been applied. It also gives a fair indication of how long the boat has been out of the water. These factors, while not important in themselves, confirm (if confirmation be needed) details supplied by the vendor or broker.

White paint, reflecting the light, is 'cooler' than dark colours, and the underlying seams may not dry out quite so fast (nor the paint line crack so noticeably); but, as a rough guide, the more visible the cracking, the longer the boat will have been out of

A preliminary inspection of the external hull might result in disinclination to take a second look (and by the way, in this case, the interior is in somewhat worse condition!) but that second look might be worthwhile. Seams gaping slightly in way of the chainplates are apparent along with evidence of a vengefully wielded power sander. The sheerline is fair however, and the fore and sidedecks are basically sound in spite of the frayed and lifted canvas covering; there is little wrong with the coachroof – apart from the second storey added at some time in the past. Even most of the deck fittings look quite reasonable. Picture this 20 foot centreboarder as she must have been 60 years ago with her gaff rig and bowsprit and the restoration has definite appeal.

the water. If there are no signs whatsoever, the vessel has probably been painted specially for your viewing. After a week or so ashore the external paint (or more likely, antifouling) on the underbody will appear dry, but on a carvel boat darker lines will be noted along the seams where the caulking retains the damp.

Presence of filler

The cynic is inclined to the belief that where there's fresh paint, there's filler beneath it. And the cynic is quite often correct! Also, where there is fresh paint with a nice glossy finish, there is a manifest hope on behalf of the vendor that a nosy surveyor is not going to ruin the surface by scraping or probing.

The presence of small quantities of stopping for cosmetic purposes (for example in the fairing of gouges and deep scratches) is perfectly acceptable. However, larger-scale evidence of filler build-up in the region of the stem, stern and butt joints, and in the area of any through-hull fittings, must give rise to the suspicion that a deep-seated problem is being concealed. Modern epoxy or glassfibre pastes, carefully applied and sanded, can remain undetected even after a series of small random explorations with a

The deadwood of a deep-keel yacht – each and every seam or through-fastening is a potential haven for wet rot!

spike, although there are specific sites on a hull worthy of critical examination. To find excessive amounts of stopping in hood ends at bow and stern is a reliable indication of consistent – and, quite likely, unsuccessful – refastening (and over-fastening). In butts it may suggest that, in an over-enthusiastic attempt to fair the planks of an old boat, the external surfaces of these joints have been savaged with a plane and then filled. This may sound an improbable case of vandalism, but I have seen it done – and to the point where mahogany measuring $1\frac{1}{2}$ inches was whittled away to little over two-thirds of its original thickness. Little imagination is needed to visualise a possible outcome of this.

Filler along the planks points to caulking carried out by a careless workman who, in raking out the old cotton, has also scraped away the timber. It is a possibility too that splits may have developed, as they frequently do in short-grained timber; these, though, would usually call for a more permanent treatment than merely ladling on a liberal helping of putty. The same is true in the case of splits, or shakes, along the length of the grain: filler is only of use for those that are narrow and limited to $\frac{1}{4}$ inch or so in depth. Any deeper shakes should be glued and splined (but not until the hull has taken up completely).

Probe carefully under external strap chainplates, for rot is commonly found in such areas as a result of water penetration through the holes of corroded bolts. Filler is no substitute for a timber graving piece and the replacement of affected fastenings. The wood immediately under rubbing strakes is also susceptible to rot.

Certainly, there are few places in any hull where there should be more than a light application of filler, so bear in mind that any lavish use is a sign of one of three basic conditions, or a combination of all three. These conditions are as follows. First, rot, in which case there will certainly be found more rot, since it has either not been accurately diagnosed not appropriately treated. Secondly, any repairs may have been entrusted to a sloppy shipwright, in which case, as with rot, there is probably going to be more of the same distributed around the vessel. (One trademark of a poor boatbuilder is the joining of two adjacent defective hull strakes with a single slab of seamless timber graved in between both. This might, theoretically, remain in place while all around it fails, but it certainly says something about inferior workmanship.) The third possibility is that of external damage, but without stripping bare large areas of the hull, injuries may only be confirmed by noting any bending, twisting and loosening of deck stanchions, chainplates and other hardware; these items are harder to camouflage than the hull itself.

Seams

Although the seams of a carvel vessel should be inspected along the length from interior and exterior (the inside view to affirm that there has been no overcaulking – a situation that arises when mastic and cotton are forced right through a seam), the general state can be gauged with a fair degree of accuracy from the external check. Ideally, of course, seams should barely be visible: in most cases, if caulked, rather than battened or splined, they are. A period of months ashore (or weeks, if the weather is hot and dry) will inevitably cause a certain amount of opening, even if the vessel is protected by a cover. While it can be disheartening to watch this happen to a newly painted boat, it does little harm so long as the movement is restricted to a mere cracking of the paint line; once in water the wood will swell in its own good time without adverse effects. Not that simply dumping the boat into the hoggin from a travel hoist, then leaving it to swing unattended on a deep-water mooring, is recommended. It is not unheard of for a piece of grit or sliver of metal to lurk unnoticed in an underwater seam, and this will prevent it ever taking up completely. Someone should be on board (armed with a bilge pump) more or less constantly until any leaks subside to a weep or two.

Where seams are uniformly gaping along the entire length of the boat, recaulking will be unavoidable and all old caulking and stopping will have to be raked out. This is a tedious but not particularly skilled operation; to be honest, the major skill lies in knowing when to leave well alone and to ensure that edges of the hull strakes do not suffer erosion from the raking tool. A situation that is potentially more serious is one where seams have opened to a greater degree amidships than at the ends, for this suggests some distortion has occurred in the past. Attention must be given to establishing whether this is in fact the case and, if so, to what extent. It may be confined to the area immediately around the chainplates and simply be the result of direct stress. This, although an undesirable complication, is at least responsive to treatment: simply distributing the load of the rig to the chainplates more effectively via heavier internal frames should eliminate the main cause. The seams can then be effectively reduced by glueing slips of compatible timber to the stakes prior to fairing and then caulking in the normal manner.

Although a clinker hull is constructed without caulking between the strakes, it is not unknown for mastic and cotton to have been forced under the lands – perhaps by an owner not inclined to trust nature and allow the boat to take up at its own rate once launched for the season. The caulking can be removed, indeed should be removed, but after a year or two in place it may have inflicted much harm upon the planking,

Not a moonscape, just wood nearly a century old. Barnacles encrust and obstruct the skin fittings (a seacock strainer can just be made out at lower left of the picture). The sap wood has eroded to leave characteristic 'tunnels' along the grain, and one lonely tingle vainly attempts to prevent water pouring in through defective fastenings.

possibly causing it to split quite severely. There is also a strong possibility that there will have been sufficient distortion to prevent the hull ever taking up again; if this should prove to be the case, glued slivers may have to be inserted under each strake. This is a fairly drastic measure and one that would call into doubt the permanent structural integrity of a cruising yacht subject to the strains of the open sea.

Ships' lifeboats have always been an attractive proposition for conversion into cruisers (a popularity that continues to this day, long after timber has been superseded first by steel, and then by glassfibre or aluminium). Some such vessels are seen with a length of moulding under each midship strake from gunwale to bilge runner. This served two purposes: first, to offer some protection from damage against the side of a vessel when lowering during boatdrill or in an emergency, and secondly, to discourage the planks from opening after months exposed to tropical sun, wind and weather. (A waterlogged lifeboat does not inspire a great deal of confidence in those who have urgent need of it.)

Since this length of moulding was general practice in ships' boats, it was occasionally copied by boatyards intent on stopping leaks in clinker vessels as quickly as possible and at little cost. Certainly it was a less-involved method than replanking or replacing a series of damaged ribs. It was thought that if it was suitable for ships' boats, then surely it must be ideal for yachts also. In some cases it may have cured the symptoms, if nothing else, but a buyer should be wary if the strakes of a clinker hull, other than a ship's lifeboat, have been blessed with these quadrant mouldings. They are almost certainly a later addition and there for a purpose.

Any major defects occurring in seams and planking are usually duplicated above and below the waterline, although areas such as the garboard strake (the plank next to the centreline keel) and, not infrequently, the tuck under the transom or counter of a sailing vessel, have (because of their sharp curvature – rarely so pronounced in the topside planking) an increased risk of splits and defects as a result of stress. At the bows, and more noticeably the stern where this curve is at its most accentuated, there is a chance of either the chamfer of taper on the strakes being sawn with less than perfect accuracy. Slight subsequent swelling of the wood, perhaps years after launching, causes seams to over-tighten. This tends to reveal each plank individually, rather than as a section of smooth curve. It detracts from the appearance, although not necessarily from the structural integrity. Since just about the only cure is replanking, the alternative is simply to live with it – although this could have a depressing effect if your goal is to restore the vessel to pristine condition.

If any planks show signs of curvature across the grain – the centre bowing out slightly proud of the edges – then suspect rot and probe gently for it. If rot does not seem to be present, the curve will, in all probability, be the result of poorly seasoned timber seeking to re-establish its natural curl.

Through-hull fastenings

All through-hull fastenings are a major cause of defects in both planking and frames since they corrode, usually undetected, and the space formerly occupied by solid metal becomes a moisture trap. And of course, where there is moisture, there will in time be rot. So not only are the fastenings, once surroundings become damp, going to corrode at an ever-increasing rate until they reach the point where they no longer contribute to the viability of the hull, but the damp will leach through the hole drilled for that fastening and encourage rot in planking and frames. It will not be long before the plank will have such a tenuous hold on the frame that it will spring outward, even without the added stress of thrashing through choppy seas. The springing of a plank or butt end is one of the greatest dangers of working to windward in an old boat and has caused many a loss.

Particularly liable to spring if fastenings are in the slightest degree defective are the highly stressed planks that form the rounded bows of such Dutch craft as Boiers and Lemmeracks; here the curvature amounts almost to a full semi-circle. The cruiser (canoe) stern, of such vessels as the Norwegian Reddingskoit and its derivatives, is also vulnerable, as is the even more curvaceous version seen in the well-known British MFV type (those built to Ministry of Defence specifications seem to suffer more than those constructed for fishing in northern seas). Repair is never easy for the amateur, and even some professional boatbuilders do not view this task with enthusiasm.

Almost certainly, some replacement of the planks will be necessary in order to provide a sound base for the renewed fastenings, and arguably the best technique is one that employs a combination of steaming fairly thin planks prior to laminating two (or possibly three) thicknesses in place, then glueing and through-fastening securely.

Any and all corrosion of nails, screws, bolts and studs is often referred to, albeit loosely, as nail sickness. There are a host of different fastenings, though, some of which get 'sicker' faster than others. Many formal written survey reports state that fastenings have been hammer tested, but this, so far as the vast majority is concerned, is impracticable. Nails or screws must first be located, which is easier said than done. Once successfully tracked down, a sizeable chunk of stopping and paint must first be removed. Any countersunk fastenings that are immediately discerned, without prior scraping, are more or less guaranteed to be in need of attention. Their presence is indicated by rust weeps or by depression and drying of the stopping at the site of the nail or screw head.

Since defective fastenings are more dangerous at stress points, these should be examined closely. It would be unreasonable for a vendor to object strongly to the laying bare of a small selection, but ensure you have permission first. When the head is bared, the slightest tap will prove sufficient to inspect for movement; an onslaught with hammer and punch is bound to move *any* fastening, however sound, and if the sale does not proceed the damage may have to be made good at your expense.

If steel or iron spikes, nails or dumps have been used and corroded beyond their useful life expectancy, the wood will be rust stained. It will also quite possibly have the fibrous appearance associated with 'wet rot'.

If screws have been employed in the construction, and the vessel was professionally yard built, expect to see the screw slots turned in the same direction, along the grain. If a few appear to be haphazardly driven, though, note the area and make a closer examination from the inside; this may be an indication of recent repair work.

Removal

The refastening of an elderly boat is a task without much pleasure or satisfaction, in spite of its importance. Even worse than the refastening, though, is the removal of the old nails, etc, which will have become more or less a part of the timber itself. Worst of all are twisted iron dumps and barbed ring nails; they require incredible perseverance because extraction will entail drilling, probing and heaving in equal proportions. Stainless steel screws should be simple as they are unlikely to break and slots do not burr easily; unfortunately they are rare, except at a site of previous repair. Brass and steel screws are far more common and both types break readily; brass is the more fragile since the zinc will probably have leached away over the years.

If a carefully honed screwdriver bit inserted in a ratchet brace is ineffective (attempt half a turn to tighten first), use an ordinary screwdriver and hit it with a hammer; this may loosen the screw sufficiently to free it. If not, heat from a soldering iron may work, but since the slot is possibly becoming burred beyond the point where it can be re-cut, drilling may still be the only answer. There are a large number of through-fastenings per foot of overall length. My 25 foot Glen class keelboat had over 5000 screws in the construction of the hull alone – and quite a few had to be replaced. In addition, every screw above the waterline had to be stopped and coloured in because she was bright varnished. So, if you have doubts as to your tenacity, stay away from a boat with dubious fastenings!

Clinker boats with copper and roves require double the effort, as the interior rove will have to be freed off by drilling and the nail then tapped out with a fine punch. Where the nail is clenched (with the end turned over into the rib), it is not difficult to straighten it. At least, that is the theory, but the copper may have become brittle and snap off short rather than bend obligingly. A hacksaw blade, carefully inserted between the lands, may help by cutting the nail in half.

Large bolts, such as those securing the rubbing strake, chainplates etc, have the single advantage of being highly visible – from the interior at least – although visibility does not automatically guarantee accessibility. Should brute force not suffice to loosen them, either the head or tail may

Shrinkage of timber from the joints is visible in this picture. If the damage is no more than surface deep (and of course if the planks are of sufficient thickness and otherwise sound) epoxy encapsulation may be one answer, though expert advice should be sought since it is an expensive operation, even though resins may still work out cheaper than skilled labour.

have to be sawn through; to facilitate this, a portion of frame or knee may need cutting away first.

After removal, the shaping of slightly tapering plugs for each hole (these should preferably be of stable hardwood such as good mahogany or iroko), followed by glueing and hammering them into position, will by comparison seem a relaxing task. A helper, even one without woodworking skills, can be allowed to work almost unsupervised, for as long as each hole is reamed to free it of foreign materials (such as tallow or mastic which will prevent adhesion of the resin glues) there is little scope for mistakes.

Holes will nearly always have to be plugged before refastening; rarely is it possible to achieve a satisfactory result merely by inserting a fastening one, or even two, sizes larger. Apart from the condition of the timber in the immediate vicinity of the existing hole, the internal ribs or frames may not be substantial enough to accept the increased diameter of the new metalwork. (If trenails have been used, it may be feasible to drill through these – in effect, using them as dowels – and refasten through; otherwise, they are all but impossible to remove except in small fragments.)

The integrity of the frames and checking for evidence of previous refastening is often overlooked; a plank should be eased away so that this inspection can be carried out. It is astonishing how frequently new strakes are nailed or screwed on to frames that are cracked, partially rotten, or which have had so many sets of nails hammered home over the years that the timber has acquired the texture of a loofah.

Condition of planking

Doubling of the planks is mostly seen in working or fishing vessels where the superimposed planking acts as protection against damage by the vessel's own gear and from the rougher aspects of life in a commercial dock. Usually this extends from just above the waterline to below the turn of the bilge, but it may reach as far as the keel itself – and sometimes a portion of the topsides may also be doubled. Oddly enough, it is not always spotted at once. Paint and time blur the sharp line of the upper edge and it can, on a larger vessel, be mistaken for an unfair plank; on a small boat it is both unmistakable and a clear pointer to past (and also present and future) troubles.

In the case of a heavily constructed working vessel, if no rot can be seen along either upper or lower seams and there appears not to have been excessive movement or undue unfairness in the doubled planks, removal of the outer skin may not be necessary. All the same, a detailed internal check should be carried out to confirm that doubling was not a measure taken to alleviate any pre-existing defects. Unfortunately, it is only possible to make a guess as to what natural processes are proceeding quietly between the two thicknesses of planking and there is a tendency to fear the worst. Removing some fastenings (best done by a shipwright with the vendor's permission and at your cost) should give an idea of what, if anything, has been laid between the two skins, whether they are in close contact, or if damp or water are present. If they are, the eventual consequence must be faced: that of stripping the doubling and possibly replacing a good deal of underlying planking also.

Rudder trunking

One of the most daunting sites in which to encounter wet rot is in the timber rudder trunking. This is difficult to detect here without removal of the rudder; this is awkward in the extreme to get at without dismantling portions of hull and deck. Wet rot here, at its lower end, is inclined to spread further into the hog and any surrounding frames. Today it is more usual to have a metal or stainless steel tube enclosing the rudder stock, but even here there exists a possibility of rot developing under the lower plate where it comes into contact with timber.

It makes little difference whether you use metal or wood with regard to ease of the remedial action, since the major difficulty of the operation is, first of all, extracting both

Sketch of the early stage of dry rot showing tendrils seeking out moisture. (The darker areas are wood previously eroded by wet rot.)

rudder and stock. This, in the case of a keel-boat, usually entails the excavation of a pit beneath the rudder into which the unit can be lowered or, in the case of a smaller vessel, jacking up the hull.

In a wooden trunking, rot will probably start at the lower end; capillary action will then ensure that it works upwards through the timber cells until complete breakdown follows. If it is certain that only isolated areas are damaged, it may be possible to grave in new pieces, but often the deterioration will be too widespread.

On a vessel under 30 feet or so in length, it may be possible to reach with a chisel from upper and lower ends, routing away all soft wood and treating any remaining sound portions with wood preservative. Once the wood has dried out thoroughly, two half-shells (simpler to laminate than one single tube) of good-quality hardwood veneer laid up around a wood or metal core can then be slid into position within the trunking; they can then be heavily bedded with glue on to the remaining timber. The core will retain the sections in position until the glue has completely cured. The core must be covered in polythene to permit later removal, which can be effected by the simple expedient of hammering at it from above. The seams can then be pared smooth using a chisel with an extended handle and the interior of the trunking can be generously treated with epoxy resin or paint. This may sound rather a hit and miss method, but the only other option is major surgery.

The keel

Next on the list for inspection is the keel, whether of timber as in the case of the majority of motor craft and unballasted craft, or of lead or iron (or a marriage of both such as occurs in the narrow fin and bulb keels of certain racing yachts). The keel always tends to be taken for granted – with just a cursory glance to ensure it is there and attached! To be honest, this is probably adequate in the majority of cases, but there are exceptions when some informed judgement comes in handy.

In a timber keel there is little reason to tamper with the dimensions; true, some inches in depth may have been added to cover signs of rot or worm action or, alternatively, a few inches may have been eroded away because of such maritime perils (or, of course, because of underwater impact!) If rust weeps are visible along the upper edge or between any joints there is probably corrosion of the fastenings, and this must be attended to as a matter of some urgency. However, as the keel is timber and therefore not subjected to strain, it is most unlikely to drop off unexpectedly!

A ballast keel, which may weigh as much as the entire hull and spars of the vessel, imposes a great loading upon the structure and the attached bolts or studs.

It is the first thing to strike solid ground if there has been an error of navigation. In spite of the attention lavished by designers on attaining the optimum ballast ratio, draft, profile and section, it is also one of the first things subjected to the whims and improvements of owners. After all, in its life span a boat may be sailed in a wide variety of cruising areas – deep draught may be a delight to one owner, but anathema to another! So do not assume that the vessel necessarily has its original underbody configuration: the keel may have been modified. It can sometimes be hard to prove this, but there are a couple of helpful clues: unfair curve to the profile from forefoot to the fore edge of the keel, or a marked difference in width between the top of the keel casting and the timber backbone.

Drastic alterations to the keel can have a disastrous effect upon sailing performance (not to mention the structural integrity), as can any relocation in the fore and aft plane. This, if miscalculated, will have an adverse effect on the balance under working sail. Should a less weighty keel than the original have been substituted, the boat could be dangerously unstable; if it is too heavy, there is a risk of excess loading to floors, frames, keel bolts and, more particularly, to standing rigging and mast. This is because the increased weight and lowered centre of gravity will bring about an increase in stiffness and will lessen the heeling moment for any given wind strength. Thus in strong winds the boat will be sailing with a far greater effective area of sail than was ever contemplated by the designer. Added weight, for which that particular boat was not intended, will also be the cause of a ponderous motion in a seaway; the boat will feel sluggish and will be extremely wet into the bargain.

Keel bolts and studs

It is very much in the purchaser's interest to insist upon a keel bolt being X-rayed or drawn whenever possible (professionally, at added expense to yourself, of course). In practice, a potential owner may rely on inspection of the visible portions of bolts, and put to one side the sum (a large sum!) needed for their complete replacement. Such a course of action presumes that a visual examination does not reveal incontrovertible evidence that the bolts are about to disintegrate without warning. If the heads and plate washers are not reduced to rusted lumps, attention to the bolts can form part of the scheduled restoration programme.

The keel may not necessarily be through-bolted but instead be fastened by studs. Such studs screw into the metal for a depth of at least 4 inches, depending on the keel's dimensions. Bolts, however, are more usually to be found in the case of a traditional yacht. These generally are drilled right through the entire depth of the keel from upper to lower edge (and their removal is only possible either with the yacht blocked up to allow clearance or a small pit excavated beneath the fastenings). Alternatively, bolts may pass through about one-third of the keel's depth; access slots are incorporated in the casting with the nuts positioned and tightened through these. Wooden plugs are then wedged into the slots, faired and painted, leaving the surveyor to fathom out the exact site at a later date! Keel bolts, while usually spaced along the centreline, may, if the casting is wide enough, be 'galleried' – that is to say, ordered in a zig zag pattern. With a steel plate keel with cast ballast bulb, a type common to several classes of small offshore racing yachts, the through-hull attachment will be via flanges on either side of the upper edge of the keel.

It is usual for an iron keel to be fastened by mild steel bolts which have been hot-dip galvanised, although originally wrought iron, now less easy to obtain, would in all probability have been preferred. Silicon bronze is used in the case of a lead keel.

When surveying the external hull, weeps of rust will often be seen emanating from the joint between ballast keel and hull. The first thought that springs to mind is bound to be that of corroded fastenings. But some seepage (which can appear deceptively widespread) is normal, although the significance of it should be investigated. An iron keel that has not been treated with the appropriate rust inhibitor and primer will always be liable to oxidation and scale, and this may be the sole cause of the staining. It is equally possible, though, for this to be the first sign of corrosion within the steel bolts, the rust having seeped through the sealant.

The keel should be checked as far as possible for evidence of wringing, which could have taken place during an unscheduled grounding. Stand at the bow and look aft to ensure the keel is more or less in line with the stem. A plumb bob can assist you when checking alignment – or rather, it can help if the vessel is built with unerring accuracy. A wooden boat, however, is a work of art rather than a work of mathematical exactitude, and it is not unknown for there to be

Sea Wraith, a fine example of the classic Windfall class. This one was built for the Luftwaffe before the Second World War and brought to England as a war prize.

anomalies in such matters as height of rubbing strakes or lines of seams (even a centreline projected down the stem may not be straight).

The forefoot should be carefully examined for it is here that evidence of straining of the keel bolts may be seen. Scrape a portion of the paint away and check for any timber packing pieces that might suggest the keel has been forced aft slightly with possible attendant damage to bolts and floors (this may be confirmed) during the internal inspection.

The forefoot, deadwood and false keel should be checked out for rust weeps as a result of corrosion of fastenings – soft spots are commonly discovered in seams and joints even if recent paint has temporarily obscured signs of seepage. All too often, replacement sections of timber are graved in without dealing with the primary cause.

The long timber keel of a motor vessel or smack may, even if reasonably fair and apparently free from the ravages of rot and borers, eventually be put at risk from defective internal bolts. An inspection of the upper edge may reveal the first signs of softening and, as with a ballast keel, rust percolating through the mastic. A similar check should be made of wooden bilge runners and attention paid to the fore and aft ends of these.

There is a possibility that the keel might not be made up of one or even two full lengths of timber, but instead be built up with extra slips amidships. This suggests hogging to a greater or lesser degree and, while the packing of the keel may have prevented further movement, planks and frames must be carefully scrutinised. Should you want to resell, there is a fair chance that a purchaser might pull out once the condition is spotted, even if the vessel, is in other respects, fairly sound.

Bilge keels

Whether or not bilge keels are original to the design (with a traditional yacht, they are often an additional afterthought), they present a would-be purchaser with an array of potential defects. Quite apart from the rust to which mild steel plate variants are susceptible, the effects of stress to which bilge keels are continually subjected (when a boat lies on a drying mooring, this is a stress that may be further increased by uneven weight distribution on rough ground) can result in twisting, loosening of the fastenings, and splaying of the keels outwards. As though these possibilities were not in themselves enough, there is also the matter of internal reinforcement. A deficiency of this may cause the keel to penetrate the hull should the vessel take the ground awkwardly and place its entire weight upon the keel.

In the 1960s when bilge keels first became acceptable to the yachting fraternity, designers were ambivalent as to whether a bilge keel should be an appendage to be ripped free in an emergency without otherwise damaging the structure of the vessel, or whether it should be heavily ballasted and form an integral part of the hull, as would a conventional centreline keel.

Although few traditionally constructed boats were designed for bilge keels (with such worthy exceptions as some of the famous carvel Hillyards and clinker Sea Kings – although there were, of course, numerous small plywood sailing craft), none of these are at risk of any structural breakdown in the normal course of events, whatever the designer's preference as to keel size and ballasting. It would take a remarkable combination of circumstances to cause damage to the keels or hull – conditions that might easily reduce any craft, however sound and of whatever keel configuration, to matchwood. But it can be a different thing altogether if an owner has decided to tack on these improvements himself, often to a heavy displacement long-keeled vessel, without bothering to seek advice from designer or boatyard. Insufficient attention may have been paid to the provision of adequate internal bilge stringers and floors – not only to provide a firm anchorage for the attachment bolts, but to distribute the loading. In a carvel-built vessel it may be considered quite enough to overlay one or more of the hull strakes with a reinforcing piece and bolt through this. (I have even seen a flange bolted across a caulked seam!) A keel of mild steel plate does not prove difficult should replacement be necessary; the bolts are nearly always both visible and accessible.

Of course, occasional examples will be discovered where a well-meaning owner has decided to encapsulate the entire keel, flange included, in composite timber and glassfibre so as to fair into what is fondly hoped will be a more efficient foil. This is a nuisance, for if remedial action is needed as a result of corrosion of the steel core and fastenings, preliminary work with a pickaxe (or, at least, a chisel) will be needed. It is also worth remembering that this same owner has probably made other unwanted modifications also – all of which will reveal themselves in good time!

Twin keels (also separate skegs) are rather susceptible to wrenching if caught across a mooring chain or warp; this takes a fair amount of force, but a strong current may suffice. As with any underbody appendages, pay careful attention to the forward edge, ensuring that there is no undue gap in the join with the hull. (Regard any protruding whiskers of Nelson rope (commonly used on moorings) with a suspicious eye.)

Centreplates

Centreplates – whether contained within in a timber housing in the accommodation or, arguably far less troublesome, working entirely through an external ballast keel – also have their problems. The main one is that they can remain obstinately retracted in spite of your efforts to lower them for inspection. Mud is generally the culprit, but it is quite possible that the centreplate may have been twisted – and consequently jammed almost irrevocably. No boat should ever be shored with the plate lifted. It should be dropped and chocked with separate blocks to allow for the possibility of slight movement in the ground or of the boat itself. Be that as it may, it is not unusual to be denied sight of the plate and pivot bolt because of strategic siting of supports (suspect that they have been positioned with this sole purpose in mind). This means that there is some uncertainty as to general condition and it is worth pointing this out to the vendor with the intention of negotiating a price reduction.

Any major problem with a centreplate vessel may arise from the fact that its construction is often somewhat lighter than that of a comparable deep-keeled yacht. This means that, although replacement of a damaged plate may not be prohibitively expensive or complicated, it is possible that damage may extend to ribs, frames and floors, and also to any wooden trunking or casing fitted.

This more or less concludes the external examination – though a would-be purchaser should repeat the exercise. This may reveal something missed on the previous circuit.

Remember not to consider any single aspect of construction in isolation; if there is a defect, try to see why it exists and whether it is linked to other anomalies. Everything noted should be thought of as a clue that might lead to the diagnosis of another fault.

Finally – beware of tingles! An old vessel may be blessed with these to the extent that the hull can look as if it has suffered a half-hearted attempt at copper sheathing (as indeed, it may have). Tingles usually cover splits, unsound fastenings, old skin fittings, or even a hole in the hull. Of course, since they maintain watertight integrity, no surveyor would strip one from the underbody without first ensuring replacement (at the purchaser's expense and to the owner's satisfaction – which means undertaken by the boatyard who will duly indemnify the owner if the boat sinks). Tingles are accepted for what they are – temporary repairs. But not only do they serve to keep water out, they also keep water in – so stand to one side if removing an underwater patch!

CHAPTER 8

Above the waterline

Deck and cockpit

Next comes the inspection of the decks, superstructure and cockpit. Normally in a written survey the watertight integrity of hatches and windows (which are expected to have undergone hose-testing) would be noted separately, but since these do undoubtedly constitute part of the superstructure they can be included in the general inspection.

As with the actual construction of a hull, there is little difference in the methods of building the decking and superstructure between a sailing vessel and a motor boat. The main divergence is the relative bulk and height of a motor vessel's upperworks, which are likely to include a wheelhouse with standing headroom.

Alterations and 'improvements' may well have been made to the superstructure over the years, especially in the case of pre-war sailing vessels where the low coachroof frequently did not extend forward of the mast. The desire for improved headroom and accommodation triumphed over aesthetics in all too many cases, resulting in ungainly doghouses and heightened coachroofs of truly astounding appearance. They were tacked on without even a cursory thought given to structural strength. Another space-increasing strategy was to increase the height of the topsides from midships to stem, a frequent feature in motor cruisers whose fuller bow sections are better able to tolerate the increased weight forward. (Of course, built-up topsides, when designed as such rather than simply being erected from any surplus materials found lying around, can look fine – as they do in Maurice Griffiths's much-respected small ships.)

Therefore, the first essential is to note whether amendments have been made to the original design and, if this appears to be the case, to be chary not only of the quality of shipwrights' work, but also of the quality of timber employed. Plywood often takes the place of solid timber and, while this does not automatically imply a bodged job, there is the likelihood that the plywood may be of shuttering quality – or worse. If the coachroof sides are painted rather than varnished, this will be difficult to ascertain – although a preference for paint may in itself be suspicious. Be on the lookout for the telltale sharp ridges along the grain which are pointers to delamination; if the ridges show signs of movement when pushed hard with a fingernail, urgent treatment will be needed. Delamination that has been noticed by an owner and filled in may be discernible as a smoother patch in a painted surface that otherwise shows some signs of the underlying grain.

Coachroof and doghouse

The addition (or indeed subtraction, although this is rarer by far) of a doghouse or coachroof does not automatically ruin the looks of the vessel or detract from the value so long as the work has been competently carried out. There are ways and means of rectifying some of the harm done to the boat's profile and reducing the height – in appearance if not in actuality. The coachroof top can be removed and the existing beams replaced by ones with a more

Some yachts of marine ply construction are nowadays regarded as minor classics – as is this modified 'People's Boat' (which would admittedly have been more attractive without such modifications as the doghouse!). Delamination of the ply is, of course, a major problem in this type of vessel; once the paint has deteriorated, water penetrates and the veneers separate rapidly. An economical restoration depends greatly on the original standard of construction (many of these designs were home-built) and the accompanying inventory.

pronounced camber; this will still give adequate headroom along the centreline, while noticeably lowering the profile. Contrasting paint has the visual effect of disguising the camber itself, and the fitting of full-length timber grabrails, suitably bright varnished, will distract the eye even further. Or alternatively, as mentioned in a previous chapter, bulwarks can be built up slightly, and varnished rubbing strakes and capping rails added to improve the appearance still further.

It is inadvisable to embark upon a programme of dismantling doghouses and taking reefs in coachroofs without considerable prior inspection, accurate measurements, and at least some preliminary sketches. Unexpected snags have a tendency to crop up. In theory, it is only a few hours' work to whip off the coachroof intact by cutting through the fastenings in the carlins, inserting scaffold tubes through the ports, and winching the complete unit clear with a hoist. Once blocked level, a slice can be carved from the lower edge and the newly elegant coachroof dropped back into the original location. But, even though barely visible, there is generally a slight inward slope to any coachroof – and I have seen one instance where an owner was left with a yawning gap between the coachroof and carlin. This method of lifting the coachroof clear can, however, be used to good effect if the carlins themselves require replacing since, with the upperworks safely out of the way, complete runs of timber can be utilised. Structurally speaking, this offers a significant improvement over the scarphing in of localised short lengths between beams.

Apart from the unattractive appearance of an enlarged superstructure, such improvements may be a functional inconvenience. A doghouse or raised coachtop erected immediately abaft a tabernacle will prevent you from lowering the mast!

It is not uncommon to see amendments to Broads boats and Dutch working craft where the coachroof is carried forward of the mast and the extended fore hatch permanently sealed shut. This long hatchway is an essential part of the design, allowing the counter-weighted mast heel to pivot clear when lowered. Without it, the mast can only be unstepped with the aid of a crane. This means the cruising range of the waterways, for which such craft were designed and built, will be greatly restricted.

Potential weakness

Both working craft and flush-decked racing yachts can be weakened where deck beams are cut to build an accommodation unit, particularly if a keel-stepped mast is replaced by one stepped on to the coachroof and the hull inadequately braced internally.

If the conversion was undertaken in the past, and neither planking, frames nor decking appear to have suffered, then it is reasonable to assume that the owner, probably working with professional advice and assistance, got it right first time. However, should the construction be very recent, and the vessel has not been sailed since, there is no way of knowing just how well the structure will take it. If there is the slightest doubt lurking in your mind, have everything checked by a designer, knowledgeable shipwright or surveyor.

Any coachroof depends entirely upon the quality and seasoning of the wood used since it is not in itself a structure of outstanding strength, being supported only at the edges and further weakened by the cutting through of windows. If there are large glazed areas, the construction should be framed up. However, cost cutting or indifferent workmanship often cause this basic woodworking tenet to be ignored, so almost invariably planks develop splits along the grain. It goes without saying that a proportion of these splits will be in the worst possible places: between the portlights or windows. Prompt attention may prevent them spreading or extending right through the timber, but glueing and splining may not be sufficient. If rot has been allowed to infiltrate the shakes, complete replacement of an entire side may be inevitable. The shakes are not hard to spot in varnished woodwork, but, if the sides are painted, bear in mind that the paint could conceal splits that may have been puttied up. If anyone has been misguided enough to replace original ports with overlaid tinted acrylic windows, there must be a reason (and it may *not* have been to increase light in the cabin).

Condition of windows

The sealant and general condition of windows, and the internal and external frames, have to be carefully examined. Windows that leak make life on board unpleasant. More important than this, though, is the fact that rot will in all likelihood get a foothold – not only around such watertraps as the lower window corners, but also under the frames. Ensure that all glass and acrylic panes are sound and, in the case of a large glazed area that has cracked across, take a close look at the superstructure. It may be that the damage was caused by a flimsy construction that has permitted excessive flexing of the sides of the coachroof.

Skylights, more particularly those of the type rather derisively referred to as 'chicken coops', evoke mixed emotions in those whose boats have them. Picturesque as they are, they are an absolute curse – indeed, the one redeeming feature is the increase of headroom immediately beneath! However, this does not compensate for their drawbacks: constant leakage. (Who remembers to put on that fitted canvas cover until after the downpour has started? And who will volunteer to get soaked doing it?) In any case, no canvas cover, however heavy or well tailored, will offer good protection in a heavy breaking sea. An even more threatening drawback is the fact that a skylight is neatly sited in the single weakest area of the deck or coachtop; or rather, the skylight *creates* this weakness since a substantial cut-out has to be made in the unsupported central zone. And it can foul sheets, make it awkward to stow a dinghy, and the panes can crack (if of ordinary glass). Despite all this, many owners still feel the charm and character of skylights outweigh the problems.

Hatches

Most irritations relating to a boat's hatches are as much a result of indifferent design as of poor construction. Not all would agree, but the most practical means of access to the accommodation, so far as a medium-sized vessel is concerned, is by way of a sliding main hatch. On a seagoing vessel this should be as small as is compatible with the size of the human frame. Although a sliding hatch, if it's well made and moves freely on suitable metal runners, is an uncomplicated and tough piece of joinery, there are occasions (usually as a result of the impositions of wheelhouse or deck space) when other variants are unavoidable. The hatch may be hinged at the fore end so as to flip up (in the case of a small sailing cruiser, the hatch when duly 'flipped' is bound to snarl main or jib sheets) or it may both fold and hinge. This latter system is less inclined to foul running rigging, but twice as liable to trap an unwary hand. No matter how the hatch opens the following criteria apply: it must indeed open and close without the application of undue effort (and to this end should possess an interior handle as well as a secure handhold outside); all hinges must be sound, as must the fixing screws and/or bolts; and the hatch must give protection against adverse weather at sea (or security against external intruders on shore). The structure is required to be robust, and free from splits or delamination in runners and coamings.

The vertical aperture of the main companion is on many sailing vessels closed with a number of flushing boards, and grooved to slot into position in a given order (which is guaranteed to baffle a new owner for a month or two). This method is simple and effective, but care must be taken that the boards can be retained in position during a knockdown and that the crew can escape in the event of such a mishap – or if the vessel completely inverts. Sometimes a translucent acrylic flushing board is carried simply for use when living on board, where daylight is more important than privacy.

If doors as opposed to wash boards are fitted, they should open outward, especially if the accommodation is entered from an unprotected open cockpit. These should be heavily constructed and, in all but larger craft of upwards of 50 feet or so (and ideally in those vessels as well), there should be a bridgedeck at the forward end of the cockpit. This storm sill, which should be of similar height to the side deck, can prevent total flooding in the event of a severe broach or 90° capsize. Since it requires a minimal physical effort to step over a bridgedeck – especially when carrying a loaded drinks tray – it is often replaced by full-length doors, and not infrequently by doors that open inwards and could be caved in by a sudden inrush of water. Outward-opening doors are far more capable of withstanding such extreme conditions but, when opened, they have a tendency to obstruct sideways vision, engine access, or even the movements of the helmsman if there is an off-centre steering position.

Motor cruisers are generally designed with the main access into a wheelhouse (or deck saloon) having more in common with a patio door than a protection from the dangers of severe weather. It is not by any means unheard of to add a sliding double-glazed door to an otherwise traditional wheelhouse. Be warned: even if this slides as it should when the boat is laid up ashore, it almost certainly will not once under way. Damp, along with any working of the hull and superstructure, however slight, will see to that.

It is fair to say that designers of motor cruisers (along with some owners) have a rather misplaced faith that the buoyant sections, broad beam and high topsides that make such spacious accommodation for overall length, will ensure the seaworthiness of the vessel, come wind or weather. This is rather a blasé attitude since a large proportion of traditional heavy displacement power craft, with an average cruising speed hardly in excess of 8 knots, are very vulnerable to extreme conditions – conditions in which either ineffective handling or loss of power at a crucial moment can provoke a disastrous broach. Should any of these occur, that secure and watertight hatchway could mean the difference between survival and the ultimate loss of the boat.

Forehatches, usually taken for granted except as a facility that provides through ventilation in settled weather, may also mean the difference between life or death – and not merely in a storm. Certainly in such weather the watertight integrity and security of closure of the unit are important and therefore should be looked at as such in the course of a survey. But do not forget to check the ease with which the latch can be released from the interior, since a forehatch serves a vital function as an emergency escape route. Should there be an outbreak of fire – and fire is likely to start aft of midships owing to the location of such installations as the engine and galley (and possibly gas water heater or solid fuel stove) – the main companion may well be impassable, with the only means of escape being the forehatch. I have experienced a severe blaze in a galley so I know what I'm talking about. It seems almost beyond belief that many small boats are designed with only one hatch. In a vessel under 20 feet or so the crew is extremely vulnerable, as a blaze can gut the entire cabin in seconds.

Lockers

The secure attachment of all on-deck lockers is also a prime concern. A large proportion of sidebench locker tops in older boats rely solely on their weight to hold them in place – which is fine until water gets on board and the lids become buoyant! It presumably has never entered draughtsmen's heads that hull, steering, rig or engine could conceivably suffer such damage as to render the vessel liable to swamping while not under control. One heavy sea shipped on board may find its way into a cockpit locker that cannot be effectively sealed shut, and then into the bilge where it will almost inevitably flood the engine.

It's not all the fault of the design team, though: some owners' demands allow ample scope for water to enter where lockers are concerned. For example, sometimes full-width bridgedecks (which may be structural components) are blithely tunnelled through so as to provide quarter berths, often without bothering to seal the locker lid! Extra-deep caverns, presumably for the stowage of inflatables, are created by removing the soles of sidebench lockers, thereby allowing unwanted water instant access to the bilge and accommodation. Some cockpit lockers are arranged so that the contents can be reached from the boat's interior, thus avoiding the inconvenience of venturing on deck.

Cockpit and locker layout are pretty well

inseparable since a large footwell means a corresponding decrease in the usual stowage areas: under sidebenches, the afterdeck, and so on. Generally favoured today, in sailing vessels at least, is a small self-draining well with a large area of seating, often separated into two areas if wheel steering is fitted. There are arguments for and against a self-draining cockpit, and it must remain a matter of personal choice (unless racing offshore, where it is a mandatory requirement). It is often argued that access to engine, shaft and sterngland is made difficult where the well is watertight since the sole must be bedded into place on sealant and thus be a more or less permanent fixture. In reality, though, a well-made double coaming hatch secured by toggles will be both watertight and quickly removable when necessary.

There is also a body of opinion that is against cutting any holes whatsoever through the shipside. This (except where a vessel has a good deal of freeboard and the sole is well above the waterline) will be unavoidable – as will the provision of crossed drain tubes (crossed in order to prevent water flooding into the cockpit when the yacht heels) and seacocks fitted to the overside discharges. Although personally not inclined towards complications for their own sake, I would always opt for a cockpit that is either self-draining (or at least watertight which can be pumped out if need be) – even where this is at variance with the original character of the craft.

Whether in the course of the survey or in later planning of alterations, do not forget to take into account such essentials as batteries, fuel and water tanks (and engines) and make certain that they are not permanently entombed! This also holds true so far as any reconstruction of wheelhouse, doghouse and all hatches is concerned. Even at the date of the initial building, due consideration may not have been given to the possibility of removal of an engine for major overhaul, which may only be achieved at the cost of hacking away bulkheads, deckheads and soles.

Also overlooked with surprising frequency, whether at the design stage or in the euphoria of general improvements, is the desirability of being able to see where the vessel is actually heading. Low sidebenches combined with a high coachroof mean that the helmsman has either to stand on tiptoe during all crucial manœuvres or perch upon a portable stool, duly transferred from side to side when tacking. Wheelhouse windows, even when they permit an unobstructed view forward in fine weather, are readily obscured by rain or scud and, in addition to wipers or a revolving clear view disc, should be fitted with at least one window that can be opened. (An opening transparent hatch in the deckhead is very useful when coming alongside a deep lock or high staging.)

A rakish slope to the fore end of a wheelhouse undoubtedly improves the lines of the vessel, but it hinders visibility as it increases the degree of reflection. This can make it awkward to judge distance accurately. The further the distance between the glass and helm position, the more marked this will be – and it can be quite unsettling. The 'trawler' wheelhouse – with reverse slope to the fore end – is by no means in keeping with every displacement motor vessel, but offers improved visibility and is less affected by flying spray.

Strictly speaking, none of these design considerations form part of a structural survey, but they should be carefully noted since they profoundly affect a vessel's handling. This in turn affects the confidence of the crew and, ultimately, the vessel's seaworthiness.

The decks

On many traditionally built yachts where tradition has been adhered to at all costs, it is the construction of the deck that all too often dampens the crew's enthusiasm for

Expense no object – a particularly lovely example of a swept laid deck with varnished nibbed king plank and varnished covering boards and margins.

the shipboard life. There are many aspects worthy of praise in the shipwright's art, but the ordinary tongued-and-grooved pine decking, built down to a price and relying on its canvas covering to impart a degree of weather proofing, is not one of them!

It is not the only method of decking, although the ease and speed with which it can be laid (coupled with the low initial cost of the timber) mean that it is the most usual type found in small to medium sailing and motor cruisers of the pre-war years – unless it has been replaced with marine ply. Marine plywood is arguably the ideal material for a deck. It is light, tough and simple to shape, and can be rapidly nailed and glued into position where, so long as it is well protected by paint, it will last for a generation or more with little further maintenance.

Laid decks, with the contrasting paid seams, enhance the looks – and the price – of any boat, but the maintenance is demanding. In order to obtain the best of both worlds, the planking is often laid over an underlying skin of leakproof and stable marine plywood. But since nothing on a boat is ever eternally resistant to leaks nor totally stable, this ultimately gives rise to deterioration that is doubly difficult to deal with.

Laid decks may be one of four types, regardless of whether they are laid on to ply or directly on to the deck beams. The first type is fore and aft, where the planks are in line with the centreline; the second is swept, in which case they follow the plan of the vessel and are curved along the line of the gunwales; the third is herringbone, which, as the term suggests, is a diagonal arrangement (one rarely seen in Britain and impossible to lay without longitudinal stringers).

In these three variations, the king plank, covering board and margins may either be straight or nibbed – that is, notched to accept each individual plank end. A swept laid deck with all structural timber nibbed represents craftsmanship of the very highest order, but on a small yacht it sometimes looks fussy.

The fourth type of laid deck could be described as 'the fraudulent', and is much on the increase as the demand grows for instant classic 'character'. The term 'fraudulent' is perhaps a little too harsh, as many of these prefabricated laid effects are very good indeed and make use of good-quality timber slips machined with great precision. Lighter varieties are veneered with a contrasting timber inlay line taking the place of payed seams, but the best do use wood of sufficient thickness to withstand reasonable wear. However, the life expectancy of this type is questionable in the 'traffic areas' of a much-sailed boat.

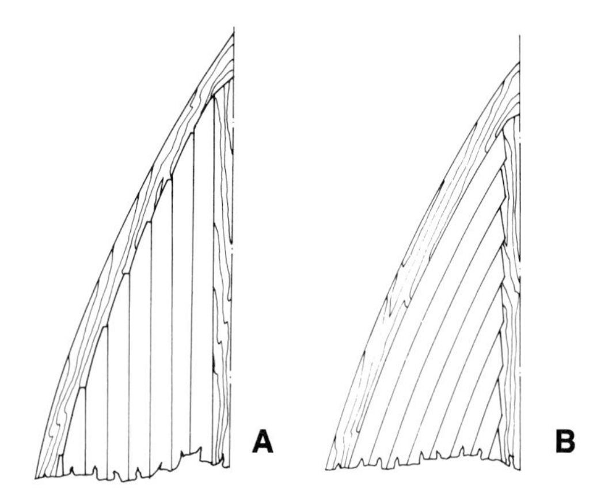

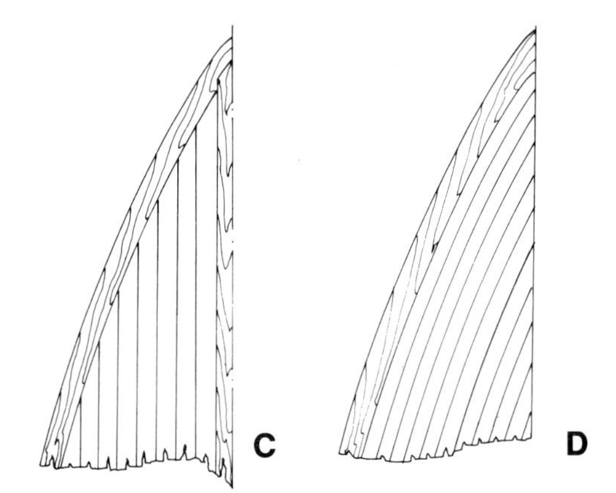

A Straight laid deck with nibbed covering board.
B Swept laid deck with nibbed king plank.
C Straight laid deck.
D Swept sprung laid deck without king plank (both this type and **C**, are often pre-fabricated, panelled or veneered on to ply and laid in sheet form).

Localised repairs to these over-laid panels call for intricate skills that are more associated with marquetry than the discipline of the shipwright. It has to be said that repairs to a good solid deck laid in the classic manner are not exactly the most straightforward either – indeed, they demand much patience and precision. The removal of a worn section of planking without causing extensive damage to a much larger area is difficult enough where the timber is fastened by means of dowelled screws, but on older boats planks are often nailed. So, along with everything else, there is the small matter of first discovering the nails. Although repairs may be needed only in isolated areas, years under the tread of human feet, to say nothing of countless scrubbings, etc, may have eroded the wood to the point where the cosmetic appearance is unacceptable. If this is so, a new deck is the only answer. As the timber wears, screws will stand proud and be ready to cut into exposed flesh. While such screws can be extracted, tightened down and redowelled once, it is not a procedure that can be repeated ad infinitum.

Prime sites for rot

Laid decks are subject to movement and will need regular attention to the seams; this applies regardless of whether they have been payed with pitch, marine glue or the modern polysulphide compositions. Obviously, the state of all seams will be one of the things checked during inspection, but don't become so enthralled by the look of a laid deck that you become oblivious to the possibility of rot. Rot – and in the case of plywood, delamination as well – is liable to be lurking beneath the quadrant moulding at the coachroof to deck join, wherever flexing has affected the integrity of caulking and stopping and in the vicinity of all fastenings.

By far and away the most undesirable place for rot to set in is in the covering board, the outer border of the decking. Decay could simply be caused here by corroded through-bolts, in which case it may not have spread far and local surgery is all that is needed. On a large vessel with bulwarks, however, rot in this area may be sufficiently widespread to render an economically viable restoration out of the question. This is because of a time-honoured unsound building practice: the internal frames are doubled, or sometimes extended, in order to protrude through the covering board and thus form the support for the bulwarks. Over the years water trickles inexorably down the frames to deck level, where

A traditional carvel-built Norwegian fishing vessel with the hull planked up and the deck beams and carlins in place. But, excellent as the workmanship undoubtedly is on this well-proven design, problem areas can be picked out even at this stage – the extended frames which support the bulwarks and the immense curvature and twist of the planking of the canoe stern impose enormous strain on the fastenings (which, in this case, are rather close to the hood end).

it will find its way through pinholes in any protective surface or defective fastening at the root of the support and covering board. This is bad enough in itself, and will start off the process of deterioration in the deck. However, as that timber suffers and becomes increasingly porous, the moisture, encouraged by the natural capillary effect of the long grain in the frame itself, will travel down the frame and instigate wet rot there also.

It is certainly not difficult to identify these ravaged areas, at least not if they remain undisguised (remember, paint and filler could have been used). If you do suspect this condition, I would regard the juncture of frame and covering board as one of the few legitimate target zones for a determined and thorough probing with the edge of a chisel, and also a site where some paint should be rubbed down to the bare wood (always assuming that there is some wood remaining, because there may not be if rot has gained a foothold).

This may sound very alarming, but consider a 40 foot smack. There will be twenty to thirty frames above deck, each of which may be afflicted on three sides by an area of suspect timber for at least 6 inches. It is possible to cut in short lengths to deal with each outbreak of decay, though an amateur would be hard put to make a sound job of it and not many boatyards would care to attempt it. In order to rectify matters satisfactorily, the entire covering board will have to be lifted along with all ancillary timber attachments. In a vessel that is already stripped out, this procedure might be worth the effort, time and cost. However, in the case of a boat with good internal joinery (assuming the quality of the interior woodwork to be reflected in the asking price), the price of dismantling fitments to avoid damage (which would in all likelihood be inflicted in the course of repairs) may make the purchase or the remedial action financially unjustifiable.

Deck coverings

It used to be standard practice to cover tongued-and-grooved decks with light canvas or Trakmark, a textured vinyl material. However, if a laid deck has been treated with such lack of respect it was probably in preference to recaulking – but even the soundest canvas may cover a multitude of sins!

A deck that is free of defects in every respect, sheathed in canvas that has been carefully preshrunk on laying and subsequently well protected with several coats of paint (the first being thinned so as to saturate the fabric), should be both watertight and able to flex sufficiently to accommodate the normal working of the planks. It should remain in this condition for a decade. This is rather fortunate as old, soundly adhering canvas can be extremely hard to prise off (indeed, removal may need the use of a blowlamp). Glassfibre used in conjunction with either polyester or epoxy resin, and also Cascover (nylon cloth impregnated with resorcinol glue prior to application of vinyl surface paint), are even more durable if applied on a carefully prepared surface.

When examining a sheathed deck, notice if the sheathing, whether it be canvas, resin and cloth or Trakmark, extends under deck fittings, mouldings and cappings. If it doesn't, suspect that it was hurriedly stuck on as a desperate means of avoiding trouble in the short term (or for the purpose of selling the vessel). All fittings should have been removed and re-seated with mastic after covering, otherwise the deck will not remain truly watertight. This can only serve as a guide, for without cutting away portions of a deck covering no more than an intelligent guess can be made as to what lies beneath. Some indication may be seen at the joins: loose canvas or fixed timber or brass strips suggest previous investigation, presumably carried out with the aim of curing weeps.

Plywood decks, unlikely to leak unless laid with exceptional lack of skill and a miserly application of glue, may rely on paint as the sole protection against the elements, so once the surface breaks down the wood is left accessible to moisture and eventual delamination. If butt joints are visible, even as mere hairlines, inspect them closely in case filler has been used to obscure signs of glue failure in the veneering. Take care to examine closely any area where plywood comes into structural contact with other timber, especially if no cappings or mouldings are fitted. Marine ply is straightforward enough to repair but, once delamination has gained a hold on the deck, considerable portions may require excision – along with all fittings in the affected areas.

Regrettably, this holds true where repairs to any type of decking are concerned; what can appear, on the face of it, a minor matter of replacing a plank or two – or perhaps a small area of rot beneath a windlass – becomes an extremely taxing task.

CHAPTER 9

Surveying the internal hull

After examination of the interior, all aspects of the hull construction can be linked together to form a complete picture. This should either confirm a surveyor's worst suspicions, or provide reassurance that all is well with the vessel. Admittedly, this internal check is complicated by the presence of internal joinery, floors, bearers, ceilings and soles, a proportion of which will prove stubbornly immovable. However, where the structure can be seen, not only can the final summing-up be made on soundness of timbers, planking and fastenings, but also an accurate assessment of the original building specification can be made. Sometimes owners who take considerable pains over painting and filling external defects omit such niceties where such basic and essential components as frames, floors and knees are involved.

Matters are certainly made easier for the surveyor if he is left alone to pursue enquiries. However, the vendor's curiosity (or even apprehension) tends to mean that there will be an uneasy presence hovering furtively in the background, wary as to the discovery of some guilty secret. Normal courtesy forbids ordering an owner off his own boat, so exploit the situation instead: suggest that an extra hand to lift berth tops and lever up (or unscrew) soles would be most welcome.

As with the exterior of the hull, the interior of motor and sailing craft of conventional construction (including diagonal) can be regarded as similar. The main exceptions are the overhangs of a sailing vessel and also the sharp tuck in the garboard, both of these parts are liable to harbour problems. A yacht, especially one designed with racing rather than cruising in mind, will possess finely attenuated overhangs subject to stress distortion imposed by the loading of the rig. Rot, too, is nearly always present, flourishing in ill-ventilated corners that are almost impossible to treat successfully, because of inaccessibility. Since the counter is most vulnerable, this is the logical place to start the inspection. The first point to establish is whether or not the counter is still as the designer intended. Often it will have been shortened, since the easiest method of dealing with widespread deterioration is simply to saw off the end section!

Such an amputation can pass without too much comment on a sturdy cruiser, but an elegant six-metre boat where the counter has suffered an expedient demise has lost much of its essential character; restoration of this would surely be one of the purchaser's first priorities. It is a good idea to construct a low profile access hatch in the aft part of the decking to permit occasional circulation of air, and thus enable a visual check on the internal condition of the counter.

With a broader counter or full-width transom, repairs are less likely to have been executed in so summary a manner. Having

The main beam of a barge yacht – wet rot and furniture beetle (a hazard not to be overlooked once a boat is laid up on shore) have made mincemeat of the timber, although bearing in mind the indignities which have been heaped upon the remainder of the structure perhaps the state of the beam is the least of the problems!

said that, it is not unknown for a reef to be taken in an unsound transom: suspect this possibility if the edges have been heavily doubled. The transom should be carefully inspected for shakes, especially at the edges, and also for rot. Additionally, it should also be checked where the gudgeons of a transom hung rudder are through-fastened. (The condition of these would be ascertained at the same time.) While grovelling around in the hindquarters, flashlight in hand, the opportunity can be taken to examine the inner seams, deck beams etc, as well as the components of the wheel steering mechanism if this is installed (not omitting to check that provision has been made for an emergency facility). Fitments such as fuel tanks, batteries, etc should not only be examined for their own sake, but the hull beneath needs looking at as far as is possible. It is these dank and generally unexplored territories that are prime sites for deterioration.

Moving forward to just aft of the midship section, inspection may be hindered by the installation of any machinery whose immovable bulk will obstruct a portion of frames and floors – and in an area where the sharp turn of the bilge tends to produce faults in frames and ribs. It is a fair bet the engine bilge will, in many cases, be filmed with oil scum and grease. Peer into the depths, checking the type and condition of the engine bearers and ensuring that the weight of the power unit is well distributed on load-bearing frames; also, ensure that the joins between the frames and bearer are

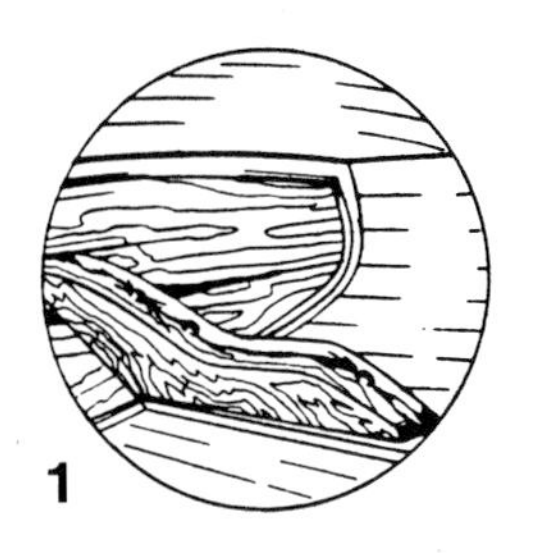

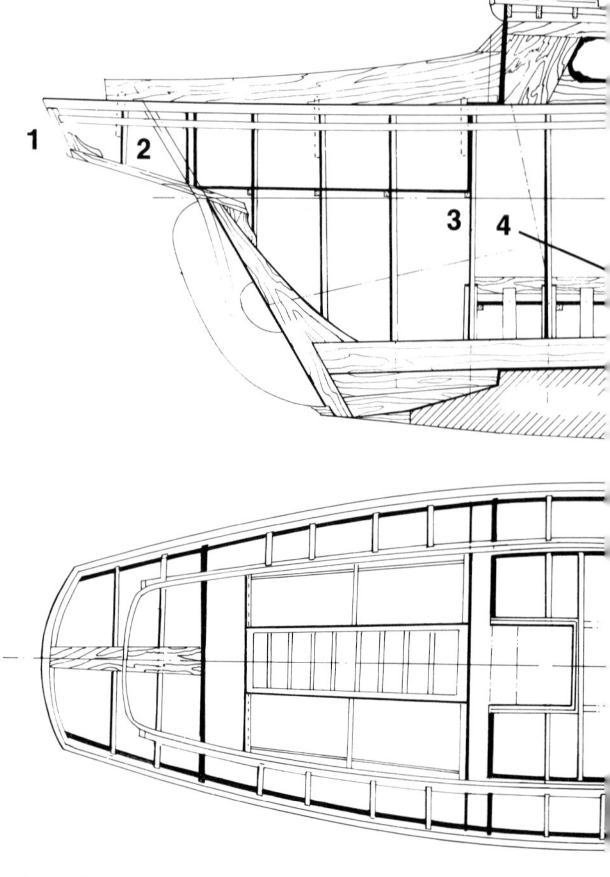

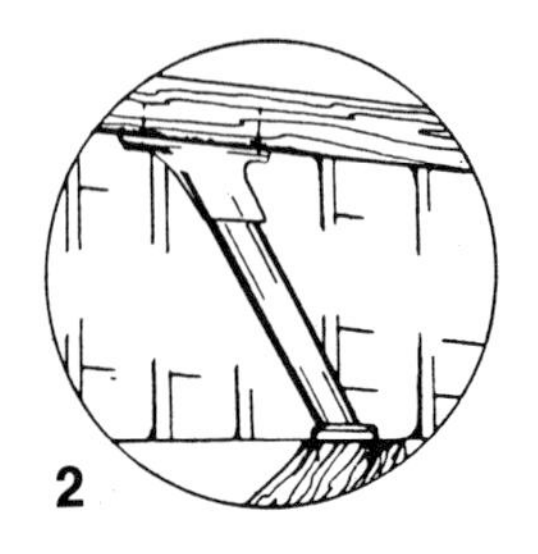

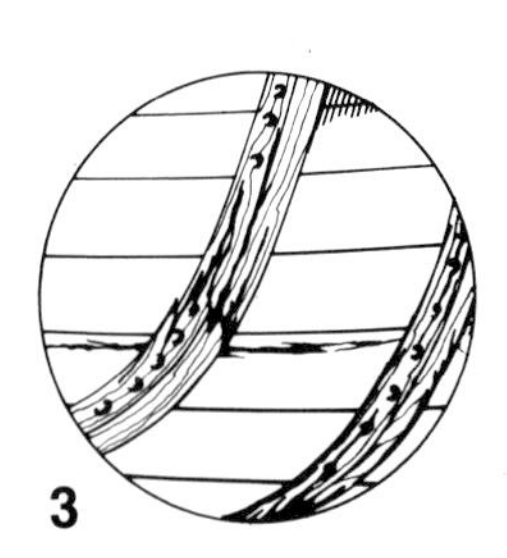

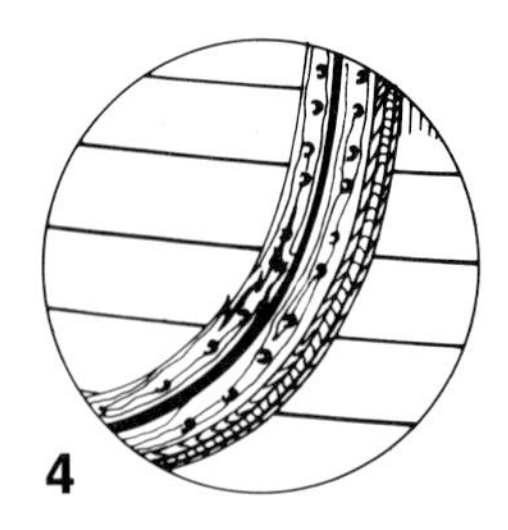

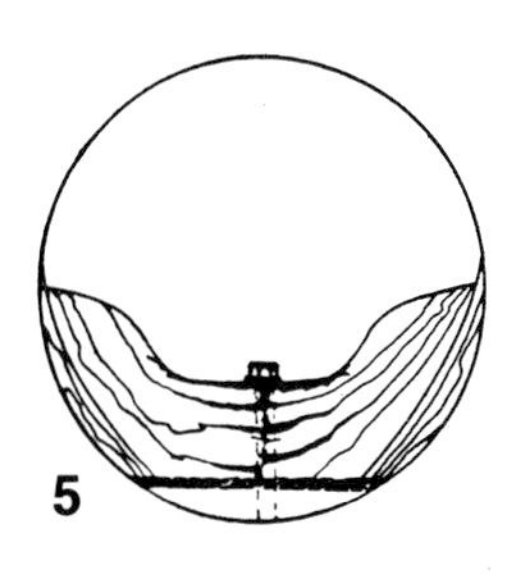

Common faults of the interior hull: timber carvel yacht.

1 Rot in archboard and stern knee: this is largely due to corroded fastenings which allow water ingress. The poor ventilation of long overhangs is usually a contributory cause.
2 Metal corrosion and wet rot in the surrounding timber at the upper and lower ends of a steel rudder trunking. Timber trunkings are especially vulnerable to rot inside, and repairs are difficult, time-consuming and liable to be very costly.
3 A fractured frame with damage to the plank in the immediate vicinity. The damage could have been caused by collision, grounding or possibly by nipping between a larger vessel and an immovable object such as a jetty. The forward frame shows signs of capilliary rot working upwards from the lower extremity, also rot caused by water penetration through corroded fastenings.
4 A laminated double frame. Laminating a frame in situ is arguably the best method of repair, but leaving the old one in place is poor practice: it creates a 'hard spot' on the hull, exacerbates the possibility of rot (between the frames) and it is, of course, readily detectable!
5 Rot in a load-bearing floor brought about by seepage from keel bolts or by bilge water left to stagnate over a period of time. Repairs will involve removal of all through-fastenings. If floors are of steel or wrought iron,

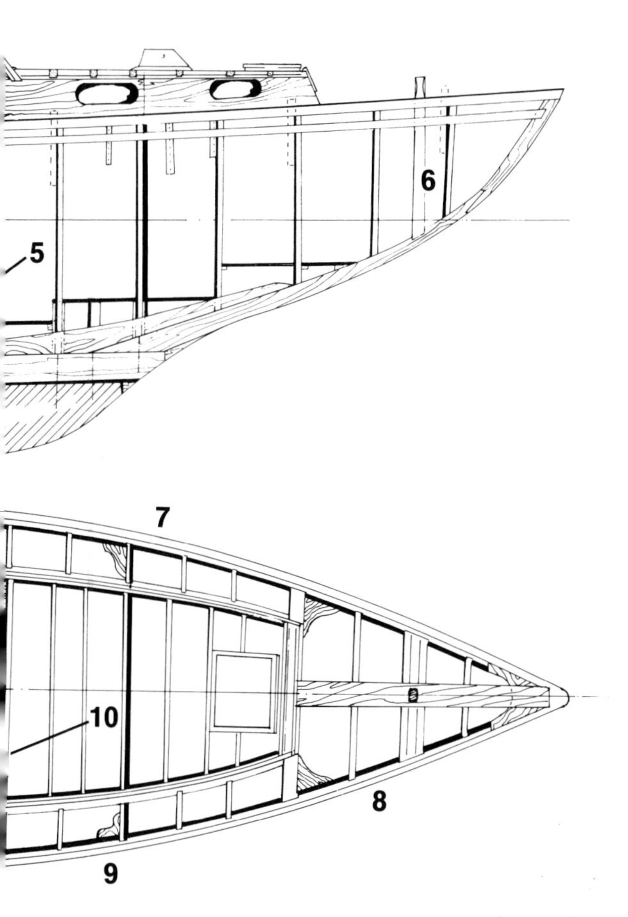

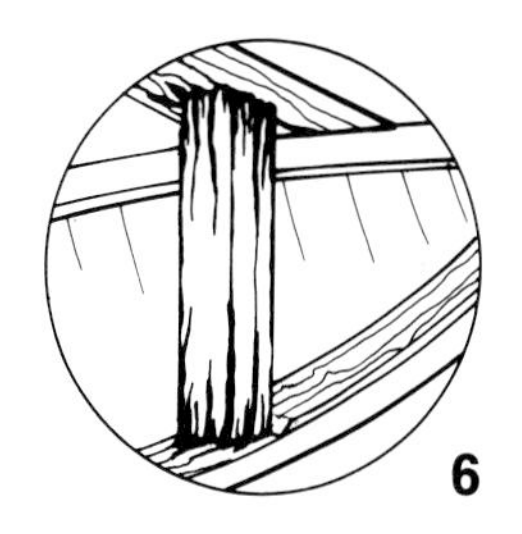

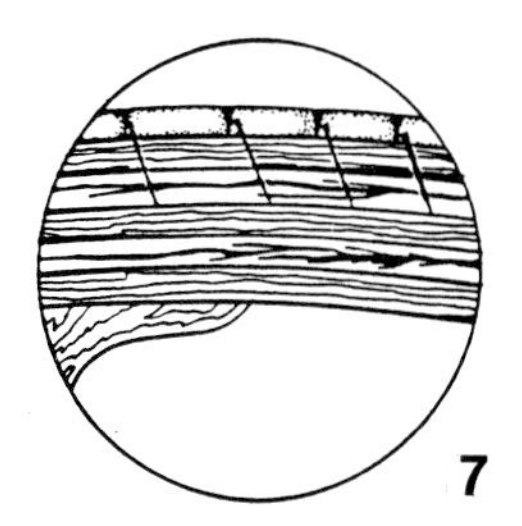

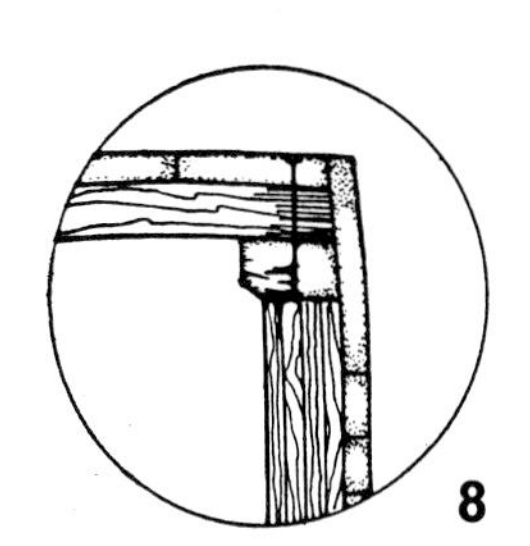

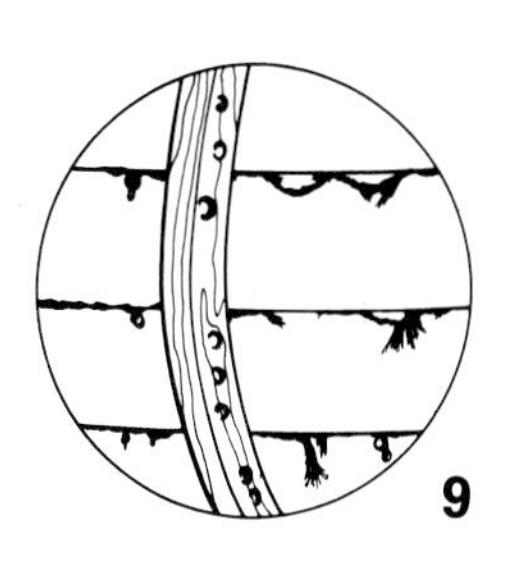

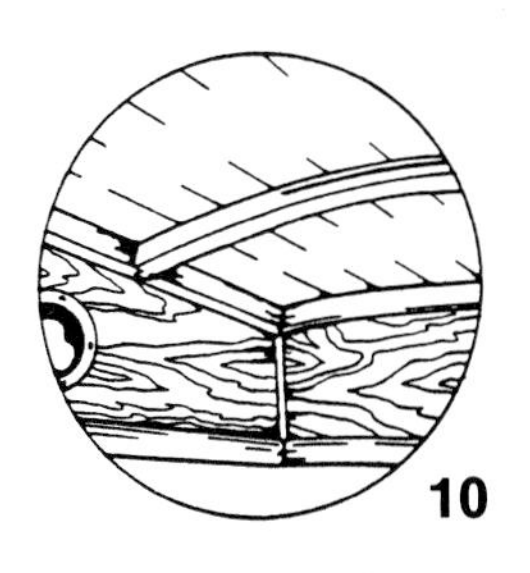

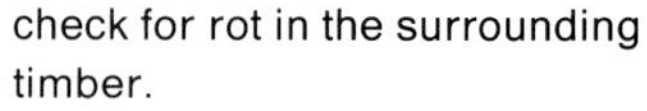

check for rot in the surrounding timber.

6 Through-deck Samson posts are always prone to rot as it is impossible to prevent a small amount of movement – and therefore water – eventually leading to severe deterioration.

7 A laid deck with secret nailing: this method of fastening lends a whole new dimension to replacing a deck, as the nails have first to be located and then wheedled out! Movement of the deck may cause the nails to work slightly, with the usual result – rot!

8 Rot frequently affects the beam shelf, once again through-fastenings and poor ventilation are the chief culprits. Replacing long sections of shelf is not a task for an inexperienced amateur, and some idea of professional charges should be gained before going ahead with a purchase.

9 Caulking cotton forced through the hull from the outside – common enough and with luck it may have not caused irreversible damage to seams. On the other hand, there remains a possibility that they will have been forced open to the point where they will no longer take up. (NB: uneven spacing of fasteners suggests that there may be later additional fastenings for a good reason).

10 Faulty deck coverings and years of slight movement allow water into beam dovetails and seams in tongue-and-groove planking.

sound, allowing no possibility of water entering.

Internal ballast

Internal ballast makes the examination of the hull even more time-consuming, not to say dirty, exhausting and frustrating. Both sail and motor vessels are often weighted down with iron or lead pigs, and sometimes ballast includes sash and scale weights, old lengths of chain, sand bags, or a combination of any of these!

If internal ballast was an integral part of the design, it may have been cast to fit into allocated spaces within the bilge and be correctly stowed on strips or boards to protect the hull timbers from damage or corrosion. This will not make the ballast any easier to take out, but it will mean that attention has to be paid to the correct realignment of each individual lump afterwards. Heavy and slippery to grasp as lead may be, iron (unless regularly cleaned, scaled and painted) will be far worse to handle since the chances are that each pig will be almost permanently rusted on to its neighbour.

Avoiding the end-of-season ballast removal ceremony has given rise over the years to a number of fascinating ideas. One of the most ingenious that I have had to deal with (without much enthusiasm, since I had the fiddly job of extracting each and every piece of the ballast) has been that which involved the greasing of all separate castings prior to wrapping each of them in brown paper neatly bound with hemp. This system helps to prevent severe rusting more effectively than might be supposed, but it does not eliminate the need to remove ballast prior to laying up.

It could be argued that a good deal of trimming ballast is not really necessary in the first place. Where small to medium-sized boats are concerned, it would make better sense simply to substitute useless chunks of ironmongery with water tanks, tinned stores or, even better, extra anchors and chain. Experimentation once the vessel is afloat may prove that all such surplus ballast can be jettisoned to good effect. There is no doubt that internal ballast can, and all too often does, damage the hull structure. This can even hold true where the ballast was initially specified. Removal for a full survey may show gaping seams and movement in frames, both of which can be directly attributed to several hundred pounds of lead resting directly on the planking. (In the case of the iron ballast, this is added to the rust scale that clogs up the limber holes. This prevents the free flow of any bilge water, which may exacerbate corrosion in the fastenings.)

Secure retention of the ballast is sometimes considered to be of secondary importance. In reality, in the event of a knockdown, half a ton of assorted metalwork slithering around the main bilge is a serious situation. The normal method of retaining ballast is to screw the soles firmly into place. The disadvantage is that if the craft suffers external damage through grounding or severe collision, immediate inspection and repair of the affected area could prove to be impossible – and this might result in the total loss of the vessel. Compromise dictates that the sole should only be fastened – although *very* securely – in way of ballast. Six three-quarter by six wood screws will not withstand the weight of one lead pig should there be a complete inversion, and adequately secured access hatches need to be constructed at regular, closely spaced intervals. It is in the area amidships that the most widespread defects are likely to be encountered in the transverse structure: the frames (or ribs) and floors. These will be largely a result of the enforced

Framing a fishing vessel in Norway; the construction is massive and such traditional shipbuilding calls for a good deal of physical strength.

curvature of the components themselves, and the stresses imposed by an external keel (or possibly internal ballast). Deterioration of fastenings, particularly of floor and keel bolts, will encourage fungal decay, and all the inherent weaknesses mentioned above will be made worse by a lack of accessibility and routine maintenance.

Frames

A few defective frames on a carvel (or clinker or diagonal) hull are accepted with a degree of equanimity. Timber is not, after all, a material whose behaviour can be exactly predicted.

Heavy frames that have been sawn from a block of sound and stable timber (generally those to be found on a vessel above medium size) may split along the grain, but are less liable to fracture across at the turn of the bilge. Steamed frames, though, are liable to dry and crack in this vicinity. Even well-seasoned purpose-grown frames may do so, although they are perhaps the most resilient. However, sooner or later all frames may suffer damage. Few older boats are without one or two cracked or doubled frames and these can constitute a potentially serious structural defect.

To an extent, a traditionally built boat has an in-built safety margin: a frame may splinter at the bow, a couple midships, perhaps one will rot in the stern, but not much will happen to the overall strength of the hull. But if a number (for example, half-a-dozen) of frames crack in one stress area – perhaps the garboard tuck, beneath the engine, or around the ballast keel – it is not hard to visualise the effect on the hull. Such localised defects in frames may have come about as a result of an accident; so, if a number of affected timbers are discovered, a second inspection of the external hull would be well advised.

Nowadays, laminating replacement frames is common practice. This may be carried out *in situ*, laying each lamination up against the inner planking – thus, in effect, using the hull as a mould. Alternatively, the frames may be prefabricated off-site around a jig or lay-up board. This is a simple and effective form of construction, especially for the heavier frames of a carvel-built craft. Steaming is certainly best for the manufacturing of the light ribs for a dinghy, especially the ribs in the eyes of the craft which have to be bent into a sharp U section.

Doubling of frames is still a widespread means of alleviating problems, if not an actual cure. Although it is obvious from appearance that remedial action has been taken, there is nothing wrong with the practice so long as water cannot run between the old and new frames. Personally, I dislike seeing doubled frames, which smack of a hasty and half-hearted job, but I certainly would not turn down a vessel on account of them. To many owners of smacks and the like, such signs of rough and ready workmanship are flaunted like honourable battle scars!

Common joints.
A Scarph. Used in joining lengths of timber such as stringers, or planking. Ideally the length should be not less than eight times the thickness of the timber to be joined. The surfaces to be glued should be planed so as to be slightly concave. Curved pads should be used when clamping (see inset of scarph cross-section) to exert the maximum pressure whilst the glue dries.
B Haunched scarph. Used where increased resistance to damage is required – as in keel, keelson or hog.
C Butt joint. Through-fastenings should be offset. Butt joints are a frequent source of problems on older craft where glue was not used. Erosion of fastenings gradually permits water to permeate beneath the butt strap, and rot often starts in the planks, where it travels along the timber drawn by capilliary action.
D Simple **stem construction** for a smaller yacht.
E Stopped **dovetail** used in deck beams etc.

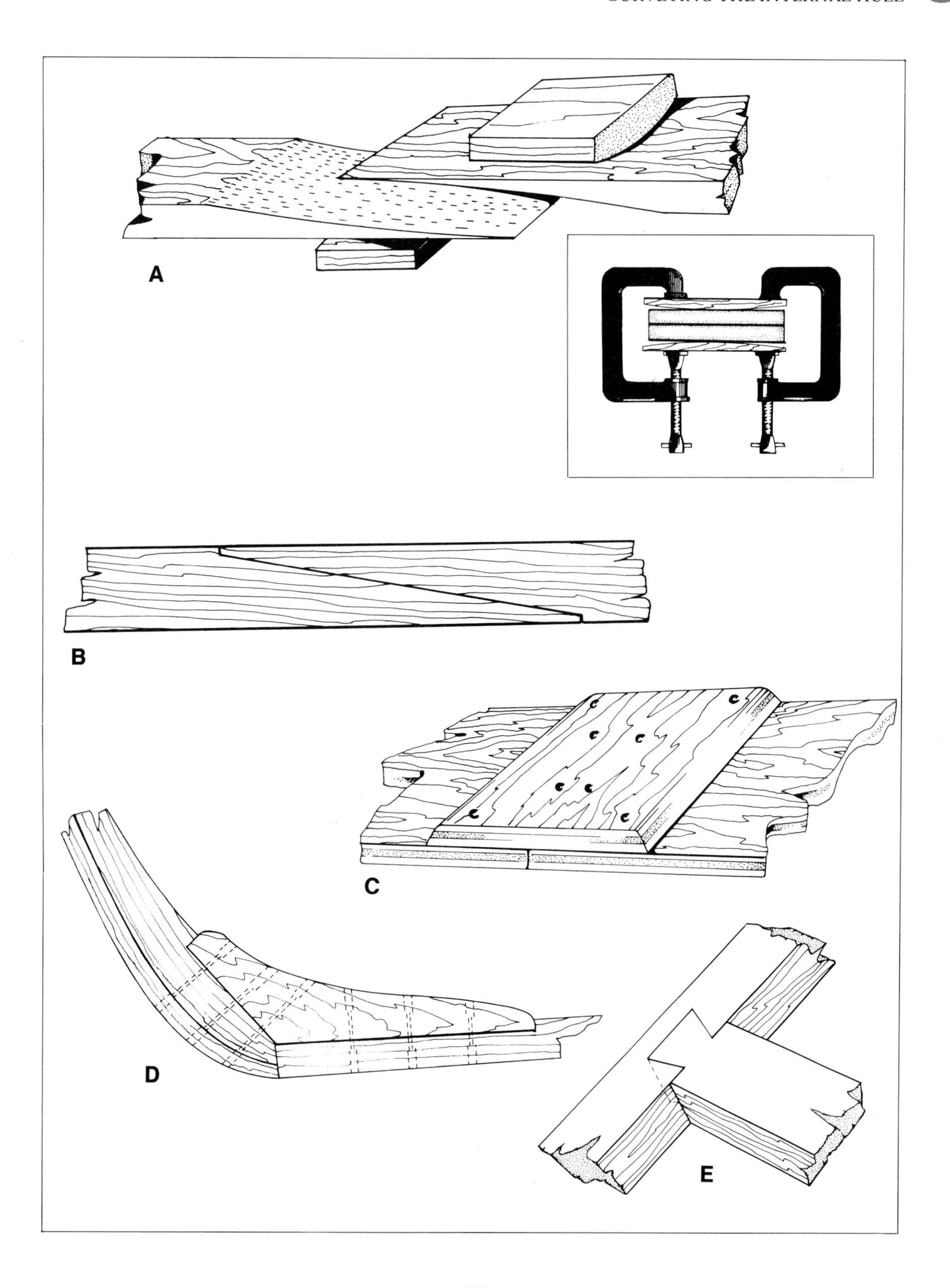
A
B
C
D
E

Whatever your feelings may be on this matter, those frames in closest proximity to the doubled members are the ones to regard most critically. The passage of time and deterioration before making good will probably have increased stresses on sound timbers, and will likely have weakened them to breaking point as well.

None of the above techniques are very demanding so far as actual woodworking skills are concerned – although the fitting and retention of an externally laminated rib or steamed timber may require two pairs of hands and spragging pieces against the hull to hold the rib in place while fastening. As usual, the most difficult part of the job will be actually getting at the repair site, which – there being no justice in this life – will inevitably be within the confines of galley, heads or engine space, and thus require the dismantling and disconnection of all installations.

The difficulty of reaching obscure corners does of course make close examination harder. In any case, the first indications of weakening, prior to the occurrence of a fracture, may be virtually invisible – no more than the faintest of horizontal cracks. Even scraping of the surface to get rid of dirt and bilge paint may not reveal anything, although a reliable preliminary sign is a subtly unfair curvature noticeable on the inner edge of the frame.

Often escaping notice is the presence of rot in the lower end of a frame or rib. This is hardly surprising as a visual inspection calls for a degree of bodily flexibility more associated with a contortionist. However, even when invisible to the eye, the distinctive open fissure or split can be felt with the finger. If left untreated, capillary action will draw bilge water upwards into the frame and eventually lead to inner disintegration.

Even if well masked by fresh paint, some idea of the soundness of the fastenings can be established from the frames: rust weeps from corroded iron nails rarely remain hidden for long, and if you see one the chances are that there are more. Corroded copper roves are not immediately apparent, but once you spot one you will be alert to the existence of others. If refastening of these has been effected, this fact should be detectable on close examination of the frames, even where previous holes have been stopped. Frequently the spacing of nails will be irregular, as sound fastenings are unlikely to have been replaced for the sake of maintaining an ordered pattern.

Floors, beams and bulkheads

Amidships, at the lowest point where bilge water finds its own level, there can exist a combination of dissimilar metals, salt water and timber. This bodes ill for the continued health of any vessel. Quite apart from steel keel bolts and through-hull fastenings of copper or brass, there may be metal load-bearing floors. These might be of stainless steel (in which case, they are probably a later addition or replacement) or bronze, steel or wrought iron. Wrought iron may have been hammered into position while hot; it is worth checking whether any softening present in the adjacent area is in fact rot, for charring is not unknown.

Inspection of timber floors in way of keel bolts will reveal the state of these fastenings and any plate washers. A corroded bolt head can be taken as evidence of more severe corrosion in the shank of the bolt – or, at the very least, viewed as a suitable case for extraction and investigation. Almost certainly, visible corrosion will be accompanied by localised rot, so this will have to be made good before refastening. Splits across are an additional unwanted complication, and a further breeding ground for rot and corruption. (It should be borne in mind that the replacement of a floor will in most cases call for the withdrawal of a keel bolt and can therefore be regarded as a major undertaking.)

Next on the list of transverse components

for checking out come the deck and coachroof beams. Of course, the relationship with all longitudinal members can hardly be ignored, since it is in joints that defects mostly occur. The actual beams rarely deteriorate to any great extent, apart from miscellaneous shakes (easily dealt with); also, if they are laminated, there is the possibility of glue failure and the opening of the timber strips.

This will entail removal and re-making, unless the area is sufficiently localised to make glueing and splining an acceptable alternative. True, rot can often be discovered where occasional fastenings (of grabrails perhaps, or items of deck hardware, carelessly dowelled or stopped) have corroded, but on the whole such defects are limited in extent and readily dealt with.

Bulkheads in a carvel or clinker boat provide an element of rigidity in the cross-section, but are not necessarily an integral component as they are with glued veneer construction. Nevertheless, their very presence can be revealing, especially if they appear to have been installed as an afterthought. Their general function is usually concerned with the interior layout, but they may suggest later design amendments such as a watertight cockpit or an enclosed engine space. In either case, ensure that the bulkhead is not restricting access to vital seacocks, or restricting the removal of engine and shaft.

Load-spreading components

Sailing vessels have been more affected than motor boats by the tendency to reposition the main propulsion unit in accordance with an altered perception of efficiency (only occasionally justified). But, equally, drastic alterations to the rig that entail re-stepping the mast in an altered fore and aft plane (or on heel plate or tabernacle instead of the keel) can compromise the boat's structural integrity.

In many older sailing craft, the mast would be keel stepped and supported at deck level by a pair of massive beams known as the mast partners. Lodging knees of massive dimensions gave an additional back-up. This was a very solid (albeit unsophisticated) method of supporting a substantial spar setting a low-aspect gaff rig. This was then largely superseded by the Bermudian rig, more or less in its present form. Like most new ideas, it was opposed vehemently at the outset. However, it rapidly became accepted by the yachting (if not the workboat) fraternity. Certainly it appeared to offer a number of advantages over gaff, not least of which was ease of handling by fewer crew.

All-round performance, though, proved the most telling point in favour of the Bermudian rig – in particular, its measurable supremacy when working to windward. But this rig necessitated a taller mast, comprehensively stayed and stepped further aft. This usually entailed cutting through the coachroof. There was in itself nothing wrong with this, so long as the appropriate internal framing was constructed at the same time. Because of spiralling timber costs, it was not long before the spar was perched on the deck, in a heel step. This saved the cost of 6 feet or so of spruce.

Except where a tabernacle is fitted which allows the mast to be lowered without recourse to a crane, this change is of dubious value. (There are arguments in its favour, though: such as that of retaining the spar in one piece if it goes overboard after rigging failure, as a keel-stepped mast usually snaps off.) As with most other alterations, a professional conversion carried out by an experienced yard should be trouble-free, since adequate internal bracing (whether a load-bearing pillar or bulkhead) would be duly provided. But of course many amateurs, of varying degrees of skill, were also hell bent on updating their rigs; the evidence of this work is sometimes visible in the form of a flattening of the deck or

A case of mistaken priorities? It does appear, from a glance at the frames, that it might have been wiser to start with these and the hull fastenings before whipping off the entire coachroof – although if actually living on board, the onset of winter may reverse the normal order of working!

coachroof beams in way of the mast, almost invariably accompanied by defects in the planking. If a bulkhead has been installed that is too flimsy or improperly fitted, a slight bow outwards from top to bottom may be noticeable. Should either symptom be seen, treat the vessel with suspicion – even if no other problems are evident. Be very wary of purchase if the boat has never been sailed with the changed rig. A hard thrash to windward may at once produce structural problems.

An integral part of the internal stiffening is in the form of hanging and lodging knees (vertical and horizontal braces of wood or metal) placed at critical points of the hull – such as under the deck, in way of the mast, at bows and stern, and also to support a centreplate case. Frequently the fastenings will have corroded, with the inevitable result that the wood will have deteriorated. Replacement of knees constitutes more of an irritation than a severe test of craftsmanship. However, this does not mean that the condition can be disregarded entirely, because evidence of previous movement or drawing away from the carlin or deck beam may indicate strain rather than shrinkage of the timber itself. For whatever reason, a gap between structural members is unwelcome, for it invites moisture.

In a carvel or clinker boat, the planking itself provides the greater part of longitudinal strength. Consequently, there are few other internal stringers, with the exception of the inner deck edges or carlins and the beam shelf, inside the gunwale, into which the deck beams are jointed. This shelf is conspicuous by its absence on a surprisingly large number of boats that are regarded as classics. The beams are merely fastened through the shipside, and the covering board over the planking, and the whole affair is then presumably considered to be adequately tied. Without doubt, this short-cut simplifies construction and pares down the timber costs. Despite this, it seems a rather ill-conceived practice. I have to admit, though, with the exception of minor instances of rot in the vicinity of defective fastenings, I have witnessed little other evidence of problems as a result of this short cut.

A hard-chine vessel will of course have bilge stringers, as will (hopefully) a yacht fitted with bilge keels. If not, longerons usually tend to do double duty in that they form part of the interior joinery as well as contributing to the overall strength of the hull.

The interior joinery

Interior fitments, their quality and lay-out, have hardly been mentioned yet in this general outline of construction. This is because so far as traditional building methods are concerned, the internal fitments rarely affect the overall strength or rigidity of the hull. However, in veneer construction, they most certainly do. This being the case, a beautiful hand-waxed and panelled interior may be a strong selling point, but it should not be allowed to blind one to the soundness – or otherwise – of the main structure. Unfortunately, all too often the heart rules the head to the extent that a boat whose hull is in the last stages of degradation, but which is possessed of a fine saloon, fully fitted galley and luxury toilet compartment may well command a higher price than a sound vessel with rudimentary accommodation – however impossible the rebuilding of the former, or worthwhile the restoration of the latter.

When assessing any wooden vessel a certain amount of latitude must be permitted regarding the scantlings, timber types, fastenings and the means of bringing all three together. For every rule, though, there are many exceptions. Perhaps it should be remembered that both designer and shipwright are individuals, and are determined to express this individuality. A few of their products are excellent and the majority are highly satisfactory. Nevertheless, there have certainly been one or two maritime abominations. Time has shown nearly all of these in their true guise, but a few remain – beckoning seductively to the unwary (and even a knowledgeable purchaser can fall victim to their charms). Thus the many hours spent in surveying the basic hull structure is time well spent. Shortcomings in the mechanical department, domestic utilities, furnishings and equipment can all be alleviated by injections of cash, but little can be done about poor design or construction.

CHAPTER 10

Modern timber technology

Ten years ago, this chapter on advanced timber technology would have been restricted to plywood and moulded veneer construction, where the hulls would be glued or laid up using resorcinol-phenol-formaldehyde or urea-formaldehyde resin adhesives. A brief mention might just have been made of some of the new resins that were emerging on to the market.

These days, even though few of the basic techniques for the building of new craft have drastically altered (except perhaps with regard to disparate types of core material and the need for stability and control of the working climate), the emergence of epoxy resins cannot – indeed, should not – be ignored, particularly with regard to the restoration of classic timber boats. It is claimed that the WEST system – the acronym for Wood Epoxy Saturation Technique – has changed the face of high-technology timber boatbuilding and repair. Not, though, that these resins are restricted to the maritime world; the use of resin composites has been pioneered in the fields of architecture, composite fire- and blast-resistant systems for oil refineries, and also in aviation. Yachts, and increasingly light commercial, life-saving and passenger-carrying craft, even now account for only a comparatively small part of the total output.

Before going further with the WEST system, it is perhaps useful to point out that the term 'saturation', when used for the treatment, sheathing or construction of timber fabrications is not strictly accurate. This is because the resin encapsulates rather than saturates the fibre of the wood. Common sense will make it obvious that, short of localised injection, it is not possible to saturate a given piece of sound timber to any great depth. However, the encapsulation, if total, does render all surfaces impervious to water. Therefore, in theory they are impervious to all forms of water-borne – or rather, water-exacerbated – decay.

Actual moulding and laminating methods with the WEST system differ little from those used in 'conventional moulding'. However, because external surfaces are coated, timbers that are light in weight, but unstable (and therefore not previously exploited to any degree for hull construction – e.g. white pine, white and red cedar, etc), can be used as a core material.

The epoxy resins, although capable of achieving optimum adhesion only to timber that has been thoroughly dried out, are nevertheless not so sensitive to atmospheric conditions as to rule out their use by amateurs. Naturally, as is the case with all boatbuilding adhesives, a high degree of care must be exercised when handling: dermatitis can occasionally result from contact. Wear protective gloves, ideally with a barrier cream underneath, and be meticulous about washing your hands afterwards.

Manufacturers' precautions must be followed to the letter. (This is equally true when rubbing down resin composites: mask and goggles are essential as the dust is highly irritating.)

The resin, depending on the materials with which it combines, has three properties: first, as an adhesive for construction; secondly, used with appropriate cloth, for sheathing the hull (internally and externally); and thirdly, as a gapfiller. For this last purpose it may be mixed with bulking agents such as microfibres, colloidal silica (which effectively thickens the resin mix and impedes penetration into a porous surface), or one of the bubble fillers – such as glass bubbles or phenolic microballoons. According to the manufacturers' specifications and advice, more than one of these fillers may be used in conjunction with another depending on the specific qualities desired.

The besetting problem for the majority of amateurs who become drawn into large-scale projects is the maintainance of a viable ambiance and temperature in which the resin can cure evenly. This alone has brought about the demise of more than one ambitious cold-moulding exercise using 'conventional' adhesives – as I know to my own cost when I bought a half-completed hull. The dissection of the glue lines and veneers proved a dispiriting experience. Small areas of glue had apparently never cured, while the remainder had done so before the veneers could be retained in close contact with one another. This was the result of errors on the part of the builders, and the resorcinol glue was not to blame.

The materials

The epoxy recommended for use as an adhesive is always of the solvent-free type (undiluted with organic solvents such as those used in paint or varnish). It is of fairly thin consistency, low shrinkage and, when mixed with the appropriate filler, has good gap-filling properties. These epoxies can be mixed with fast or slow hardener to vary the working times according to expediency. When cured, the resin and hardener react and form a rigid polymer plastic. Working with resin is straightforward, but a perfect end product can only be arrived at by accurate measurement of all components and the maintenance of recommended temperature levels. But there is one advantage over many conventional adhesives: the actual minimum temperature level required. Except at the time of pouring and laying on the resin, a warm atmosphere is not necessary: a thermometer reading of 15°C is perfectly acceptable. If it is unavoidable, the mean temperature can drop as low as 5°C and still permit total curing of the resin. In this case, though, the time taken at all stages from touch dryness to gelcoat – and thence to complete cure – will be considerably extended.

The major difficulty encountered with low-temperature working conditions will be in the handling of the resin – in the pouring, mixing and application – since the cold causes the chemicals to thicken. An acceptable solution is to warm the resin, either by placing containers close to a safe source of heat (not, of course, an open flame burner), or standing them in buckets of hot water. A current of warm air directed at the resin will ease the mixing process and, when coating the wood, warm air directed over both the faces to be glued will ensure a free flow and an even coating. Once the joint is together and air excluded, the epoxy can be relied upon to cure safely in spite of a less than ideal ambient temperature.

Epoxy composite systems have produced some outstanding 'state of the art' fast cruiser/racers, multi-hulls and power boats. All of them are light and tough, although not necessarily guaranteed to delight the eye of a traditionalist. But the technique is rapidly finding favour in the construction of craft, whether day boats, power craft or blue-water cruisers. For small boatyards the advent of epoxy makes it both feasible and commercially attractive to construct 'one-offs' with that distinctive character of a bygone era and all its nostalgic appeal. Although these highly individual craft command high prices, demand appears to be growing. A few of the designs, though, might be regarded by the cynical as carrying traditionalism to the point of self-parody.

Challenging and exciting as the technique of epoxy and timber may be to a builder of boats, to the amateur restorer it is presented as little short of wondrous. There is no doubt that its usage has saved many an elderly vessel from demise. Complete restoration of some virtual derelicts can be contemplated with greater confidence by an amateur with little experience, and therein rests a potential drawback to the system: possibly the only drawback. The use of epoxy resins is shrouded with something akin to the awe generally reserved for miracle cures, but in reality the 'magic' of the product lies in the skill and dedication of those using it. While no manufacturer of such chemicals would suggest that short cuts are ideal working practice, the guidelines as to the use of these materials can give the lazy the impression that yawning craters, rotten planking, frames and floors can simply be filled, sanded down and painted over and the problem is solved. And who will know the difference – in the short term at least? Unfortunately, there will always be some unscrupulous character who is out to make a quick killing by tarting up an old vessel. This boat may look wonderful for a year or two, but it will then resume the process of gradual deterioration. It is marvellous to see classic boats restored to their former glory, but a purchaser should be wary unless regular inspections at various stages of restoration have been carried out by a surveyor. It is not wise to rely solely on photographic evidence. The camera may not lie, but it certainly can distort things – whether by accident or intent.

Sheathing for strength or protection

Although the use of glassfibre cloth and epoxy resin for external sheathing provides almost total protection against rot and marine borers, it can also be used as a means of greatly enhancing overall structural strength. The process itself is straightforward, but a great deal of preliminary preparation will be needed; just how much is dependent on the initial state of the timber. Although this stage is time-consuming, it should on no account be skimped. A carvel hull, which flexes slightly, will require the seams to be either filled with epoxy and the appropriate bulking agent, or by splining and sealing prior to sheathing. All surfaces to be treated must be very low in moisture content and completely clean. Grit blasting may sound a drastic way of cleaning off, but in fact the epoxy benefits from the porous surface thus created. The greater the absorbency, the more effective the penetration of the resin – thus the greater its ultimate efficacy. Admittedly this is not a process well suited to a hull that is merely to be treated with oil-based paint rather than sheathed, as the sapwood is stripped away leaving the harder heartwood areas to stand proud. But although the external sheathing will provide great strength – indeed, it can to all intents and purposes produce a new hull – the interior should also be encapsulated with resin and cloth. Because of the strictures imposed by the original construction, this is not always practical; therefore, at best, a liberal coating of resin may be all that can be realistically hoped for.

Ideally, the interior should be completely stripped: with all ballast, fittings and engine removed prior to the commencement of work. However, for one reason or another, this may not be possible. Sheathing by itself will achieve a measurable improvement in the hull, but will not completely restore integrity if there are a number of seriously damaged or rotten frames and load-bearing floors. While it may be impossible to replace every frame, great efforts should be made to replace those defective members that are accessible. In some instances – but not near the mast or chainplates – it may be acceptable to treat partly rotten frames by drilling and injecting the affected sections with resin. This, it is claimed, will restore a considerable amount of the original strength. Since this is less troublesome than laboriously fitting new frames, the temptation may be to resort to this method throughout the hull.

On larger yachts and working craft – where the frames are often over-sized to start with and can tolerate a small amount of deterioration here and there – it is not uncommon to see encapsulated frames which have thus been hardened and rendered solid, but which nevertheless retain the weathered and battered look associated with mock Tudor beams. Even when the resin has successfully penetrated each split, crevice and all areas of carroty grain (and this will not be easy to ascertain), I would prefer not to see such signs of antiquity. Personal whim it may be, but I am inclined to look more favourably upon frames that are more or less in accordance with the original contours and dimensions. More to the point, I think any surveyor would wonder whether other labour-saving tactics had been considered expedient during the course of refurbishment.

However, no such half measures can be tolerated in the case of load-bearing floors. Without question, those found to be defective must be replaced – either by sawn or laminated timber, or metal fabrications.

Innovative use of epoxy systems

The accommodating properties of modern resins do render possible some quite remarkable – if unorthodox – projects. One that stands out in my memory is the transformation of a once handsome Whitstable smack from an assemblage of rotting and blackened timbers into a vessel that might just have been launched. Indeed, the finish was in most respects far superior to the original, while at the same time remaining faithful to it. The metamorphosis had been achieved by bonding what amounted to a complete cold-moulded outer hull on to the ravaged original planking, while also encapsulating the interior and stabilising the structure. This notable piece of craftsmanship was the work of a skilled shipwright – he was, however, greatly assisted by limitless funds and no-holds-barred attitude of his client.

There is the caveat, as with all forms of moulded construction, that voids and cavities may lurk between the laminations; and, in a case such as this particular one, between the old and new hulls. Unlikely as this may be, the possibility cannot be dismissed. Unfortunately, though, unless a number of core samples can be taken, judgement has to be based largely on the standard of other, more visible, workmanship. While such a limited inspection is far from ideal, it will give a general indication of the thoroughness with which repairs have been carried out.

This pragmatic approach is not an unreasonable one to adopt towards most timber boats when assessing the refurbishment or rebuilding that they have undergone. The rule is equally valid when applied to vessels built of ferro-cement, steel, aluminium or glassfibre, each of which has its own peculiar strength and limitation. It is especially relevant, though, to all forms of composite or glued construction. Resin composite systems, as now marketed, have been around for a fairly short period of time, and therefore there are only a limited number of examples with which to make comparisons. The most useful attribute to a would-be purchaser is arguably an open, but discriminating, mind (not accompanied by an equally open wallet).

Contacting one of the leading suppliers and manufacturers of epoxy systems would be a sound move. SP Systems of Cowes are most helpful and, not surprisingly, take a keen interest in the past and present building and restoration projects of their customers.

Before purchasing, ferret around boatyards and brokerage lists for as long as possible, make notes, and check out back copies of yachting magazines and old nautical books if these are to hand. You can then embark upon a programme of what is now known euphemistically as 'shopping around'. It is obvious that there are limits to this, though. Should vendors and/or brokers get together and compare notes, don't be surprised to detect a certain frostiness in the atmosphere!

Come to think of it, my own presence in a boatyard may no longer be welcome with open arms. But then, I am not altogether sure that it ever was!

CHAPTER 11

Glassfibre

Development of the glassfibre yacht

Although by the end of the Second World War boatbuilding methods had improved enormously (catastrophic as wars are, they advance techonology at high speed), the search for new materials and techniques was unremitting. Naturally, research was targeted mainly towards military and commercial vessels; yachting at that time was regarded as the pastime of a privileged few – and, as such, was barely given a second thought.

It is sometimes suggested that the upsurge of interest in sailing and boating directly resulted from the advent of glassfibre; this made mass production possible and the consequent lowering of price. However, closer investigation does not altogether bear out this statement. By the late 1950s marine plywood had come into being and fleets of affordable knock-about plywood power craft, racing dinghies and sailing 'pocket cruisers' in the 18 to 22 foot range had appeared on the market. The earliest glassfibre competitors of these craft were in fact no cheaper (although a high-quality carvel-built yacht did command a substantially higher figure). Glass-reinforced plastic, in spite of its much-vaunted advantages – impact resistance, negligible maintenance, imperviousness to rot and marine borers, etc – met with considerable consumer prejudice. It is, after all, hardly surprising that an owner who has worked hard to pay for a bilge-keel sloop, the design and construction of which, so the builder assures him, is the finest and most up to date that money can buy, is going to be less than delighted to learn that a few yards of fabric woven-form glass filaments and a bucket or two of polyester resin are about to confer instant obsolescence upon his pride and joy!

The writing, however, was deeply inscribed on the wall. From the moment of arrival of the first unsaturated polyester resins into Europe in 1946, it was a short step to the first craft produced in 1950–1. The myriad yachts and powercraft in evidence today took less than half a century to achieve. The last fifty years have undoubtedly seen an eclipse in boatbuilding.

But can a boat created on a production line, rather than individually crafted, ever be seriously considered as a classic? Each vessel within its own class was, after all, almost identical to the next, except in differences in such fripperies as the colour of the deck paint and the fabric of the berth cushions. The truth is, though, that there were greater variations than is sometimes realised (arguably more than nowadays). In the first place, production runs were usually shorter (and not infrequently curtailed by the insolvency of the builder), with perhaps as few as fifty boats moulded to any one design; however, there were wide differences of style and function between designs even within the same size range. Also, increased competition led to outlandish attempts to break through the cost per berth barrier. Undoubtedly, although there are exceptions, a lot of the smaller, mass-produced sailing and motor cruisers were ungainly high-volume dormitory units

Several production glassfibre yachts of the late 1960s and early 1970s have come to be regarded as classics. This may be due to their construction, eye-appeal or performance – or all three as with this Hustler 25 cruiser-racer.

which really do justify the deprecatory terms by which they came to be referred.

One reason that the looks of such vessels suffered – apart from this obvious stress on extra accommodation – seems to have been the result of the determination of certain designers to ensure that their boats looked as though they were moulded from reinforced plastic. They did not *want* them to be mistaken for timber. Ugly as some of these little boats were, some of them don't seem so bad when compared to today's equivalents. Furthermore, a significant proportion of them are still soldiering on, having required no more remedial attention over the years than, perhaps, the occasional facelift and possibly an updating of rig or engine. This seems to suggest that they were in fact better constructed (certainly, many were far more heavily laid up) than today's production boats which, surveyed after five years or so, are rarely without one or two minor structural defects at best, or – at worst – osmosis. (Osmosis is actually a misnomer as it describes the process that produces the blistering rather than the blistering itself.)

While the smaller craft of those days were similar, many of the medium-sized or larger yachts and motor cruisers had a crisp and unfussed line to both hull and superstructure. This was directly derived from timber vessels; indeed, the timber trim was often lavish with all possible attempts being made to conceal the fact that the vessel was actually moulded glassfibre. The actual lay-up often followed the hallowed tradition of some timber boatbuilders: the heavier, the stronger. The knack of paring down specifications of mat and reinforcement to save weight (or rather cost), however, was rapidly acquired. Particularly attractive examples from the early 1960s were the Alden Challenger and some of the smaller Phil Rhodes designs; also, there were fast semi-displacement offshore motor cruisers such as the 48 foot Perpetua, launched in 1954 and claimed to be the first large glassfibre vessel built.

Class identification

But are these boats classics? Well, certainly a number qualify on the grounds of age alone. Thirty years is a respectable length of time and many look set to last another generation or so. Age is not the sole criterion: some of the yachts and power craft in the forefront of today's technology have a strong claim to be considered as classics: they are innovative, efficient and, in the case of the larger yachts, very beautiful.

Within the accepted meaning of the term, though, there is a hard core of vessels produced by famous designers or well-known yards, the majority being direct derivatives of their timber forebears. In essence, the purchaser is paying for a name and, since the asking price is likely to be high (it may even be double that of an essentially similar boat considered unworthy of the classic label), it is important to ensure that what you pay for is in fact what you get. This may seem to be stating the obvious, and so it will be to, for example, a purchaser who is set upon a Nicholson 32 and has been so ever since the design was first moulded. For someone less experienced, it is not impossible to confuse a Nicholson 32 with a Morgan Giles 30 (I have known this to happen, which is why I am using the example). Apart from the overall length (not easy to verify by eye alone), the similarity is great. To the casual observer, the main differences would be the absence of one window per side in the coachroof and the sparsity of the external woodwork in the slightly smaller boat. True, there would be variations in such things as the accommodation and cockpit layout, but many Morgan Giles 30s were fitted out by amateurs and the Nicholsons have been around long enough to have had considerable modifications made to them.

There is a faint possibility that from time to time a deliberate attempt is made to deceive, but usually it is more the case that it is just not possible to classify each production glassfibre yacht or motor vessel with absolute certainty. Since business acumen and boatbuilding skills did not inevitably go hand-in-hand, the moulds and plugs for various classes were sold off and so made the rounds of smaller builders' yards and, occasionally, backyard moulders. By no means were all of the boats thus produced inferior to the original. In fact, some were actually slightly superior as far as the overall finish was concerned, although the exact specification and details of the lay-up may remain a mystery. But the one thing that one of these boats will not possess is the plaque of a famous yard – the designer label, so to speak! Perhaps it would be more accurate to say that the boat *should* have this, since it is not unknown for a batch of the previous builder's plates to be sold along with the moulds and tools. In many cases, the brand name of the vessel was also part of the package deal. But often the new builder altered it, perhaps desirous of a new image. Therefore it is very hard to be certain.

One of the most difficult types to classify with any degree of certainty is the Folkboat – or, rather, its numerous kinsmen. I can think of at least half-a-dozen small boats that are closely related to the Folkboat. These include (and I am bound to have omitted some) the Contessa 26, Invicta, Folksong, Nicholson 26, Diamond, and Halcyon – as well as three glassfibre Folkboats conforming with the One Design rules. These all have in common a graceful curved bow and raked transom stern with transom hung rudder, but not a lot else (apart from the brochure descriptions harking back to their illustrious ancestry). Even so, it might come as a shock to learn that both the counter-sterned Warsash One design and the Wing are described as Folkboat types (though not, I am certain, by the designers). And even the Hamble One design, a cruiser with chopped counter, built-up topsides and a short coachroof, was re-launched in the 1960s as the new Folkdancer class.

Naturally it is not only sailing vessels that sometimes defy classification: the many Watson and Nelson types, fine semi-planing power craft whose hulls are in demand by commercial organisations, harbour patrols and as pilot cutters, also are wont to have their name taken in vain. All have certain features in common, but the major apparent difference is often mainly between engine models and installation, moulders' specification and, of course, the fitting-out yard. It is the latter that may have the most influence on the price, raising it (or reducing it) by as much as a third even when two vessels are outwardly similar in condition and inventory.

The dictates of fashion as well as utility also play a part in establishing the neo-classicism of some craft, and it is not immediately obvious to the uninitiated why one class is so highly preferred to another – occasionally even in the face of a known propensity for certain structural problems. The entire business of nomenclature and terminology is a minefield, so it is probably safest to employ a surveyor (although occasionally even surveyors are confused by species look-alikes).

The classic replica

Deservedly or not, replica craft have to be considered as classics, if only because there does not seem to be another category into which they will conveniently fit. By replica, I mean just that: a warts-and-all moulding that has taken a traditional working boat or yacht as the plug. In extreme cases of salesmen's hyperbole, the craft from which the copies have been lifted is purported to be the very last of its type in existence.

Personally, I do not believe that copying the original lines of a boat – often to the extent of leaving signs of irregular seams, indifferent paying, etc visible in the moulded hulls simply because the original boat was afflicted by them – is an especially meritorious concept. It suggests the nautical equivalent of reproduction Chippendale; however, as with copies of antiques, there is a demand. Each type of replica vessel must, though, be accepted and judged on individual merit: the quality of the laminating and internal and exterior joinery.

In some cases, the substitution of timber by reinforced plastic can have an adverse affect on performance. Admittedly, this will hardly be noticeable on a craft over 20 feet. Nor on one that has a fairly high ballast ratio carried in an external ballast keel, for the amount of ballast can be adjusted at the design stage to compensate for discrepancies in the altered centre of gravity that construction in plastics entails. In smaller craft, though, where form stability is of paramount importance, the weight distribution may have undesirable effects. An increased amount of internal ballast may be needed to offset the heavier topsides and this may reduce freeboard to an unacceptable, or even dangerous, level. The amount of positive buoyancy, in the form of foam-filled areas or watertight bulkheads, must be adequate; often it is not. Unlike her timber forebear, though, a glassfibre boat will rapidly swamp and founder.

These criticisms are not levelled at those glassfibre designs based on the traditional as opposed to cloned. The former craft select and enhance the best characteristics. Many of these delightful cruisers – such as the Cornish Crabber and well-known daysailers such as the Drascombe Lugger – retain a traditional appearance, while at the same time making the most of modern techniques. They are not perhaps classics in the strictest sense, but they are excellent compromises: they handle smoothly and are easy on the eye. The secret of their success lies in the fact that any potential faults (and most of the vessels that provide the inspiration for these newer designs had their unpredictable little ways) have been anticipated and eradicated at the drawing-board stage. Some concessions have to be made for today's somewhat overcrowded coastline and harbours: manœuvrability, adequate power and an easily managed rig are essential. And as far as is concomitant with the vintage character, the accommodation has to reflect today's desire for comfort below – something that would have appalled the skipper of an old-time working boat!

Construction methods

Glassfibre techniques, in common with timber boatbuilding methods, can be roughly divided into two categories: traditional and innovative. To some extent, as with

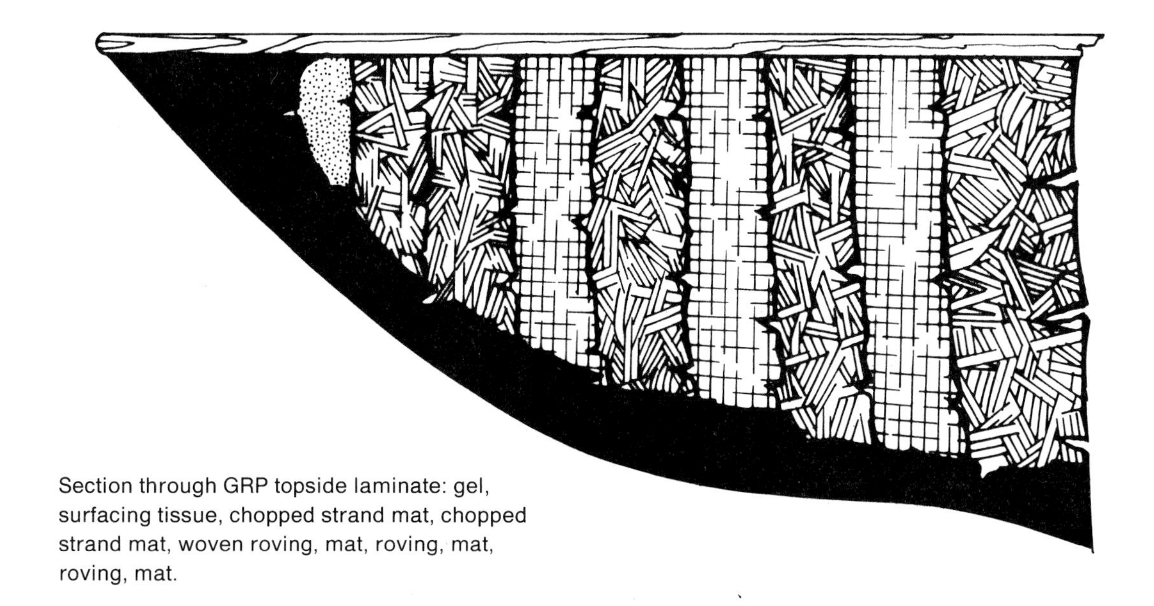

Section through GRP topside laminate: gel, surfacing tissue, chopped strand mat, chopped strand mat, woven roving, mat, roving, mat, roving, mat.

timber construction, the latter systems tend to be favoured by the home builder or a yard in the business of producing custom-built racing boats. Strictly speaking, a classic glassfibre yacht is laminated (with the cloth usually laid and impregnated with resin by hand) inside a female mould. Longitudinal stiffness is imparted to the structure by encapsulated paper ropes and timber bulkheads, with additional cloth providing reinforcement where necessary. All deck fittings are backed up by hardwood plates. However, the alternatives to 'conventional' construction from a female mould have also to be considered.

In order to produce the female mould within which such a glassfibre hull is laid up, a plug has to be made (unless an existing hull is used, as occasionally is the case). This plug dictates exactly the finished hull's condition on release from the mould. All blemishes, imperfections, unfair bumps and hollows have to be smoothed away, or all future production craft will be stuck with them. The construction of these two items is both time-consuming and expensive and requires a large working space).

The hull is laid up from the outside in, with the gelcoats first (following prior application of a release agent and, possibly, a surfacing tissue whose function is to ensure that the texture of the underlying mat is not visible through the gelcoat), and then successive layers of alternating chopped strand mat and woven roving. The chopped strand mat (often, in a cost-conscious modern production factory, fed as strands into the chopper gun, mixed with resin and catalyst in the barrel, then sprayed directly on to the mould) is in effect the backbone of the lamination. This material is readily saturated with resin, easy to lay since the random fibres interlock and 'stick' to one another. For its weight, chopped strand mat possesses acceptable multidirectional tensile strength.

In order to further increase strength and flexion tolerance, this mat is interlaid with a woven roving. As its name implies, this is a glass fabric, of varying degrees of coarseness and weight that bonds readily to the mat – though not to itself or anything else. Unwoven rovings (although all cloths have the lengthwise warp and the transverse weft at 90° to one another) consist of filaments running parallel and linked by cross stitching, a unidirectional roving providing the greatest strength along the length of the strands. Unlike chopped strand mat, rovings do not readily accept a compound curve: unidirectional cloth, for obvious reasons, being the least adaptable.

There are variations on unwoven rovings to accentuate the strength characteristics across or diagonally to the weave. These cloths, in common with all other rovings, may be used in order to reinforce a given area or to effect repairs. Sometimes used in the basic hull lay-up is a bonded composite of chopped strand mat and woven roving. This can reduce lamination time, especially in the case of a small- to medium-sized vessel.

The alternative type of hull fabrication is that of sandwich or single skin laid up over a male mould or, as it is sometimes known, a batten mould – a term that well describes the construction and form.

To build such a mould is both simpler and quicker than it would be with a female mould. It also obviates the need for a plug, but it is still a comparatively large undertaking – particularly where just one boat is to be constructed from it (or rather, over it). But a sound and sturdy mould, used for foam sandwich construction, can in many instances be lifted clear of the finished hull and reused. Lofting the sections to full size and correctly aligning them is the single most important part of this operation; fixing the longitudinal battens into position is then quick and easy. Any premature feelings of self-congratulation should, however, be dispensed with, because what is not revealed, at least not until the lay-up is completed, is whether or not the hull is fair. This is hard to assess just by looking at the mould itself, even when covered by its protective thin polythene skin. One drawback to construction over a batten mould is the amount of filler and fairing required to produce a first-class external finish; indeed, it is this that so often gives away the fact that a hull was built by an amateur.

Foam cores

The core materials for sandwich construction are nearly as numerous as species of timber, but many of these are restricted to ultra-light, highly innovative, and fiendishly expensive performance craft that do not (yet) come within the compass of this book. Those most usually encountered in the normal course of events will be foam (generally polyurethane or a PVC/polyurethane mixture) or end grain balsa, which is supplied on a light fabric backing. This enables it, like the closed cell foams (supplied in strips or sheets according to type), to be eased into place around the curvature of the hull. Quite large areas can be tacked into position at one time. (The technique employed in foam sandwich construction, by the way, should not be confused with filling the cavity between the premoulded inner and outer skins of a hull with foam, injected in order to impart stiffness and positive buoyancy to the structure.)

Foam or balsa sandwich construction has few inherent problems; this is true even for the inexperienced builder, so long as two basic tenets are adhered to. The first is to accept that some form of shelter from the elements is vital (as is a portable heater to keep the ambient temperature well above freezing point: polyester resins cure at approximately 18–20°C). The second is to be patient – not only to help in enduring the physical processes involved in laminating, but also to cope with the seemingly endless initial stages: lofting, building the mould, reading and re-reading, and then finally memorising the procedures involved in handling the core and the resin. (Polyester resin is not a substance to be trifled with. It is quite safe if handled in accordance with the manufacturer's directions, but there is some risk of explosion if the peroxide-based

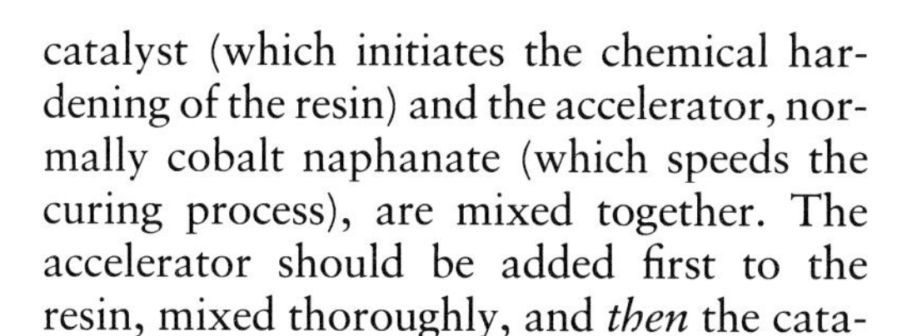

catalyst (which initiates the chemical hardening of the resin) and the accelerator, normally cobalt naphanate (which speeds the curing process), are mixed together. The accelerator should be added first to the resin, mixed thoroughly, and *then* the catalyst added.)

A core or sandwich construction consists, in simplest terms, of a resin-saturated foam or balsa sheet which is first laid over the mould form (this core being usually stitched with thread or tagged into place over the mould battens with copper wire). Over this, inner and outer skins of chopped strand mat and roving are laid and impregnated, with the exact laminating schedule varying according to the designed specification. So long as the core is saturated as deeply and evenly as possible (though total saturation is not always achieved) and the laminates adhere to one another, the external hull should emerge with an acceptably fair finish: this can be perfected by sanding and filling (and possibly using a surfacing tissue) prior to applying a gelcoat. It must be a gelcoat specially formulated for use on an exposed surface, or, alternatively, an epoxy or polyurethane coating, sprayed or brushed. Usually this last stage will be very labour intensive, but a first-rate finish to the hull is more than cosmetic: it provides much-needed protection against later deterioration.

It is, incidentally, quite feasible to build a 'skin-only' hull over a male mould, although this form of construction may have no significant advantage either in money or time. This is because the mould has to be rather more closely battened and will require covering with a non-structural foam in order to achieve a fair and smooth hull finish.

The deck and superstructure of craft that are constructed commercially within a female mould follow similar moulding practices to the hull lay-up. However, nowadays, even where the hull is constructed of mat and rovings, it has become common to use foam or balsa as a core material for the upperworks because of the improved strength to weight ratio. Quite a few amateur-built boats, possibly in an attempt to maintain some pretence of traditional appearance, prefer the decks and coachroof to be of timber. Even this could be said to negate one reason for building in glassfibre in the first place: to produce a rigid monocoque structure with no seams to work or leak! (Although hull to deck joints, whether overlapped or flanged, can certainly do both if not adequately bonded in the first place, or if subjected to external forces.)

Assessing the structure

Superb as the external finish of a glassfibre yacht may be, the surveyor is faced with a certain amount of uncertainty when testing the integrity of the moulding. Frankly, tapping the hull and listening for ominous echoes will not reveal much, unless the vessel has suffered damage (evidence of which will, most likely, be obvious anyway). Thus the general appearance of the workmanship as a whole has to be used as a guideline. Before internal joinery is installed, a fair impression can be gained from examining the manner in which interior stringers have been fashioned – whether laid up over a foam core, timber, or pre-formed over an individual mould – and the care with which they have been bonded to the hull.

Another reliable indication is the manner in which major load-bearing elements, such as bulkheads, floors and engine bearers, have been glassed in. Once the interior fitments are fixed, access to these vital structural components is restricted. Despite this, the standard of the woodworking should reflect to some degree the skill and thoroughness of the builder. It will suggest as well whether materials have been skimped: erratic cash flow bedevils some

Kept in a mud berth over a period of time, a glassfibre yacht is not immune to damage from abrasion, blistering (the warmth of the mud and shallow water may increase this possibility) and silted-up skin fittings. About the only depradation to which it is immune is that of marine borers. If purchasing a yacht which has been laid up in this manner, have it hauled out – or at least dried out alongside – for a close inspection.

building projects from the outset, but real crises tend to arise once the basic construction has been completed and the hull readied for fitting out.

Osmosis

Now for the subject that is arguably the greatest single cause of doubt and worry to those who own glassfibre vessels: osmosis.

Controversy is rife, with opinions sharply divided between those who reckon osmosis to be a case for the undertaker rather than the doctor, and those who are equally convinced that the repairers and sprayers (surveyors, too, I regret to say) have created a cure for which there is no disease! Tending towards the latter view will win me few friends, but it must be said there does exist an 'osmosis industry') and it plays on the worries of its customers. Hyped-up fear of the dreaded 'boat pox' can make the most level-headed person over-react. In some cases, this over-reaction can turn out to be very costly, with as much as a quarter of the actual resale value of a boat expended in order to grind out and fill a handful of localised gelcoat blisters; to dry out the laminate (if indeed it actually showed an unacceptable water content in the first place); and to treat the underbody with solvent-free epoxy paint.

There are cases, and they do unfortunately seem to be increasing, where the blistering is so severe that the hull has to be re-gelled – though these are still relatively uncommon. Normally the blistering, if only affecting the gelcoats, is restricted in area and may never spread, or produces a deterioration so gradual that it can be dismissed – at least, in the short term. This is not to say that regular checks on the underbody should be omitted, since there are certain factors that can hasten the process.

Such is the pre-occupation with osmosis that, no matter what other serious defects the boat has, after completing a survey I await the nervous enquiry as to whether the vessel has 'got it'.

Whatever it may have, it will not in the strictest sense be 'osmosis'. This is the term applied to the process rather than the product of that process. General usage has come to signify that 'osmosis' is the actual blistering of the gelcoat (or between the gelcoats) and the ensuing plague of unsightly eruptions. These will, if large enough and sufficiently widespread, eventually allow water to penetrate the underlying laminate – where it certainly will cause serious damage. But the word itself describes 'the tendency of a solvent to diffuse through a porous partition into a more concentrated solution'. This is exactly what happens when water and a gelcoat, which for any reason is permeable, come into contact with one another. The process can be insidious: blistering may literally have been built into the vessel, but not manifest itself until several seasons have passed.

Polyester resins are not, in spite of recent advances, totally impervious to water, though the isophthalic type, expensive but durable and with superior water resistance, is generally favoured for use as a gelcoat over the less costly orthophthalic; this latter is more economical and acceptable for the hull lay-up where water resistance is not (or should not) be a primary requirement. Vinylester resin is rather permeable, although it does form an excellent bond with foam cores. Epoxies are highly resistant to water, but this increased performance comes with a correspondingly high price tag. (It is worth pointing out that even the highest grade of gelcoat will be liable to porosity if not put on with due care and attention, as no substance is unaffected by poor or slovenly application.

Cause and effect

Faulty, patchy or insufficient curing is a major reason for the depradation of the gel: careless mixing can result in some portions of the resin receiving too much or too little catalyst. Contrariwise, too rapid agitation and stirring of the gelcoat in order to disperse the catalyst may result in the formation of bubbles; these, once the curing is complete, remain as air voids.

Improper curing is not always detectable during the laminating stages, and, there is a nagging suspicion that even if it is suspected, not much is done about it. The partially completed hull laminate should be allowed to cure in its own time before the next layers of mat are applied (the resin, even without the addition of the catalyst, will eventually cure by itself – hence the short shelf life of the product). Some mass-production boats are rumoured to be specifically liable to defects caused by under-curing.

Too low a working temperature and inefficient control of humidity can be a contributory factor causing the eventual deterioration of the gel, as can the temperature of the mould itself. This mould may well have been loaded on to a transporter at the weekend, spent a couple of days exposed during transit, then offloaded at the yard where it remains hanging around for several days – growing damper and more chilled by the hour. It could take five or six days to warm up to the point where the laminating can safely begin.

If the humidity in the mould shop is too great, condensation will form on the highly polished interior surface of the mould. Equally possible, since the resin generates heat during the cure, any damp present in the atmosphere can result in condensation forming between the gelcoats or layers of laminate.

The rate at which the osmotic process takes place is not entirely predictable. Like most natural phenomena, though, it is unrelenting. Whether water penetrates the gelcoat after launching or is unintentionally included on the factory floor, the end result will be the same: it will dissolve the chemical residues contained within the hull (and inevitably the accelerator and solvents do leave traces of free chemicals) and will thus form a denser liquid that 'attracts' external water at an increasing rate. The accumulated water expands in a warm temperature (or in frost), thereby forcing the laminate and gelcoat apart and causing blistering.

Blisters are usually detectable once they have formed (the sizes vary, but most are about $\frac{1}{4}$–$\frac{1}{2}$ inch diameter, often in localised outcrops), but failing to discover any at the time survey does not, regrettably, guarantee their absence in six months' time. Admittedly, the onset of widespread blistering is unlikely within such a short time span.

Ugly as gelcoat blisters are, they are not necessarily prejudicial to the structural integrity of the hull. The risk is that, by allowing water to penetrate the substrate – which may well incorporate some incompletely saturated fibres, it can attack the laminating resin and cause a serious breakdown within the hull. This, luckily, is not as common as one is sometimes led to believe. However, if the hull has suffered damage from an external source, the process of water penetration may have speeded up; the possibility of subsequent delamination cannot then be dismissed.

Use of the damp meter

Like the majority of surveyors, in the course of my work I use a non-destructive damp meter whose high-frequency radio waves measure the change in capacitance produced by the presence of water. I have considerable faith in the information imparted, but I am also aware that this information can be misconstrued. Either as a result of careless handling or deliberate design, the machine can be persuaded to utter fearsome and ear-splitting warnings of laminate saturation – to the utter consternation of interested onlookers. This propensity to mislead can of course be exploited. Damp meters *do* record moisture content accurately, but the readings have to be carefully interpreted.

The damp meter is a tool, and its effectiveness is dependent to a large degree on the experience of the operator. Certainly it will indicate moisture in the immediate area of the scan, but what is not revealed is the reason for its presence. This may well be a result of water penetration of the gelcoat and saturation of the substrate, but it is equally possible (indeed, much more likely) that water is trapped beneath successive coatings of antifouling. Unduly high readings may also be caused by the water tanks, pipes or timber bulkheads – or they may simply be caused by a wet cloth left lying on the internal hull surface. Moisture penetration is frequently the result of gelcoat damage or crazing: hastily executed repairs to an insufficiently dried-out surface, which may be imperceptible to the naked eye, are shown up by the scanner and can be subsequently confirmed with the aid of a powerful magnifying glass.

I have recently encountered one or two insurance companies that request moisture content readings of their clients' hulls. This is odd since merely knowing the moisture percentage alone, without taking into account the reason for it (such as the vessel having been in commission until the previous day!), seems pretty irrelevant.

Some yards and independent operators will – for a fee charged according to the boat's overall length – record moisture readings of the hull. I would be a bit chary of such operators as they do not explain the reason for any measurements, and suspiciously the readings often seem to be at 'danger' level.

If all other possibilities can be ruled out, and moisture content remains high even after a period ashore, the existence of acid-filled voids within the laminate or delamination is a possibility.

Glassfibre construction certainly has the propensity for latent defects, some of which are difficult to track down and eradicate. Much repair work can be undertaken by a careful amateur, so long as an acceptably controlled temperature can be maintained in the work area.

As with all types of construction, though, some defects are almost impossible to eradicate except at an unrealistic cost. A careful eye should be able to pick them out at the time of survey or, at the very least, suspect their existence and take appropriate advice before purchase.

CHAPTER 12

Surveying a glassfibre yacht

Glass-reinforced plastic, notwithstanding its many good points, does have a fair quota of defects that are peculiar to it; tracking these down in order to ascertain their extent and importance is not a process that should be hurried. Knowing *where* to look on the external hull is just as important as knowing *what* to look for. There is really no reason why anyone who has examined a timber boat with a view to purchase should find a vessel of glassfibre totally alien. In almost all respects, the basic precepts of design are similar: attach the ballast keel (or install a power plant), pay attention to the distribution of stress; and ensure that all hull fittings are of a size and type commensurate with design and intended purpose (and preferably attached to something stronger than the skin or planking!). The areas associated with structural faults in glassfibre vessels are much the same as those found in traditional craft built of timber or, for that matter, those of steel or ferro cement. Problem areas are in the vicinity of the mast and chainplates, where through-hull or through-deck fittings are located (shaft brackets and separate skegs being especially vulnerable in fibreglass craft), and in the region of the hatches and windows. But the greatest contributory factors to breakdown of gel and laminate are bad design and workmanship.

There is one essential difference between a glassfibre boat and a traditional wooden vessel: the former can be considered as a single integrated unit. The hull, deck and superstructure are bonded together, except in rare cases of composite build where only the hull may be laid up of resin and glass. Although a written report would necessarily devote a separate section to hull, decking and coachroof, for the purposes of this book they can be dealt with as one welded structure – with resin and glass replacing the welding rod! The deck and superstructure are nearly always moulded in one piece, although such extras as wheel shelters, hatch garages and the like will be laminated separately and bonded on at a later stage in the building process. (It is impossible to incorporate any double curvature in a moulding unless the mould can be dismantled to facilitate release after lamination.)

Without question, glassfibre keeps it's secrets well. Unless a vessel has been involved in an incident (a euphemism for a fairly serious grounding or collision) or has very pronounced blistering, external indications of defects can easily be missed – at least on first inspection. Unlike a timber boat, unless the 'incident' has been of horrendous proportions, there is no guarantee that there will be any evidence to be garnered from the internal state of the hull. (There may be even fewer visible signs of damage in production yachts of the 1980s and 1990s where interior modules almost completely preclude access to the shipside and bilge space.)

A meticulous check of the interior of the vessel, in so far as this is possible, must be carried out. The condition of all domestic and mechanical systems must be scrutinised, and there may be localised deterioration around components such as keel bolts and gate valves. Trouble can lurk unnoticed under flexible plastic water tanks where constant condensation can lead to water permeation of the internal gelcoat, with the attendant risk of blistering (however small a risk this may be). As with any boat, minor problems can be obliterated with paint and filler; these are especially hard to detect in cases where the interior moulding is randomly textured with an uneven gelcoat.

Following an identical procedure to that adopted for a timber vessel, first take a long view of the hull. If distance does not lend enchantment it may be that the sheerline is unfair. In the case of a glassfibre hull this is less commonly the result of strain than of amateur construction (consider the possibility that the vessel in question might even be the original plug for the class moulds – this is not unknown). Minor cosmetic fiddling with capping rails and rubbing strakes is all that can be really contemplated without giving away the purpose of the alterations – but be suspicious of any shipwright who is incapable of achieving a reasonably smooth concave line from stem to stern (if, of course, that was the intention in the first place). Some modern designs, hardly classics yet but may be in the future, are so broad in the beam and flat along the gunwale that they look unfair, if not actually hogged!

Undulations in the moulding will also show up markedly from a distance. Unfortunately there is nothing that can be done about this, although such tricks as double rubbing strakes with alternating colour bands or contrasting double boot-tops may draw the eye away from unsightly bumps and hollows. Hard spots, which show as vertical lines, usually where a bulkhead is installed, should be noted and then examined for possible crazing.

Paint or gelcoat?

It should be immediately obvious whether or not the hull has been painted (especially if synthetic enamel has been applied by brush) since the brush strokes (and, regrettably, the occasional run or dribble) rather give the game away. It is possible to achieve an excellent finish with boat enamel given good surface preparation, time, and fairly stable weather conditions. Unfortunately, though, there is a tendency to slap paint on almost as an afterthought, a day or two before commissioning. Epoxy or polyurethane paint that has been applied by a skilled professional sprayer is quite difficult to detect in many cases – particularly once the hard surface has been burnished to a high, smooth gloss.

But, one may ask, if the surface is fairly good, does it matter if the boat has been painted? The answer is probably not, but it is helpful to know why the paint was applied in the first instance. Was it for purely cosmetic reasons – such as a dark-coloured gel taking on a chalky appearance (which is not unusual after several seasons' weathering), or was it put on to obscure severe gelcoat damage or abrasion? Be alert to the presence of any other anomalies – bent stanchions, damaged rubbing strakes etc – which might help to support a pessimistic viewpoint. Be wary if the vessel has go-faster stripes, self-adhesive logos or stuck-on graffiti. Is there something hiding beneath the plastic trim that the surveyor is not intended to see? In reality, not even such drastic attempts at disguise will prevent underlying damage from showing up eventually. It may take time, perhaps half a season or so, but crazes will gradually reemerge. As with newly applied paint, treat any such artifice with the suspicion it may deserve.

The topsides, whether painted or in their

It can be very difficult to decide if the topsides have been spray-painted or if the original gel-coat remains.

original state, will have sustained a fair share of bumps and bruises over the years: we are, after all, dealing in the main with vessels over twenty years of age. Some surface defects will have been repaired, more or less competently; some will still be on display; and a few the owner may be blissfully unaware of. Most will hardly be of any consequence except perhaps from a cosmetic angle, but some may hint at severe defects.

Although some of the darker pigmented gels will have faded or discoloured over the years, white is the hardest colour in which to detect faults. (Dark gels are in fact relatively rare on older boats because of this tendency, and the majority of early hulls were white or pastel coloured.) This is particularly so when the surface is clean and free from grime or polish build-up. But, no matter what the colour, it is all too possible to overlook on several occasions an imperfection that positively leaps out on the final tour of inspection. This is often a result of changing light conditions; as the sun moves on its course, either glare or shadows bring defects sharply into relief. It is for this reason that it is important to examine a hull immediately on arrival at the yard; make a later inspection some hours later.

This initial visual scan ought to disclose the most obvious blemishes and such localised repairs as are pretty much unavoidable once a boat is in commission: chips in the gel around the stem where abrasion is frequently caused by the chain or mooring buoy, and also on the vulnerable edges of the transom. These areas are 'resin rich' and the minor blemishes sustained are rarely a matter of great importance. Gouges in the topsides should be taken more seriously as here the gelcoat is a good deal thinner; even surface damage in this area can facilitate water penetration. Deep scratches above the waterline should, after being cleaned back, be filled and faired to profile. If the laminate is exposed, the affected portion should be covered and dried as thoroughly as possible prior to remedial action. Larger areas may necessitate controlled conditions for the repair; this of course will entail undercover storage and the employment of professional labour.

Crazes and cracks

Crazes to the gelcoat can never be dismissed without question. True, they do not automatically signal anything more sinister than over-rapid curing of the resin (not unusual in the rounded gel-rich areas of the coachroof and toerail, though apt to cast doubts on the quality of the lay-up procedure when occurring in the hull laminate). On the other hand, they just could be indicative of widespread damage. This could possibly be the result of collision – perhaps caused by crushing alongside a wharf, pontoon or larger vessel, or indeed during craneage if the slings have not been sufficiently spread. Early glassfibre cruising boats were heavily laid up and are rather less subject to the two other main causes of crazing: namely, excessive flexing and 'hard spots'. Flexing in the topsides is all too commonly seen where through-hull windows have been fitted. These, to my mind, are anathema in any small- to medium-sized vessels, but in a glassfibre sailing craft they are an invariable source of worry since the hull is rarely reinforced sufficiently to prevent movement around the window, and frames are often non-existent with the acrylic panel simply bedded on to mastic and bolted directly through the glassfibre. Flexing around these edges quickly causes crazes that then spread outward; the window sealant will deteriorate and leaking occur, a process speeded up by the tendency of a yacht to heel under way and, from time to time, immerse the window completely.

'Hard spots' occur around an internal bulkhead or, less frequently, longitudinal components such as berth supports; the crazing, often quite fine, will be seen above and below the line of the internal stiffening. Often overlooked is the possibility that crazing may actually have started in the fitting-out shop, where a team of hefty joiners stomped thoughtlessly around the inside of a bare hull!

Usually, attempting to discern the first area of crazing, the first tell-tale hairline, is the most challenging bit; after that, perception seems to sharpen and, if crazing is present, the surveyor will in all probability discover it (just the same, the use of a magnifying glass may be helpful in distinguishing between crazes and fine scratches). Those cracks that are the result of collision with a small but unyielding object tend to radiate outwards from the impact point and are aptly described as star crazes. Lines that are long and closely spaced suggest damage from grounding or nipping (or descending abruptly from trailer or boatyard trolley), depending of course on the situation and extent. When nipping or crushing is suspected, the crazes will not uncommonly be discovered on both sides of a vessel in exactly the same place.

Small cracks in the topsides do not normally justify the expense of repair. They are easy enough to grind back and fill, but the gelcoat or paint match may be less than perfect and the cosmetic appearance of the hull will suffer. Larger areas may well require remedial action, though, as there is a strong possibility that the underlying laminate may have suffered. The crazed portion should be checked over for moisture penetration and, if the moisture meter reading in the vicinity is significantly higher than in surrounding areas, professional advice should be sought. It goes without saying that the asking price be adjusted in accordance with the finding.

Assuming that a given injury was inflicted by external forces, such as the bows of another yacht, a repair to that locality will settle the problem once and for all, with no further expenditure required. But where the crazing has been caused by flexing, either around a through-hull fitting or an internal bulkhead, the original cause has to be eliminated. This may mean reseating the item (or, in the case of a window, doing away with it altogether) and could run into quite a considerable sum of money.

Extensive damage in the hull to deck join can also be expensive to put right, not only because the laminate may have become saturated and therefore require some time to dry out, but also because there is a possibility that the hull itself might have sprung slightly from its original shape. Furthermore, often the extent of the injury cannot be established by surface inspection. It is quite conceivable that delamination or splitting of the substrate will have occurred: once again, professional advice really is essential. The same degree of caution should be applied to other visible damage to the hull laminate. Large-scale repairs are

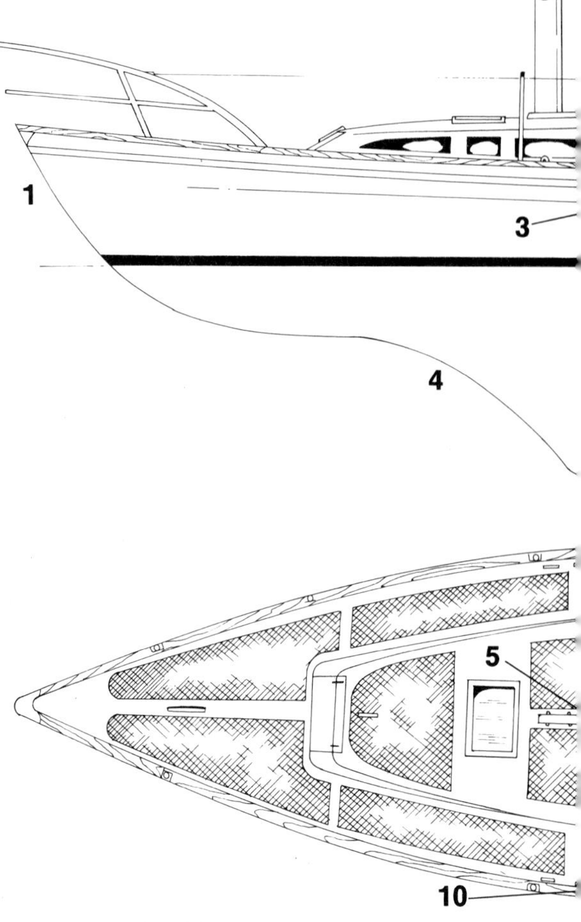

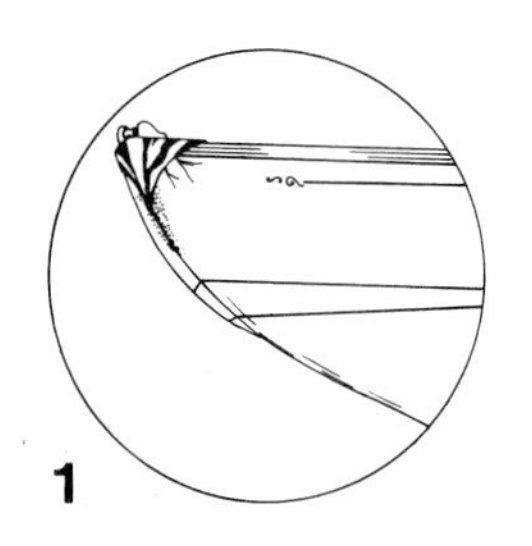
1

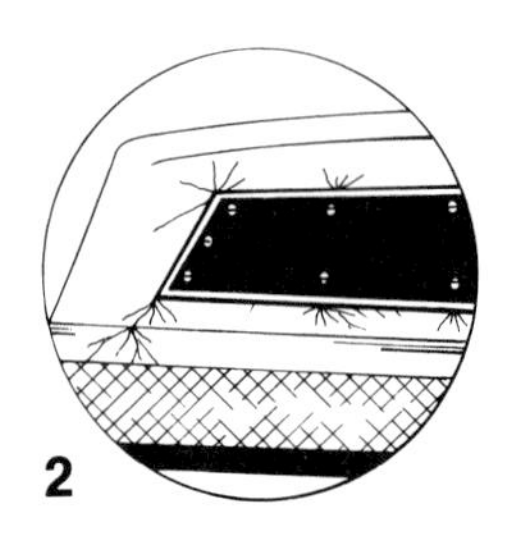
2

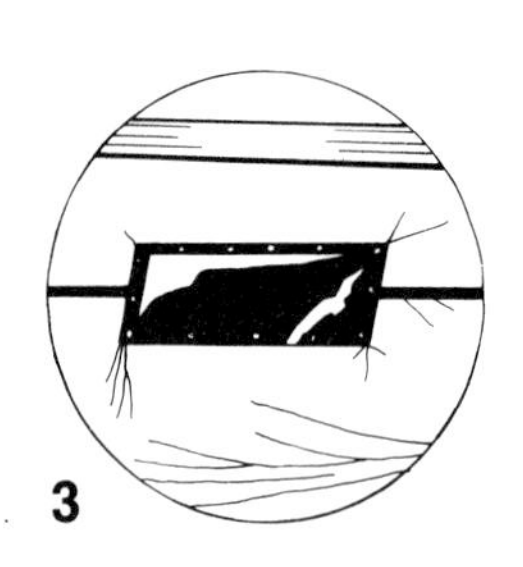
3

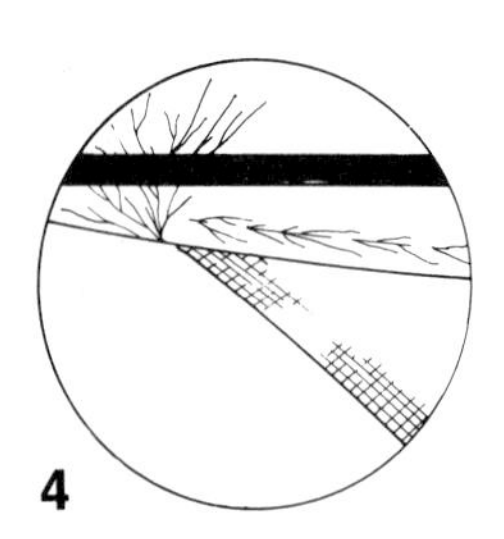
4

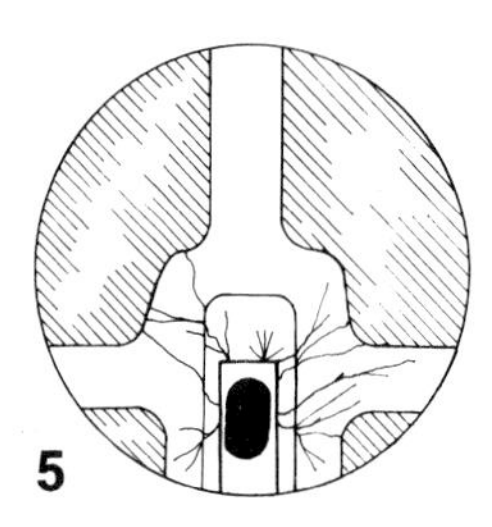
5

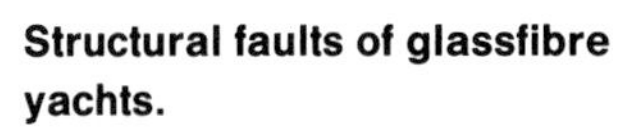

Structural faults of glassfibre yachts.

1 Few yachts escape without damage to the resin-rich area of the stem. Flash lines along the fore-edge of the hull suggest that the mould was split to facilitate removal of the finished hull.

2 Stress crazes around windows are not uncommon especially in lightly built yachts. Overlaid acrylic windows are likely to craze around fastenings (and in some cases, on examination, those fastenings will be found to be self-tapping screws as opposed to bolts!).

3 Windows in topsides are a constant source of trouble. Even when adequately framed, the laminate is still liable to flex, and crazing is the inevitable result. Applied plastic cove lines may obscure evidence of crazing, so beware!

4 Cracking at the fore end of the keel root is generally a sign of inadequate reinforcement to accept the mast loading. It may also occur as a result of grounding. Crazing along the root of a narrow fin keel may indicate nothing more serious than shrinkage of the filler employed in fairing, but should always be carefully investigated.

5 Crazing under the deck step of the mast often has serious implications, the most obvious being that the mast support is not strong enough for the job. Often the crazes appear within the first couple of seasons and never worsen, but if there are cracks extending to the coachroof or deck edge, major remedial work will be involved.

6 Flex or damage crazing in the root of the skeg is very common although it may be masked by a build-up of anti-fouling paint. Remedial action

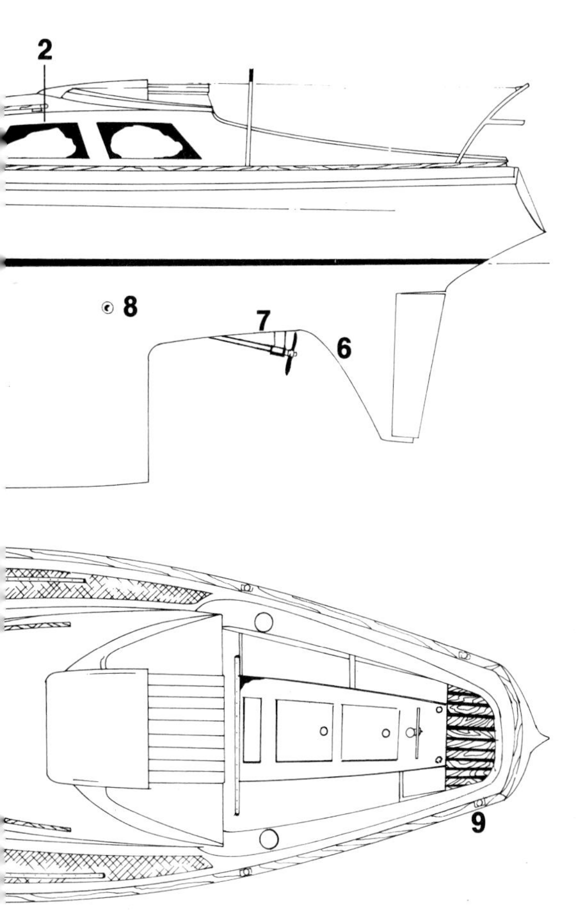

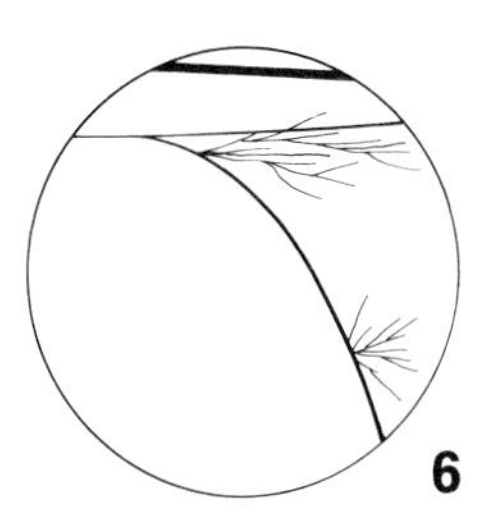

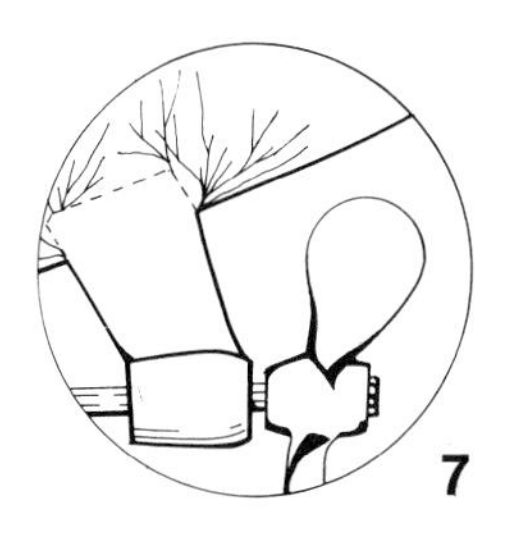

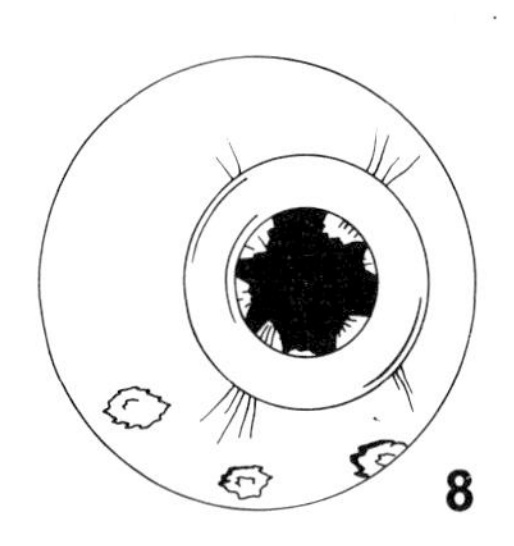

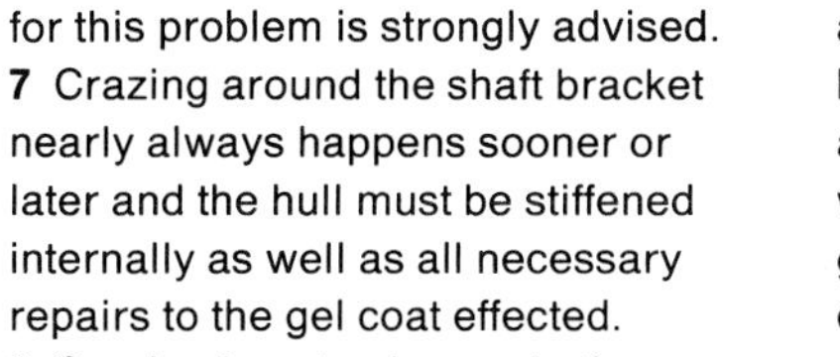

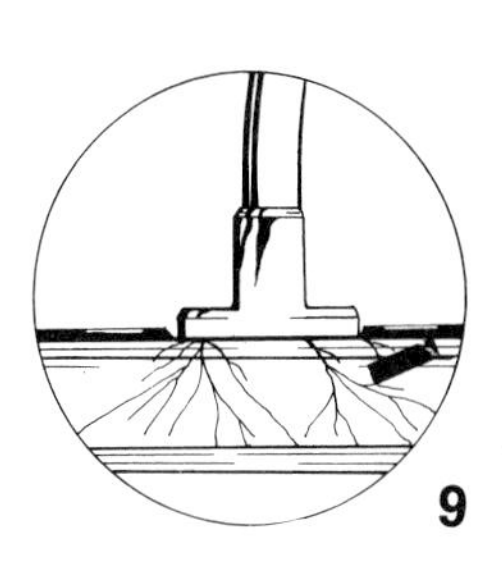

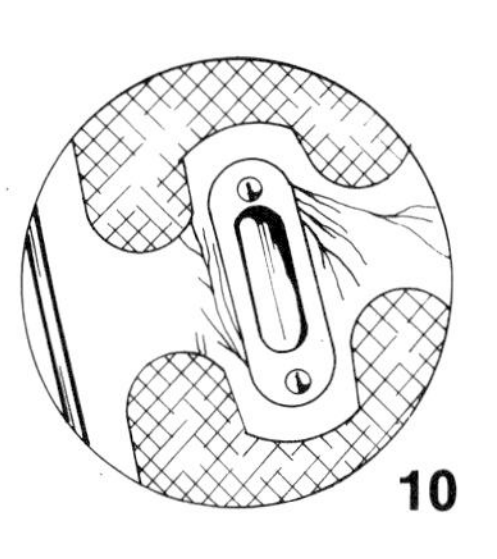

for this problem is strongly advised.
7 Crazing around the shaft bracket nearly always happens sooner or later and the hull must be stiffened internally as well as all necessary repairs to the gel coat effected.
8 Crazing is not unknown in the vicinity of skin fittings, and an internal examination of the hull may show that it has not been reinforced or provided with a backing pad for the units. Remember to clean out shell debris from inlets. (Areas of the underbody where molluscs have fastened themselves often show what appear to be small craters indicative of burst gel blisters – a magnifying glass may be needed to determine the exact cause.)
9 Crazing usually occurs around stanchion bases and so long as there is access from the underside, re-fastening is not particularly onerous. Where the stanchions are attached to the upper edge of a bulwark moulding, however, matters are more difficult. A packing piece of wood will have to be forced into the gap and glassed in (after first extracting the old fastenings of course).
10 Crazing around shroud attachment eyes is one of the most frequently encountered problems and one where the symptom is more easily treated than the cause. Far too many yachts rely on nothing more than the laminate of the deck to withstand the loading of the rig. In any case, a direct upward strain is just about as ill-conceived a concept as could be. The loading will have to be distributed to a string point such as a bulkhead, or bonded to a stringer. Metal straps under the deck are better than nothing – but only just – and not for long either!

not out of the question for the amateur, but often the assessment and implications are a matter for an experienced investigator.

Blistering can be virtually discounted so far as the topsides are concerned – but not entirely. This is because it is just conceivable that it could occur as a result of deck or tarpaulin run-off over a very long period of time. Pin holes in the gel should be noted, as these are sometimes a pointer to an indifferent gelcoat and to an increased risk of moisture-related defects in the underbody, which should therefore be scrutinised with extra care. A vessel that spends its life moored in fresh water may also run a higher risk of blistering because of the lower density of the fresh water which allows it to permeate the gelcoat within a shorter period; warmer water too has the effect of speeding up the process because the higher temperature softens the gelcoat slightly.

Underbody inspection: likely trouble spots

Whether it is because a vendor is apprehensive as to what may come to light during the course of a survey, or because he is disinterested in the outcome, inspection of the underbody is not necessarily made easy for the surveyor. Of course, the boat must be seen ashore and ideally should be stripped of marine growth prior to the examination; indeed, in the case of a glassfibre craft, this is a stringent requirement as hull and gelcoat deterioration are, by their very nature, easily obscured. And obscured they often are, not only by years of antifouling, but by accumulated submarine flora and fauna. Although a build-up of antifouling is a nuisance, at least small areas can be stripped with minimal effort and mess.

Far less pleasant is coming face to face with a fronded expanse of dripping weed, slime and creeping things. It is surprising to what extent such species flourish in our comparatively cool summer waters, although it is nothing compared to that resulting from a sojourn in the Mediterranean. A high-pressure hose will clean off much of this growth, but regrettably there is not always one available. This gives rise to a strong temptation simply to cast a cursory glance over the hull and utter a fervent prayer that all is well. Unfortunately, in a vessel so neglected, the odds are rather weighted against such an assumption! Unappetising as the prospect may be, a serious attempt must be made to clear some sort of pathway through the weed otherwise you cannot get a realistic idea of what exactly does lie beneath it. Boring as this chore may be, it is, after all, in the purchaser's own interest. (A professional surveyor might conceivably be rather less interested and issue a report containing a caveat as to damage undiscovered due to the state of the surface). Most of the muck can usually be removed with a hoe, followed up by vigorous scraping with a plastic spatula (a glassfibre or tuphnol sail batten, held in a curve by manual pressure at each end, is also effective for clearing flat areas). The greatest precautions should be taken to avoid damage to the gelcoat, even when time is limited and scraping turns into a race against the incoming tide. Concentrate on stripping small areas, about 6 inches square or thereabouts, variously distributed around the hull where structural damage and blistering are most likely to be encountered.

If physical damage does exist, the forefoot, and the leading edge of the keel, skeg and shaft brackets are the first places to look for it. Blistering and wicking (another, rather insidious, by-product of permeation; here water is drawn along imperfectly saturated fibres by capillary action, where it expands and forms blisters under the surface).

Blisters can and do form anywhere, and as is the case with crazing, it often takes a while to make the first confirmed sighting;

after that, if more are there, they will positively clamour for attention! It is because of this tendency for blisters to disperse themselves around the hull that as many small separate areas as time permits should be scraped for examination – thus increasing the chance of detecting even the smallest eruption.

Before any serious search for blemishes can get under way, it helps to know what each successive layer removed actually consists of. In a perfect world, the hull would be cleaned back to the bare gelcoat, but this is too much to hope for. It is now common for antifouling to be, in effect, self-priming, but other coatings may be revealed. The original etching primer, applied at the time of building, may still be intact and, if so, it can be hard to distinguish it from the gelcoat. Within the last few years solvent-free epoxy coatings have gained in popularity; they provide a barrier not only to water permeation, but also to a scraper. Removing this immensely hard substance is a thankless job and, quite frankly, not one for which a surveyor would be thanked – not at any rate by an owner who has coughed up a considerable sum for the product.

It may be that the gelcoat is unpigmented. Contrary to a first impression, this is not evidence of an economy drive on the part of the builders; it is, indeed, rather the reverse. Clear gel is used with minimal filler and employed for the most part in boats whose construction is monitored by a surveyor, either for the purposes of a moulding release note, classification, or as the subject of specific requirements.

Surface defects

With as much of the surface cleaned back as seems reasonable, it may be immediately possible to identify surface defects. I am inclined to look at the hull before starting to strip any antifouling to see if there are any particular suspect areas; if there are, it is these that I check out first of all. Far and away the largest number of blisters are in fact contained within the layers of antifouling, rather than the underlying gelcoat, but it is possible to probe a hundred of these and then finally discover a single blister as a result of osmosis. When found, these do not invariably gush forth acidic and astringently perfumed liquid since many do eventually dry out once the chemical action has worked itself through. Should they do so though, take a careful note of the position, mark this with a wax crayon or chalk (and on a diagram drawn in a notebook), but on no account spear them with a sharp implement before consultation with the vendor or broker.

There are one or two tricks that help in locating minor blisters. The first is, quite simply, touch. Lightly trace over an area with the fingers and imperfections can sometimes be felt where they cannot be seen. Running a straight edge down or along the hull may reveal irregularities in the surface, so occasionally will the brass-rubbing technique with a soft pencil and thin paper. But if an hour spent searching over the underbody of a 30 footer (an hour being about the minimum necessary for this size) does not reveal blistering, its presence can be discounted – for the moment at any rate. On the other hand, if one blister is found there are almost bound to be more present – or others latent within the gel.

If defects as a result of the osmotic process are discovered, a sense of proportion should be retained. Most cases do not impair the hull structure (although even one outcrop provides useful ammunition for the would-be purchaser) and can therefore be dealt with by grinding out, drying, filling and fairing. A case that calls for instant and drastic remedial action will be self-evident, even to an inexperienced eye.

Having uttered reassuring words about the misapprehensions regarding osmotic blistering, it has to be said that a really severe case is expensive to put right. The

A glassfibre hull after light sand blasting of the gel. The lighter areas would have been visible as blisters prior to the removal of the first or second gelcoat, although they might have been obscured by a build-up of antifouling.

affected gelcoat – which usually means the entire underbody gelcoat – will have to be removed by grit blasting, grinding, use of a heat gun, or specialised gelcoat peeling. No method is free of drawbacks: grit blasting can cause damage to the laminate and leave air traps; grinding produces vast quantities of dust and fumes; and a heat gun is laborious and can seal the GRP, thus hindering eventual drying-out of the hull. Peeling, a less traumatic way of removing the gel, appears to be the most satisfactory method. It could conceivably supplant other stripping procedures, although – like grit blasting – it is impractical for the amateur and requires the services of a specialised and highly skilled professional.

Having removed antifouling and affected gel, the hull must be dried out (and remember the necessity for undercover storage, dehumidifiers and heat lamps adds to the high overall cost). The surface must then be filled, faired and resurfaced, generally with a solvent-free epoxy. If inspection reveals any breakdown of the laminate, additional layers of cloth may have to be bonded to the hull in order to restore the original strength. Having completed the task, though, the boat will be structurally as good as new, and – with skilled workmanship – should have a finish to match. This being the case, there is really no question of turning down a purchase merely on the grounds of gelcoat blistering. But the price should accurately reflect the remedial work necessary. It should also be adjusted to make allowance for any uncertainty that must exist until the antifouling and gelcoat have been removed and the full extent of blistering and/or deterioration of the substrate has been revealed.

Crazing in the underbody is almost impossible to detect if you search randomly. If the hull has not been completely stripped, the best that can normally be expected without other confirmatory evidence is to find crazing in the commoner problem zones. Take note of the angle the vessel would adopt were it to ground unintentionally, and hunt around that section of the bilge. If bilge stringers or spray strakes are incorporated in the moulding, examine the areas in the immediate vicinity. One of the more usual causes of underwater crazing is flexing or wringing around the propeller brackets; this will be clearly seen once the paint is removed from the area surrounding the attachment flanges. Filler may be visible (indicating that the problem is a longstanding one), but this is no cure; the internal hull must be stiffened and brackets refastened.

Skeg and keel

The skeg, even on soundly and heavily constructed sailing boats, does seem to be a prime site of trouble, often as a result of much of the vessel's weight bearing directly on it when grounding. Sometimes, however, fouling a hawser or mooring warp may be enough to cause the damage, though poor design is still a major culprit. The basic purposes of a skeg are to support the rudder and to improve the water flow to it. This second purpose is more or less effective, but the first is often totally negated by the actual design of the rudder, which often, on a sailing vessel, has a portion of the blade projecting below the lowest point of the skeg. This renders the rudder vulnerable as well as the skeg itself. If damage has occurred, it will usually be noticeable at the fore part of the root; this therefore is the first area to investigate for tell-tale hairline cracks, though the trailing edge must also be examined. Some skegs are bolted through the hull rather than moulded as an integral part, so with this type it may be obvious from weeps through the sealant that reseating is necessary. (By the way, it is always worth checking that the skeg is in fact in line with both yacht and rudder. Surprisingly often it may not be, and though this may be a sign of previous damage, it is equally possible that it is a building fault.)

The majority of yachts nowadays have fibre-glass keels with the ballast encapsulated within, so even where the underside and forward edge of the moulding are eroded, no immediate harm will come to the vessel. The surface wear should be made good as soon as possible though, because sooner or later water will penetrate and work its way upward through the laminate, by capillary action.

Many of the older cruising vessels did have full-length keels, through-bolted, as they would have been with a timber vessel. Often the retaining nuts or boltheads, depending on the method of attachment, were encapsulated in resin. The keel can be regarded as it would be in a wooden boat: if there are signs of rust seeping from the visible portion of the fastening or from the resin, budget for the drawing of (or the X-raying of) bolts and also for the additional expense of renewal.

Modern, light displacement boats do have a tendency for the hull to flex in way of the very deep and narrow fin keels. With some classes, this just has to be accepted as an inherent part of the design. There is little that can be done but watch season by season and ensure that the attendant minor crazing does not worsen to the point where considerable water permeation occurs. The usual procedure seems to be to fill and fair on an annual basis and then sell the boat on when this becomes tiresome! It is standard practice with some more extreme racing boats to fair the root of the keel with overlaid glassfibre or epoxy putty; this cracks during the course of the season, but is simply renewed for the next year. This process may be reprehensible, but does not necessarily imply any great structural defects; however, on a light hull problems will undoubtedly develop, in time. Racing craft are, though, quite specialised, and generally an owner is well aware of what is involved so far as upkeep and maintenance are concerned. This said, it can be confusing to a would-be purchaser, who perhaps has not had much experience with glassfibre construction.

The greatest difficulty is deciding just how serious crazing around the keel root actually is. Certainly, in a fin-keel yacht of the less extreme type, it is in all probability a sign that something is very much amiss. Once again, a hard grounding or violent collision with an underwater obstruction is a likely cause. Conceivably, the floors are inadequate or perhaps the bolts too short for the leverage imposed by the ballasted fin. Then again it is not impossible that the downthrust of the rig is improperly distributed, or even the rig wrongly positioned either at the time of building or as a result of later attempts to improve performance or balance. Without additional evidence to supplement intuition, it is not easy to make an authoritative judgement as to the exact reason for any cracking. Quite recently I surveyed a 35 foot fin-keel sloop, of fairly moderate design, with the accent on cruising rather than out-and-out performance. Although completed internally by an amateur, it was moulded by quite a reputable yard and offered for sale by a brokerage firm of good standing. There was considerable crazing around the keel, with the cracks being most numerous at the fore end; the moisture content of the laminate was high and filler was much in evidence.

One hundred per cent certain in my own mind that the flexing was a direct result of a wrongly sited mast, I sounded off to the brokers who were, to put it mildly, unimpressed. So unimpressed were they in fact that they announced their intention of consulting the designer, a threat that was easy to carry out since his office was only yards along the road. A period of deepest apprehension followed, during which I wished I had restricted all comment to the platitude of 'requires further investigation'. Mercifully, the designer agreed with my expressed opinion, and airily pointed out that although he had designed the vessel he had no control over the misguided soul who fitted her out. This person had, in an attempt to create a more spacious saloon, simply moved the mast 18 inches further forward without first fitting additional load-bearing floors.

Problems with bilge keels

Unquestionably, so far as their proud owners (and vendors) are concerned, certain mass-produced bilge-keel yachts are being dignified with the 'classic' label. I suppose to an extent some can lay claim to a certain uniqueness – if being the first to boast a particular hull configuration, being constructed on the most efficient production line, or wedging in the largest number of berths per foot of waterline can be construed as unique. (This is a cynical view, albeit a common one. Most of these small boats are very able cruisers, with the majority being constructed to a good standard and neatly fitted out. Many of these will eventually be classics no matter by what criteria they are judged, but then, I suppose, so will most twentieth-century artefacts!)

The hulls of these small vessels can be judged by the same standards as their deeper-draught cousins, but the twin keels can be troublesome. Faults certainly can be put right, but actually getting at defective studs is not made easier (or cheaper) by the amount of moulded interior units that may have to be operated on.

Twin keels are more susceptible to damage than a single long ballast keel. They are less substantial, narrower and, as a result of their low aspect, cannot be through-bolted as strongly because bolts or studs must be shorter and of reduced diameter. If the boat goes ashore in a storm, which is not uncommon since bilge keelers are most sought after in regions where the ability to take the ground safely on an exposed mooring is essential, the keels are liable to be twisted or wrenched – if not broken away completely. But, then, this sacrificial action may prevent severe structural impairment to the rest of the hull.

Most keels are through-fastened on to appropriately sized bearers. Some, though, do have the ballast totally encapsulated, and occasionally, just by way of variety, the keels consist of a hollow moulding, integral with the hull. This is left for the owner to fill in with whatever weighty detritus takes the fancy. The idea seems to be that the ballast is glassed in permanently the moment an optimum ratio is arrived at, but I have seen several boats where this never did take place: presumably, the vessels in question were never laid flat in a sudden squall.

Keels that are splayed outward (as opposed to those that are vertical to the boat's lengthwise centreline) do need to be looked at most carefully, especially if the craft has been kept on a drying mooring where the bottom is hard mud or sand. The constant pounding (compressed mud is nearly as hard as cement) tends to accentuate the splaying and play will begin in the studs. This will worsen, and gradually water will find its way in and matters will deteriorate further. The weeping is usually visible (assuming the area has not been treated with a new coat of antifouling or some such) and can be seen at the juncture of keel and hull and also from the interior (if it is possible to inspect the bolt heads; the internal mouldings may be an obstacle to this). Removal of these mouldings to facilitate access makes any repair expensive (although not difficult). However, looking on the bright side, most up-to-date boatyards have become adept at re-fastening splayed bilge keels. If it seems probable that the keels will need professional attention, get several estimates and do ensure that the sum includes making good the internal mouldings that have been hacked about.

Where encapsulated keels are concerned, defects are generally confined to erosion at the lower edges. Repairs are straightforward and can easily be dealt with by an amateur. But all bilge-keel yachts having a skeg-hung rudder should have special attention paid to the condition of both these components: three-point landings on a drying mooring with uneven ground can impose a strain, particularly upon the rudder if it has been allowed to veer over to one side. Should the boat have a transom rudder, which would normally be unshipped after sailing, don't take it for granted that it necessarily has been. Check for signs of damage underneath the transom, but also be wary of signs of strain around rudder hangings; remember too, that the outboard or shaft bracket, rudder, outboard or propeller may have occasionally seen service, albeit unwittingly, as a tail skid!

One last point deserving special attention in the course of the underbody inspection is the gelcoat around any skin fittings. It is not unknown for the exits of through-hull discharges to be drilled, and the gate valve and attendant external fitting fastened over a bedding compound without any thought given to sealing the core laminate with resin. Given adequate mastic, water should never penetrate, but it can and does with subsequent damage to the gel. (Attention should be paid to log and echo sounder transducers.)

Deck and superstructure

Having given the exterior of the hull a thorough going-over, next in line is the deck and superstructure. At a glance, these may appear quite free of defects, except perhaps for slight crazing in places where the curvature means that there is a thick build-up of resin that could have cured too rapidly or, worse still, unevenly. Such fine cracks may be visible near the lower edges of the coachroof, around the moulded hatch coamings (take care in this vicinity not to confuse them with stress cracks caused by the hinges). They may also be seen in any faired corners, and in the region of the toe-rail or bulwarks – a prime site for impact damage in any case. Unsightly as such crazes can be, they are rarely of much structural significance; ideally though, some action should be taken to prevent water seeping into the core material (in the case of the decks, often balsa or foam). Wholesale eradication means grinding out affected portions, filling and re-gelling, but to bring about a really good cosmetic repair it may be necessary for a complete respray above gunwale level.

Small cavities known as air voids are

occasionally seen in those regions susceptible to cure-related crazing; these should be filled and faired to profile for the sake of appearance if nothing else.

Crazing in other areas of deck or coachroof can, without exception, be directly atttributed to stress or uneven flexing. It can constitute a major problem, especially in decks. These structures have little intrinsic strength: their stiffness resides almost totally in the reinforcement of the hull to deck joint and the lengthwise curvature along the coachroof. If trouble develops (and it is usually the result of a deliberate attempt to save weight and materials), decks may split right across. Repair and reinforcement will, in such a case, be very costly. Beware of an inherent defect if there are two patches of adjacent crazing, perhaps one at the toerail and the other at the root of the coachroof; the chances are that eventually they will meet.

A certain amount of cracking is common on an unsupported area of foredeck and is not unknown on the coachroof top; provided there is no pattern to the cracks and no confirmed cause, their presence can be tolerated. Crazes around window frames are also frequently encountered, and may simply mean that the frames have been badly fitted or there has been careless drilling for the bolts.

While on the subject of windows, it should be noted that those in metal frames may have been replaced by panels of overlaid acrylic. There is nothing essentially wrong in this practice so long as the coachroof sides retain the designed rigidity, but usually removal of the metal frames greatly diminishes it. The result is that the lower edge of the panel may work loose, especially in cases (not unknown even on some production craft) where this type of window is retained merely by self-tapping screws instead of bolts. This may occur after a period of months rather than years, so it is wise to squat down and squint upwards at the lower edge to ensure that this has not happened.

If conventionally framed windows seem sound, take into account the possibility that the compression of a deck-stepped mast has not been compensated adequately and that the coachroof sides have started to crack as a direct result of this. Carry out a painstaking search on deck in close proximity to the mast heel; further crazes or depression of the surrounding area will serve to confirm this. The purchaser then has to decide whether the strain occurred years ago, perhaps even when the vessel was first sailed, and is showing no further signs of worsening, or whether the deterioration is an ongoing matter. This is virtually impossible to ascertain unless at some time the surface has been painted. In this case, it can be determined whether or not the crazes have shown subsequent signs of movement.

The crew on board a sailing craft tend to be more active on deck than those on board a motor vessel (at least, that is the popular conception), but all adult bodies galloping around impose quite enough strain to account for minor deck crazing here and there. The crew will not, of course, move nearly so fast if unsure of their footing, so the provision of an effective non-slip deck surface in traffic areas is most important. Such a finish is usually provided by incorporating textured areas in the moulding, but these are of varying effectiveness and are often eventually coated with sanded paint. Overlaid panels of Treadmaster or one of the similar materials provide an excellent foothold, but they can also hide evidence of heavy footwork in the past – so look carefully at the surrounding gel surface for hairline fractures that will probably continue underneath the panel.

Deck fittings

All crazes in the vicinity of through-fastened deck fittings must be taken seriously. Not only are they a potential cause of delamination between gel and core material, but the ultimate security of the hardware is questionable.

The secure attachment of cleats, jackstay eyes and hand or grab rails is of prime importance on both motor and sailing vessels: a weakened deck and loosened fitting could, in an extreme case, result in the boat breaking adrift or a member of crew going overboard. Even without the sudden snatch that could precipitate fracture or failure of the fastenings in an emergency, a fitting will continue to move and the crazing on the deck will become more noticeable. Admittedly, this will be a gradual process and one that may, regrettably, be insufficient to rouse an owner into carrying out repairs.

In a sailing yacht, the moment cracking can be detected around the deck eyes to which the standing rigging is attached, action must be taken before rig and deck fitting part company with the hull – with considerable risk of injury to those on board. Over-dramatic as this may sound, it can and does happen.

Apart from fashion and the exaggerated beam of some racing craft (which can preclude efficient headsail sheeting on some points of sailing), there is no sound reason why the practice of mounting strap chainplates on the outer topsides has declined. With this practice the loading of the rig is correctly distributed with stresses imposed upon the portion of the boat best fitted for them. Signs of deterioration of the chainplate or fastenings are immediately visible and, in such a case, are easy to replace. But with deck eyes the pull is exerted directly upwards and, since both eyes are fastened through the deck, so the deck is also pulled upwards. Naturally, the strain is distributed via an internal strap fastened to a strong point inside the hull that will counteract this upward force, so where is the problem?

The problem is that quite often this is not the practice. Even more frequently, there is no way of telling for sure when it is not possible to inspect the shipside internally. Many perfectly reputable boats, even if not exactly classics, simply put all faith in a steel backing strap beneath the deckhead and have no vertical attachment whatsoever. This is bad enough in itself, but a minority rely only on the bolts through the deck plate. This is hard to believe, but quite true nevertheless. (Since these latter are often found in the most lightly constructed boats, the potential for dismasting or a delaminating deck moulding is self-evident.)

Should there be any hint of crazing with such structural implications, do pull back from hasty purchase in order to consider the cost of removing linings for an in-depth inspection, of reinforcing the fittings, and also of restoring the interior to its original standard of finish after repairs have been carried out. True, there is a chance that, as with mast compression strain, the problem may have occurred at some indeterminate time in the past and may never progress further; however, a pessimistic viewpoint is more realistic. A moisture meter reading will usually confirm the presence of a considerable build-up of damp within the deck laminate.

Indications of crazing can be suppressed in the short term – but only in the short term – by the careful application of thinned paint. After a week or two, assuming that the vessel is out of commission and the mast is unstepped so as to avoid further strain, a film of grime over the paint will perform a remarkable cover-up. It may be possible, though, to feel a difference in the surface, as it is difficult to achieve a surface that is as smooth as the original – especially if the work is done in the open air.

The interior

With all external points duly noted, the time comes to examine the internal hull and seek confirmation of defects discovered or suspected from the external scrutiny. Attention has already been drawn to the difficulties of access, but it should be feasible to inspect at least a section or two of the hull to deck fastenings and those bolts (or, occasionally, self-tapping screws!) that attach the deck fittings. These will probably show some signs of rust even though they are made of stainless steel. It is remarkable how often, even in vessels built to a high specification, inferior grades of stainless steel are employed. Physical weakening of the fastenings will take some time to occur, but rust weeps can discolour head linings and permanently stain berth cushions.

Any survey is really only a preliminary measure: many faults will be hinted at, but few will be proven. A final decision can sometimes only be based on intuition or the wholesale dismantling of the interior of the craft in question. The balance of probability is weighted in favour of major structural defects being pinpointed at the time of survey, although it might be recommended that the hull be stripped for further investigation – suggesting perhaps that internal mouldings or tanks be taken out if damage or inadequate repair work are suspected. With glassfibre vessels it is usually the ancillary items, such as hatches and windows that prove to be defective; but these must be regarded as part of the physical structure in as much as they can endanger a boat at sea.

There is relatively little in the way of cosmetic work and joinery alterations (or, for that matter, quite extensive repairs) that is beyond the capability of a thoughtful and reasonably competent newcomer to glassfibre construction. But, a word to the wise: do not buy an unsound or run-down production vessel that has a clearly defined price according to year of manufacture, layout, mechanical propulsion, etc, in the hope of smartening it up and selling it for the price of a more recent example. No amount of spraying, reupholstering nor updating of electronic gadgets will do this, as quite a few optimists have discovered to their cost.

The prices of most mass-produced reinforced plastic craft are fixed between defined parameters, although, as has happened with timber boats, true classics in glassfibre are subject to limited supply and increased demand. There are bargains around, but once on the open market these are rapidly snapped up. However, if you have enough confidence in your own judgement to make an offer on the spot, you may well make a profit in the long run.

CHAPTER 13

Alternative construction materials

The steel vessel

Although timber and fibreglass enjoy a near monopoly in boatbuilding in Britain, aluminium and steel are widely used in Europe. Holland, with its vast interlinking network of canals, has an almost insatiable demand for motor cruisers suited to these inland waters and steel vessels are very much the norm. Such boats can shrug off physical punishment that would have a timber or reinforced-plastic yacht reeling back to the nearest boatyard for repairs!

With such experience of steel construction, the hulls should be (and generally are) soundly built. Also, the overall finish is little short of excellent; it is rare to see an uneven chine or unfair sheerline. It might conceivably come as a shock to those contemplating the purchase of their first steel boat – and accustomed to oak frames like harbour pilings or reassuringly solid mat and rovings – to realise just how thin the hull plating of a steel vessel actually is; 4 mm (only a little over $\frac{5}{32}$") is not unknown in a 70 foot barge. To be sure, though, steel is immensely strong and impact resistant, and anyone contemplating a meander through uncharted reefs and atolls would stand a far better chance of ending the voyage with the yacht in one piece if it were constructed of steel.

The bugbear is corrosion, with the corrosion occurring from the inside out. This means that the process carries on unsuspected underneath paint (and also beneath the internal insulation needed to combat a second disadvantage: condensation). Sand blasting and epoxy paints will all but eliminate the risk of serious oxidisation, but, unless there is documentation and a builder's specification available for inspection, it cannot be taken for granted that sufficient attention was initially paid to this aspect of the finishing work. If there is marked corrosion within the plating (and this may have been filled, faired and painted over prior to a purchaser's or surveyor's inspection), then things have almost certainly got rather out of hand!

Dutch traditional craft

There are, at the time of writing, an increasing number of traditional Dutch sailing and motor barges imported into Britain, some of which have been stripped, de-rigged and have had engines removed for use as houseboats. A fair proportion, though, are still complete with original rigs and power plants and appear at first glance to represent a lot of boat for little expenditure. Indeed, for those with a mooring – preferably owned outright since most of the imports are at least 55 feet in overall length and rent of such a berth could be extortionate – they are excellent value. Few examples, though, were designed for the full strength of the open sea and their use would be restricted to inland waterways or sheltered estuaries.

Apart from small dents and possible

minor wrinkles along the welds as a result of flexion in the steel plates (occasionally, the older vessels may be iron built), many of these ships look to be in first-class condition. Often they are colourfully, even garishly, painted, with a good deal of brightwork – and some still retain their carved nameboards and rudderheads. The British find these Tjalks, Lemmeracks, Klippers and Botters irresistible, and there is no doubt that the curvaceous bows, sweeping coachroofs and broad varnished leeboards of such Dutch traders do have considerable period charm. Any remaining resistance to such boats is promptly swept away at first sight of a typical interior with its 'olde-worlde' charm (I personally find the lace curtains and potted plants, essential as they are to capture fully the atmosphere of such a craft, a little over the top for my own taste.) Regrettably, from a survey point of view, the 'olde-worlde' charm tends to be thoroughly screwed into place and therefore quite immovable. Thus inspection is impossible, unless hammer and screwdriver are used – and this would be regarded as nothing less than outright vandalism by most proud owners.

These craft, when operating in their country of origin, sail within sight of land; therefore they are rarely fitted with any electronic navigation aids beyond echo sounder, log and VHF (neither do they venture forth into salt water as a rule). This means that the risk of electrolytic corrosion is reduced to an acceptable minimum. If kept in British coastal waters, though, unless action is taken at once to prevent it, corrosion could quickly start. The fitting of cathodic protection in accordance with the specifications of the manufacturers (who are more than happy to give individual advice according to the type of vessel, machinery and so forth) should be undertaken without delay. This will mean slipping the vessel, which is an expensive procedure for such a large craft. So if purchasing an ex-trader that has been in Britain for some time, it is vital to check that anodes have been fitted and correctly bonded protection has been installed. If not, remember to budget for this work and inspect the hull beforehand with extra caution.

Steel, being heavy for its volume, is regarded as impractical for any sailing yacht under 30 feet or so in length – although I can think of one or two rather smaller ones that manage to sail quite delightfully, and the Dutch habitually build knock-about dinghies in steel.

The majority of smaller craft nowadays are constructed of welded steel, although older trading vessels may be riveted. If they are, examine all rivets for traces of cement; this would indicate a time-honoured way of dealing with any seepage as a result of wear or corrosion. In Britain, most steel yachts are of hard-chine hull format; this is because such a form of construction is far and away the easiest, calling as it does for nothing more complicated than flat sheets of metal for frames and external plating. There is no need to roll the steel since there is no compound curvature involved. Some beautiful round bilge vessels in the classic tradition are now produced in Britain, but the method tends to be financially prohibitive so far as the home builder is concerned.

Amateur construction

This preponderance of amateur builders has on the whole done little for the reputation of steel boats. While there are craft whose standard of build and finish approach (or exceed) that of a commercial yard, there are numerous less successful attempts. Worse still, some of these are downright dangerous as a result of being constructed from designs intended specifically for marine ply. The consequent weight increase cannot be counteracted by a simple reduction of ballast since the centre of gravity still remains far too high for safety. Such a craft would of course be avoided like the plague if the truth

A well-built steel hull can withstand a good deal of abuse. So far this casualty, beached during flooding in the Norfolk Broads, has suffered no structural damage although scale is clearly visible, especially along the deck edge. Ultrasonic scanning can measure the thickness of plating, but the fairness of the hull can best be judged by eye, possibly with the assistance of a fairing batten over large flat areas of hull or superstructure.

were known, but with the vessel stationary, the appearance will provide no clue as to its behaviour at sea.

Basic quality of construction, or the lack of it, may be glaringly obvious – the give-away signs being similar to those witnessed with timber or glassfibre craft. If a hull is fair, there is an excellent chance that the builder could read a set of blueprints and build accordingly. Judgement, though, should be suspended until all other aspects have been examined, and preferably some sort of evidence been provided to the corrosion proofing of the bare shell.

There should be less cause for concern when buying a boat built professionally, but there is still bound to be an element of doubt regarding a yard that has gone out of business. Yards do cease trading for reasons other than pure inefficiency, though. Partners die or retire, or the property value far exceeds the manufacturing profit and developers move in. But is is by no means unknown for a quick-witted amateur to form an instant company, complete with letter-heading etc, and declare himself a boatyard. Not that this automatically condemns the vessel, and it should be easier to insure as a result; however, it could be regarded as sharp practice.

Steel boats are sometimes composite structures with either the deck and superstructure (sometimes both) made of timber. There is some controversy as to this, since protagonists of steel hold to the view that it is pretty pointless using such a strong material and then sacrificing one of its greatest advantages: that of the construction of a totally integrated and seamless vessel in favour of nothing more than mere aesthetic appeal (and a true devotee would probably deny any such appeal in any case). Neither would the purist consider for one moment overlaying the steel deck in teak solely for appearance's sake. I am inclined to think this argument has a sound basis and, although I prefer the warmth of laid teak to the functional starkness of painted metal, I can see no logical reason for drilling unnecessary holes that will inevitably prove to be a source of later corrosion. Much the same holds true where deck fittings are concerned: such hardware as stanchion and pulpit sockets, cleats and sheet tracks can be welded and form a permanent and integral part of the structure.

Scale and corrosion

When inspecting the hull and decks and coachroof of a steel vessel, the presence of corrosion must be suspected along the length of rolled and turned rubbing bands – and especially in such water traps as deck scuppers, window surrounds and all areas where fittings are through-fastened. One British yard of high repute fits backing strips of stainless steel under all such components, a far cry from the days when cotton impregnated with tar would have been employed.

Surface scale is all too familiar to anyone who has owned a motor vehicle and watched the tell-tale bubbles of rust eat away the resale value! This rusted surface, a layer of porous iron oxide and air, does actually feed upon itself because it soaks up moisture, air and its own by-products.

Surface rust can be removed by chipping and scaling. This must be done lightly for closer inspection during the course of a survey, and continued in deadly ernest after purchase. If a substantial quantity of scale has formed and remains so stubbornly bonded to the steel that chipping really does require a strenuous effort, a penetrating agent such as Owatrol applied to the surface will help a great deal. After half an hour or so it begins to work its way underneath the oxidised layer to form a crust that can then be cleaned down with minimal exertion. In most instances, application of the Owatrol will leave underlying surfaces sealed, ready for fairing and priming.

The presence of surface corrosion is a nuisance and clearing it is essential in order to prevent further deterioration. But so long as scale is restricted to the surface (inspection will reveal the depth), removal along with the subsequent finishing and painting can be looked upon as cosmetic work. It is messy and laborious, but not exceptionally skilled.

A salt atmosphere is a natural enemy of many manmade materials, particularly mild steel hulls. Salt drastically cuts short the life expectancy of steel – and at a fast rate too, unless all possible steps are taken to combat it. Its depradations are usually visible as corrosion flavours oxygen-rich areas subjected to a degree of water flow (i.e. on or just above the waterline). You might be inclined to restrict your inspection to that area along with the topsides: these are, after all, the most easily seen; and the cost of slipping, particularly in the case of a large flat-bottomed craft which will have to be blocked up high to complete the survey, can run into hundreds of pounds. However, temptation to settle for a cursory check with the boat afloat should at all costs be resisted, especially if the vessel is known to have been in a mud berth or half-tide mooring for any length of time. Normally, the immersed underbody, in the absence of oxygen, would remain relatively corrosion-free, but the process of oxidisation can be greatly accelerated by the bacteria and microorganisms that find the sea-bed a most congenial habitat.

The integrity of the welds is a common cause for concern, and in truth it is not easy to ascertain. Breakdowns in mild steel due to poor welding practice are actually quite rare. The welding process is virtually foolproof and can be easily checked by the builder on a continuing basis throughout construction. Certainly, if the seams are not ground perfectly flush with the surrounding plating, there is an increased likelihood of corrosion: this is because the paint coating may be less dense, especially in the case of a hard-chine craft.

The tedious business of hammer testing welds does very little to improve the surface paint, and in most cases it doesn't expose suspect welds either. A weld would have to be so badly executed or corroded that it is hard to credit that the vessel would retain more than a passing semblance to its original self. On the other hand, thin flakes may occasionally be seen after hammer testing; in this case, a detailed examination, with paint removed, must be considered, although the outcome of this would be regarded with pessimism by most surveyors.

Although there is less scope for originality of design in steel yachts since many are custom built, clipper bows, poopdecks, trawler wheelhouses and other traditional (and less traditional) touches as dictated by the client are everywhere. Many vessels to some extent owe their appearance to their trading ancestors and replicas are very popular. While most are designed with the lines nipped and tucked in order to fit in with modern demands, a few are exact copies down to the last deadeye. Dutch small craft feature prominently among these (a first-time visitor to the main Dutch boat show in Amsterdam would be taken aback at the sheer variety of these), but British coastal craft are widely copied too: the Thames spritsail barges, Humber keels, and narrow boats. The originals of these inspire unbridled enthusiasm among devotees, who take endless pains in tracing the boats' histories and re-creating liveries and primitive paintings of roses and castles. It would also be hard to ignore the number of 'replicas' of Joshua Slocum's circumnavigating *Spray*, though most bear little resemblance to the vast-beamed unballasted sloop.

Advantages and disadvantages of aluminium

Aluminium (or rather aluminium alloy, as most grades suitable for marine use are in fact alloyed with a small proportion of magnesium – which adds nothing whatever to the tensile strength) is a reasonably versatile material, and ideal for high-quality yachts where light weight is of prime importance. The success of this material in offshore power boats and ocean racers (and of course the 12-Metre boats, which are constructed in aluminium) is well known.

Aluminium is, however, prone to several forms of corrosion, one such being pitting of the surface with an accompanying formation of a white powder. This is unsightly, but is of little real importance.It is not by any means unusual to see aluminium boats with the topsides left unpainted and apparently cleaned off at regular intervals with soap pads (although use of any steel cloth or brush is to be deplored, since tiny particles of the steel may remain on the surface of the alloy and lead to pitting). So-called poultice corrosion, because of the rather nasty hydroxide effusion that spreads from contact between a bare edge of metal and any wet substance capable of capillary conductivity (thus acting as a wick), is most undesirable. However, it can be prevented with care and appropriate barrier sealants. This form of corrosion tends to be noticeable within the interior and is seen around bolts in deck beams or through-mounting pads (also, where fibres from the upholstery come into contact with a damp area of untreated alloy).

The last form of corrosion – and potentially the most threatening by far to the structural integrity – is also the commonest:

corrosion resulting from galvanic and/or bimetal action. Aluminium reacts adversely to most metals that come into direct contact with it, in the presence of salt water. Therefore only certain metals can be safely used as fastenings or fittings. The most widely used nowadays is stainless steel. Some fastenings and fittings are plated with chrome or zinc, although often the plating is too thin to rule out the risk of an eventual reaction. (Similar care must be taken when selecting paint, especially for antifouling purposes; copper and mercury must be totally avoided.)

The welding of aluminium alloy is a highly specialised process: the argon arc system is generally used, but not all yards have the equipment or the trained personnel to undertake this. Thus repairs can be expensive and may involve transporting the boat some distance. An amateur contemplating carrying out welding would certainly need both training and experience before laying the torch to the metal. Bearing this in mind, unless an aluminium boat is exceptionally cheap) and they rarely are), the chances of acquiring a classic are very remote. However, it is always worth keeping your eye open, because, apart from a few production classes in the 20 foot and 30 foot range, most aluminium craft, whether power and sail, are indeed genuine high-technology classics, and are equipped and furnished accordingly.

Ferro-cement

Although ferro-cement is not a new invention – boats have been constructed of it for over 150 years – it has been hailed as the ultimate low-tech boatbuilding material, ideal for the amateur with designs upon a world cruise in the largest possible yacht for the lowest outlay. This resulted in a few builders having a slap-happy attitude towards ferro-cement. Sadly, as happened to a lesser extent with steel, this outlook ultimately brought discredit upon both the material and the building technique. To my mind, the problem lay with neither, but resulted from a minority who sailed off into the sunset with insufficient funds to fit the vessel out and inadequate skill in handling the craft once at sea. This has made home-built ferro yachts almost uninsurable, and you will probably have to produce a builder's certificate even for those built by specialist yards.

As with all forms of construction, there are good and bad examples produced; and, like glassfibre, steel or aluminium, most defects remain invisible until they require urgent repair. But, in the case of a boat made of ferro-cement, repairs resulting from poor building are almost impossible to put right since they are by their nature seated at the very heart of the structure.

On the face of it, there should not be any inherent problems with this material: the cement encapsulating the armature (the steel frame and mesh infill) prevents it from rust, with the steel reinforcing the cement. The finished product is almost impossible to crack; highly resistant to compression; and does not spring out of shape in the event of localised damage (and is therefore easy to repair without sophisticated tools or engineering procedures). It can also be highly finished, has reasonable insulative properties, and is resistant to attack by marine chemicals and corrosion.

This all sounds excellent, but unfortunately the passage of time has proved otherwise. The weak point in what could otherwise come close to being the ideal material for the construction of both power and sailing vessels is corrosion of the armature, whether through slow curing and retained moisture or just through one or two defective fastenings. And there are almost always one or two somewhere.

I have found that evidence of armature corrosion leading to total disintegration of the hull is almost entirely anecdotal; the majority of ferro-cement boats I have inspected have, even after many seasons in commission, appeared in good order and free from visible external cracks or other signs of breakdown. Those defects that did exist tended to be concentrated in the areas of external and internal finish, but installation of the machinery and electrics did on occasions leave something to be desired. The largest proportion of these faults were the direct consequences of impatience (eg the urge to weigh anchor and head for more congenial climes) or of strictures imposed by a dwindling bank balance.

Thus, there is a possibility that stories regarding the negative side of ferro construction are exaggerated. However, I do know of one example. This was a yacht which, after the successful completion of a transatlantic voyage, spent a couple of years pottering around the West Indies prior to a leisurely return to its British home port. During passage, severe weather was encountered and the crew prepared to abandon ship. A container vessel took them off the endangered yacht, and an attempt was made to lift the vessel on board. Once slung in the derricks, the hull promptly broke in half. On examination (at least a segment of the casualty survived to be craned on to the deck), the cause was attributed solely to corrosion of the framework. Word spread like wildfire, as such things tend to, and this may have had an adverse effect on the insurance coverage that now affects craft made of ferro-cement.

Whatever the cause, there are certainly a number of bare hulls and partly fitted abandoned yachts to choose from on the market. Bear in mind, though, that the ownership of a completed hull and deck still leaves two-thirds of the total work before commissioning to be done.

If considering buying a ferro-cement vessel not constructed by a professional yard, the only unbiased advice that can be given is to check before purchase whether or not the vessel will be insurable. If you cannot get insurance cover at any price, this does not necessarily mean that such a vessel should not be bought, finished off and cruised quite safely. Unfortunately, though, most marinas and boatyards require at the very least third-party cover, and eventually comprehensive cover could become mandatory.

CHAPTER 14

The ship's systems – mechanical propulsion

Assuming that examination of the hull structure has been satisfactory, or at any rate failed to reveal any incurable defects (and assuming that the agreed price is realistic, with due allowance being made for repairs or restoration), the serious business of checking through the ship's systems can begin. Naturally these vary in complexity according to the size and purpose of the vessel concerned; the domestic department of a working smack might consist of a galvanised bucket with the auxiliary propulsion provided by a pair of sweeps – although such a limited inventory is improbable in this day and age. Even if the intention, when purchased, is to strip the boat out, replace all machinery, plumbing, wiring, etc, it would be a mistake not to examine these systems individually. Each item may, after all, have a residual re-sale price.

For the purposes of the survey, the systems can be divided into mechanical propulsion, domestic, lifesaving and fire-extinguishing equipment. It is easy to visualise the manner in which the systems overlap to a large extent: engine, cockpit drains and a marine-flushing lavatory all have to be fitted with seacocks; and electrics are essential not only for engine starting, but also for navigation and domestic lighting – as well as such modern 'essentials' as auto-pilot, radio and satellite navigator! Since the majority of components interact, the accepted way of verifying their status is to run through a list methodically.

The steering (and structural soundness of the rudder and hangings) is generally reckoned to be worthy of a paragraph or two in its own right in a survey – if it is not mentioned routinely in the report of the external hull inspection. Where the craft is fitted with wheel steering, the mechanism can be highly complex; a sailing vessel under 30 feet, though, would almost certainly be tiller steered, and this does rather simplify matters. Of course, in the case of a sailing vessel, the rig is a major element of the survey and has to be examined and assessed carefully. Not only must the mast and spars – and the associated fittings – be inspected for damage or wear, but sails, running and standing rigging must also receive close attention. Some thought should also be given to the size and probable balance of the rig, since this influences both performance and ease of handling.

Deficiences in one or more of the ancillary systems are popularly held to be a more common cause of total loss than structural failure of the hull as a result of collision or latent defects. In truth, any grave mishap is more likely to be the result of a combination of unfortunate circumstances, any one of which might prove embarrassing, humiliating and alarming, but not fatal to the boat or crew. It may be reassuring to reflect that virtually all major defects can be picked up in the course of a survey, although accessibility will, as always, impose some restrictions. Without a shadow of a doubt, there does exist what is sometimes referred to as Murphy's Law or the 'X' factor: the random chance of something malfunctioning simply because it is there!

Insurers lay down ever-stricter rules as to siting and plumbing of gas installations, specifications for fire-fighting equipment and electrical specification; these rules alone can turn an apparently simple and straightforward substitution of old for new into a needlessly complicated obstacle course. However, official requirements should always be complied with when planning a new galley, hot water system, etc.

The mechanical propulsion is the largest single item of this last section of the survey, and it is also the one with the greatest number of interdependent components. Therefore it seems logical to start here and trace everything outwards from it. (Some yacht owners scoff at an auxiliary engine, but most yachts today do have recourse to an alternative source of power – even if it's only an outboard that is barely capable of stemming a foul tide.)

An owner's attitude to the engine has a direct bearing on its condition. To some, it will be an unwelcome and intrusive beast which crouches amid rust and oil scum under the companionway and refuses to cough into life when requested. To another owner it will be seen as a reliable friend and lovingly maintained in clean and dry surroundings. If there were any logic in the world, the former engine could at once be identified as the auxiliary to a sailing vessel, an object tolerated with great reluctance as emergency motive power only, and the latter would be clearly recognisable as the mechanical propulsion unit of a fine classic motor yacht. Ironically, things often turn out to be completely the reverse!

From the point of view of the potential purchaser of a neglected classic, the difference may well be academic since any engine is, in all probability, going to be in a similar state to the hull fabric. The first difficulty may be locating the engine! It is by no means inevitable that it will be situated in what is now regarded as the optimum position, slightly aft of amidships and, in the case of a sailing vessel's auxiliary, hidden from the public gaze by the discreet positioning of the companion steps.

In quite a few sailing vessels of flat section and therefore restricted space, the engine may be installed right forward in the eyes of the boat. Occasionally, in vintage high-speed semi-planing power craft, such as patrol vessels, it will be mounted in the fore part in order to obtain the optimum weight distribution and allow for large-capacity fuel tanks without an adverse affect on trim. The accepted view today is that such an installation is undesirable because of the tendency of the very long shaft to whip under load, but, in practice, adequate spacing of plummer blocks will prevent this. Plummer blocks are, though, items calling for precision machining and the cost of the four or five necessary for a 25 foot run of shaft is high. Since modern engines are lighter and smaller for their power ratio, it is likely that a replacement engine could be re-sited further aft; however, the positioning of tanks, banks of batteries, etc would have to be carefully calculated beforehand, as would the installation angle of the engine and shaft.

The provision of an inboard auxiliary in many vintage sailing craft, which were not originally designed to have one, led to many awkward compromises. These were inevitable given the section of a pre-war small cruiser (and those, even more extreme, of a performance yacht). This, especially when combined with a flat run aft, made impossible the normal practice of drilling the deadwood to accept the propeller shaft because, in order to obtain a workable angle, the engine would have to be almost literally sited under the deckhead itself. Often, where a centreline engine was installed, this was of such proportions as to

markedly reduce space in the saloon.

Although the accent on accommodation was not so pronounced in those days, there were many occasions when it was preferable to minimise the space taken up by the iron topsail and mount it off to one side of the centreline, the propeller emerging through the planking of the quarter and carried by an A-bracket. The disadvantages are easily seen: efficiency is greatly diminished in anything of a seaway since the propeller regularly pierces the surface with attendant cavitation, racing and possible vibration damage when underway. When motor sailing with the propeller on the weather side, any noticeable angle of heel may bring it clear of the water altogether and render it completely useless. Also, so far as the interior layout is concerned, an engine that is too bulky to fit under the bridgedeck may not so easily be tucked away beneath a quarter berth or other joinery. And, from a structural viewpoint, an off-centre installation is hardly good news since the shaft passes directly through the planking. Admittedly this can be strengthened with fairly massive frames and bearers, but these will raise the total height of the engine considerably – and also raise the centre of gravity (as well as realigning its lateral plane). All the same, replacement of the engine with a modern, more compact counterpart should be feasible, although the expense of drilling deadwood and making good the previous shaft exit in the planking has to be allowed for.

Merely because some sort of engine is discovered to be on board, it should not automatically be taken for granted that it was intended as the power unit or, for that matter, that it is in fact propulsion machinery of any kind. Naturally, a check to ascertain whether or not it is coupled to a shaft will confirm that this was indeed the original idea, but if it is simply lying there bear in mind that it might be a pump or possibly a generator. A manufacturer's name plate is not necessarily informative, as many firms such as Listers and Petters marketed pumps and generators in addition to their well-known marine engines.

After sinking on her mooring this 40 foot ketch is a sad sight as she awaits first the insurance assessor and then a lengthy period of fitting-out prior to re-commissioning. Damage to machinery and electronics will be extensive and sails and upholstery will almost certainly be ruined by oil and fuel leakages – do not underestimate the work involved in buying such a casualty.

Identification of type, as opposed to manufacturer or model, should present few problems. The permutations, after all, are hardly endless: petrol, two-stroke, possibly paraffin/petrol, diesel or, rarely (fortunately), the obsolete semi-diesel. As a basic guide, if it does not possess spark plugs and leads, it is not a petrol engine, but do not confuse the injectors of a diesel with plugs. Superficially, especially when observed through layers of rust, the appearance is similar.

Internal combustion engines

Most people realise that a petrol or petrol/paraffin engine works by means of an electrically generated spark which ignites the fuel, whereas in the case of a diesel engine continuous ignition occurs as a result of compression of the fuel. Actually, this is rather an oversimplification of the process, because the diesel fuel is warmed by compression, then atomised, before being mixed with fresh air drawn into the inlet manifold. The resulting mixture is then reheated to facilitate combustion of the fuel (injected under enormous pressure) into the engine cylinders. The necessity for the diesel engine to withstand the forces generated by the immense compression is the main reason for the higher weight and increased bulk compared to a petrol engine with equivalent output. However, this gap is narrowing as sophisticated alloys are widely employed in the casting of components.

The semi-diesel, should a purchaser be so unlucky as to come face to face with one, is a hybrid in which the compression is much lower than that of a full diesel; thus the compression temperature is lower and the fuel is ignited by directing the fuel on to a hotspot of the cylinder. This would be heated to about 600° C (often by the simple expedient of blasting away with a blowlamp) and, once it rumbled into life, this temperature would be maintained to combustion heat. The effort of firing up, especially in a confined space and possibly in an emergency, is best left to the imagination! Rare as these engines are, one or two are still installed in converted working craft and one or two still thump along in pre-war boats. If you discover one, replace it without a moment's hesitation!

Because of the high compression of a diesel, the force required for the initial start-up is considerably in excess of that called for in a petrol unit; so, where electric starting is relied upon, a heavy-duty battery is advisable (or even essential). Some larger diesels are started by compressed air (others have a once-only emergency facility for using an air bottle in the event of battery failure), but many engines, whose size places them in the category of yachts' auxiliaries, can be turned over by hand once decompressed – and this, to my mind, is a most desirable attribute.

In the course of a survey all external aspects of the engine would be examined by the surveyor: installation, condition of mountings, hoses, clips and seacocks, exhaust and cooling systems, sterngear and propeller (and the general state of both engine and bilge). However, for an in-depth assessment, a marine engineer should be called in since some checks require specialised techniques and tools. Certainly, it would be foolish to purchase a large motor vessel without such an examination, although this constantly happens.

The majority of marine engines are based upon car and commercial vehicle motors, and fitted with an altered system of cooling and reduction gearbox. In truth, they have an easier time of it afloat for they are subjected to far lighter use than if fitted in a vehicle. That said, they are also subjected to indifferent maintenance, or even a total absence of it.

This being the case, it hardly comes as a surprise to learn that in nine out of ten cases the engine itself is basically sound, but all ancillary systems are defunct.

The first item to check is whether the engine is installed on fixed or flexible mountings, the latter now being almost universal for yachts and small motor cruisers since they do permit a degree of latitude in the mounting. It must be emphasised, though, that the coupling fitted has to be strictly in accordance with the manufacturer's specifications and, even where a flexible coupling is used, there is no excuse for failing to align the engine and tailshaft accurately.

If an engine is flexibly mounted, small metal feet, each underlaid with a compression pad of hard rubber, will be visible – although they are often partly obscured by an accumulation of oil and dirt! With a rigid mount, steel pressure pads or a length of steel reinforcing may be visible – (and possibly heavily corroded) under the mounting bolts. (Ensure, if at all possible, that the bolts are in fact bolts and not coachscrews, which they just could be. These will loosen under vibration and eventually result in misalignment of the engine and shaft.)

Cooling

The angle at which the engine is installed should also be considered. In a sailing vessel it is not uncommon for the motor to be run while heeled – if the yacht in question is motor-sailing to windward for example. Most engines can function at a horizontal inclination of up to 30 degrees provided that, from time to time, the vessel is allowed to come upright to ensure adequate circulation of the lubricant to the valve assembly. But an engine that has been installed in a 'nose-down' attitude is liable to suffer an air-lock in the water jacket at the rear of the cylinder head.

A malfunction in the cooling or lubrication system is a singularly effective way of bringing an engine to an abrupt, noisy and – if not at once detected – permanent halt. Next to a failure in the fuel supply (or a warp tangled around the propeller), it is also the commonest problem.

Basically, there are three methods of cooling marine engines. The first and most often encountered method on smaller yachts and power craft is by direct intake (raw water cooling); the second method makes use of a closed freshwater system with heat exchanger; and the third, not usually seen except in some fishing vessels and craft operating on inland waterways, also employs a closed freshwater circuit around the engine, but with long external keel pipes acting as a primitive form of heat exchanger.

The first method is the simplest and therefore the cheapest, although the principal drawback is corrosion when operating in salt water. Because of the lower operating temperature inevitable with this type of cooling, scale also tends to build up in the water passages. There is an additional slight risk of particles of debris in suspension being drawn in with the water, although the fitting of the appropriate strainer to the inlet ought to eliminate this (more likely is the inlet growing foul with weed and shell so that insufficient water reaches the engine: the result is overheating). Indirect cooling with freshwater and heat exchanger is clearly superior on all counts, except that of cost, but the indirect keel-cooling system is not to be recommended if contemplating the installation of a new power unit. It will to some extent prove detrimental to performance, even on a large, heavy displacement power boat. And, of course, the external runs of piping are susceptible to damage from an accidental grounding.

A small proportion of marine petrol and diesel engines are air cooled. This is a dubious practice since, except on a very large boat, it is not usually possible to maintain an adequate flow of air without resorting to the use of mechanical blowers. These are an increased complication and mean a higher initial cost – and yet another component capable of malfunctioning at a crucial moment! In the case of a small craft, sufficient air flow is usually incompatible with sustained watertight integrity.

Seacocks and hoses

Dissection of the engine does not fall within the scope of a normal survey, but a fair idea as to the efficiency of the cooling system can be obtained from scrutiny of all hoses, clips, seacocks and gate-valves, as well as connections to the engine. In spite of the undisputed importance of all of these items, many owners seem to develop a 'blind spot' with regard to them; an otherwise well-cared-for engine may be relying upon hoses that are worn or cracked and barely connected by terminally rusted clips. The neoprene impellers of water pumps rely on the circulation of water for lubrication, and if allowed to dry (as they will have if the vessel has been left standing) they may stick – and the blades snap off – once the engine is started.

Seacocks and gate valves suffer badly from neglect. Since the ability to close these fittings off in an emergency is absolutely vital, it is hard to understand why their condition tends to be ignored. Admittedly the positioning may have something to do with this – it might also explain why it is quite common to leave seacocks in one position (permanently open) regardless. Both types of fitting are generally to be found on board any boat with through-hull discharges: a gate valve (which may also be fitted between lengths of hose) is operated by means of a wheel on the top, while a seacock is always lever actuated and fitted with one inlet/outlet to a hose and one direct to the ship-side. Seacocks are almost invariably precision manufactured from high-quality marine bronze. Beware, though, a gate valve may not be! The results of severe corrosion could result in the loss of the vessel, so check not only the fitting itself, but also its fixing bolts. Where a seacock is fitted to a glassfibre hull, ensure that the base is positioned on a bonded-in timber pad, or at least that the laminate has been strengthened in order to accept it. A good deal of strain can be put upon the base, especially where the seacock has been left unused (and without grease) for any length of time.

During the inspection of engine plumbing do not overlook the exhaust system and the bilge pump (also the cockpit drain hoses). As with all hoses, ensure that there are no cracks or signs of leaks, and make certain that there are no kinks or tight bends that would restrict the water flow (the hose to a diaphragm bilge pump should be of a reinforced type, otherwise the pressure exerted in use can cause the pipe to collapse inwards upon itself and so restrict or prohibit the flow of water). In the case of the exhaust, see that there is sufficient bend to create a swan neck: this precludes any chance of water entering if the vessel is overtaken by a heavy following sea. Fortunately, this is a rare occurrence, but one that has nevertheless caused the loss of several vessels caught out in severe conditions. Nearly always there was water already aboard in large quantities; this causes the stern to drag, which allows more water in through the exhaust – thus killing the engine. By this time the vessel would be helpless and, without outside assistance, at risk of breaking up or foundering.

Of course, at some point in the course of the survey the external skin fittings must be examined, not only to check on the accumulation of weed and shell growth that may block inlets (though this is at least easy to see and quick to remove), but also to note the slightest sign of breakdown in the bronze or nylon from which the fittings are generally fabricated. Also look closely at the hull in the immediate vicinity: in a wooden boat, a poor seal may lead to rot; in the case of a glassfibre vessel, there is occasionally evidence of stress crazing.

The engine space

One thing that will have become pretty obvious by this stage in the proceedings is the state of the engine bilge since investigation of engine mounts and seacocks brings the surveyor into close proximity to any oil and grease deposits. True, there is a school of thought that holds firmly to the view that a nice all-enveloping scum of oil acts as a protective barrier to the engine and, perhaps so far as a road vehicle is concerned, there is a germ of wisdom in this belief. But it is not a state of affairs to be tolerated within the confined area of the engine space on board. Not only is it a positive deterrent to routine maintenance, it also constitutes a very real fire hazard. (And an overall film of oil obscures signs of any continuing oil leakage.) The fitting of fire-retardant insulative linings within the engine space was frequently overlooked on older vessels – even where the main propulsion was by means of a cumbersome and clanking piece of oil-covered machinery that usurped the crew accommodation and made all conversation impossible when under way. Once the bilge area has been thoroughly cleaned, an oil-repellent lining should be installed as a matter of course. This will not only reduce – or at least partly contain – an outbreak of fire, but it will go a long way towards damping out engine noise.

Even if there is no obvious reason for oil in the bilge (and, apart from thoughtless spillage, its presence is usually the result of a failed oil seal – which may require removal of the engine to remedy), its presence does suggest that little attention has been paid to the vessel's mechanical side. Thus inspection should proceed on the assumption that if matters external look doubtful, those things hidden from view may be far worse!

A well-oiled bilge does little to encourage a close look at the sterngear; in any case, this is often rendered virtually impossible by lack of access. Sailing vessels are common offenders in this respect as the cockpit sole is often screwed firmly into place, bedded on to hardened mastic and, to all intents and purposes, irremovable for survey. Glassfibre boats tend to be even more awkward, with access to the sterntube sometimes limited to a small nylon hatch – barely large enough to insert a hand.

Sterngear

Considering the importance of the sterngear, it is difficult to explain the inclination to hide it from view. In theory it requires little regular attention; in practice, especially in older craft it can be a source of irritating – though minor – weeps.

A marine engine transmits the drive to the propeller by means of the shaft, coupled to the gearbox and exiting through the hull via the sternbush or shaft log (although the latter term is rather anachronistic as it originally applied to that portion of a tree that was bored for the shaft). There are exceptions such as inboard/outdrives, saildrives and water jets, all of which are quite specialised. (In any case, relatively few would be found in classic yachts.)

Unless the vessel has been damaged or tampered with by an inept mechanic, few problems are necessarily going to be discernible merely by inspection (with the exception of the sterngland and its greaser). In a vessel that has been neglected or laid up it is as well to condemn the coupling as a matter of course and budget for a replacement; a flexible coupling can deteriorate if not in use. Do not automatically replace like with like, for it is not impossible that a coupling incompatible with engine and gearbox has been fitted.

The majority of sailing and motor vessels under 30 feet have a comparatively short run of shaft and this will, in almost all cases, be straight and free from play. However, there is always the possibility that a slight misalignment of engine and shaft may be corrected by the fitting of a pair of universal joints. If an extended shaft is installed, see that it is supported along its length and check whether the plummer blocks have been maintained in a greased condition during the engine's running time. The difficulty of attending to this necessary operation is one major drawback to a central- or forward-mounted engine. It is possible to have a shaft that is only slightly out of true straightened, but if there is evidence of corrosion it is better replaced. With stainless-steel shafts the problem of crevice corrosion is rife, and never more so than when a vessel has been laid up for a long period. If the engine has been operated in salt water, some residue will remain trapped between shaft and sterntube: this has the effect of starving the stainless steel of oxygen and causing a breakdown in the protective surface. This leaves the way clear for pitting, which could weaken the shaft or even lead to the abrupt detachment of the propeller itself. The bending forces exerted abaft the sterntube, which are increased by the vessel's motion in a seaway, are to some extent neutralised by the bearing. Clearly, though, excess wear or pitting cannot be tolerated in the vicinity since this will exacerbate the forces imposed and, in an extreme case, the shaft could snap.

This bearing may be made of anti-friction white metal (a mixture of tin with small quantities of copper and antimony added), of rubber or, in the case of a vessel of considerable antiquity, of lignum-vitae. Nowadays, the water-lubricated rubber or polyurethane bearings are widely used in spite of being relatively short-lived compared to metal bearings lubricated by a manual or remote greaser.

Bearing wear can be brought about by a number of things: the scouring action of sand or mud particles in the water, a misaligned shaft or damaged propeller, as well as a degree of wear in the coupling. The exact amount of wear is not usually easy to assess without dismantling the fitting: it has to be quite advanced before it can be detected by shaking the propeller.

Water entering at the point of the shipside exit of the shaft is prevented by the sterngland or stuffing box. Although the basic principle is simple, there are variants – with some types requiring professional overhaul in accordance with the specifications of the manufacturer. Occasionally the internal grease can harden to the point where it actually impedes the revolution of the shaft. It will then have to be cleaned out and fresh grease applied. From time to time a stuffing box may need repacking, either with Teflon cord or soft cotton impregnated with grease. Leaks can be almost undetectable once the boat is afloat; it is only by the amount of bilge water quietly accumulating after a period of disuse that a skipper will be alerted to the fact. It is therefore a wise precaution to have all seals professionally examined prior to launching, especially where the boat has been out of the water for more than a month or so.

The propeller

At least defects in the propeller are highly visible – though this being the case, it is astonishing how often a vendor protests (feigns?) shock and horror on being informed that either corrosion or physical damage has wrought havoc on the performance of the boat. This applies equally to propellers fitted to power boats or to sailing auxiliaries where use is only intermittent. On a very high-speed run-about, the vibration would be impossible to ignore, but in many cases it is difficult to see how it could be dismissed even on a displacement vessel – except perhaps where an owner would rather not admit it, even privately!

The majority of propellers for cruising boats are manufactured from bronze, although most outboards are fitted with nylon or light alloy. Determining the diameter and pitch of a propeller ought to be a matter best left to the experts. Given the dimensions of a vessel, type and intended use, the manufacturers of the power unit should be able to come up with an accurate specification. It would be wise to verify this before removing the existing propeller for re-profiling or re-metalling (and certainly before replacement since a new bronze propeller is very expensive – even in the case of a vessel's small auxiliary engine). A slight deviation from the optimum might in reality not be all that noticeable in the case of an auxiliary, but with a motor yacht it will prove detrimental to both performance and fuel economy.

In sailing craft, where the performance under sail is considered more important than wheedling the last quarter of a knot from the engine, the reduction of drag is more highly regarded than maximum engine efficiency. With this end in view, racing craft in particular tend to favour either a feathering or folding propeller: the former 'feathers' the blades so that when under sail they fold so as to be in line with the deadwood, keel or skeg, and the latter folds to form a streamlined unit (rather resembling clasped hands). So long as neglect does not allow an accumulation of weed, both types function adequately under load. Simpler by far is the fitting of a two-bladed prop which, when the engine is in neutral, is simply stopped vertically in line with the keel; the shaft may be marked so

A quarter installation showing how close the propeller is to the waterline. This means that if motoring in a seaway, waves will fling it clear of the water from time to time. It cannot be employed on the weather side if motor sailing, and it may also make manœuvring in tight corners difficult.

that the crew can carry out a quick visual check as to whether this has in fact been carried out.

No matter how severely damaged, a propeller will more or less fulfil its function and drive the boat through the water. It will only do this for a limited time, though, unless it is securely attached to the shaft. A loose keyway, a missing castle nut or, more common by far, a split pin which is partly or wholly absent, can lead to an abrupt termination of power. Mud and weed often combine to look like nuts or pins: always scrape away the accretions and have a close look.

Erosion or bending of the blade tips is common, and in many cases it is due to collisions with underwater obstacles. Corrosion is not entirely unknown – in particular, where the propeller is of manganese bronze. Strictly speaking this is not a bronze at all, but a form of brass (an alloy of copper and zinc), and as such it is prone to a gradual leaching out of the zinc content as a result of electrolytic action. Considerable pitting and almost complete breakdown of the tips will be visible should the corrosion be severe; should the bronze appear bright and polished as the boat is craned out the water, this indicates electrolysis has probably been at work (suspect it elsewhere in the vessel since cathodic protection cannot be adequate). The effect of cavitation tends to be seen as deep and quite regular shallow gouges.

The fuel system

Restricted access can make inspection of fuel tanks and lines most awkward. From the point of view of weight distribution, the tanks should be installed as low as possible in the vessel, but, in the case of a small yacht or motor cruiser where space is limited (and the quantity of fuel carried is not, in any case, likely to weigh more than an extra member of crew in the cockpit), the usual site is under the aft or side decking. And once installed at the time of building, bulkheads are then fitted and sidebench tops permanently fastened into place! There are occasions when his sense of smell will cause a surveyor to suspect that all is not well either with the tank or the fuel lines; even when the vendor offers a cheerful assurance that this is the result of recent spillage, check the tanks and connections either by hand – or with a wad of absorbent cotton on the end of a stick if items are (as they almost certainly will be) just out of reach.

Any fuel constitutes a fire hazard, with petrol being particularly volatile. The slightest evidence of a leak in the tank itself should be sufficient to condemn it. But the possibility of corrosion from within is not one to be ignored, especially if the tank is not suitable for the fuel that it contains. This is fairly common with older boats that have been re-engined – often having exchanged a petrol engine for a diesel model. A petrol tank can be fabricated from a variety of metals (or glassfibre). These include aluminium (although no brass or copper fittings must be used in conjunction with aluminium to prevent galvanic action), stainless steel, brass, copper or steel (preferably galvanised). The latter two must not be used for the storage of diesel fuel since it is 'allergic' to them and will react adversely. Particles of corroded metal inside the tank will sooner or later find their way into the fuel lines and clog them. Starved of fuel, the engine will splutter unceremoniously to a halt; since the sediment is most likely to be disturbed in bad weather, the resultant stoppage could have serious consequences.

Stainless steel does seem to be the nearest to ideal for all fuel types, although this is reflected in the higher cost. However, even this metal is not free from the risk of corrosion pitting if condensation forms pools in the tank. To avoid this, it is normal practice to top up the diesel in the tank before a winter lay-up (not to be recommended where petrol is concerned, though; apart from the fire hazard, gummed deposits can form within the tank).

The engine controls should be examined for full and free movement and all pins, bolts, etc should be checked to ensure that this continues. Some ingenious lash-ups are seen often where the boat has been previously owned by an engineer – often such engines are excellently tuned but fed and watered by the most unorthodox systems imaginable. Such systems, efficient though they usually are, seem to have been evolved expressly to baffle surveyors!

If an engine can be turned over, whether by hand or on the starter motor, the chances are that it can be saved however decrepit it looks. If it refuses to budge, it has probably seized either partially or irrevocably and will therefore have to be lifted out – either for inspection by a marine engineer or to dump at the scrap yard. And this is where the real problems start: it simply may not be possible to remove the machinery without first taking out bulkheads, joinery and, not infrequently, a section of deck – or even part of the coachroof or wheelhouse. Such large-scale structural upheavals may far exceed the cost of a new engine.

Where an engine does not seem to be totally beyond hope and yet cannot be turned over (either because a manual starting facility is not fitted or as a result of failure (or absence) of battery and/or starter motor), some idea – though it will be little more than guesswork – can be gained from a look at the exhaust outlet. If the surrounding area is completely free of soot, this may suggest that the engine, when last in commission, ran reasonably well without burning excess oil and with acceptable fuel combustion. On the other hand, it may simply be an indication that the engine has not been run since the hull was last cleaned or painted. In the case of a petrol engine, it is worth taking out the plugs to check whether or not they have oiled up; an oil deposit indicates wear of the pistons or rings.

Starting up

If the engine can be started (having *first*) ensured that a supply of cooling water is on hand and that there is oil in the crankcase), the exhaust will once again provide a clue as to its condition. A small quantity of smoke is universal when the motor is cold (and, in the case of a two-stroke, also when it is operating at normal temperature), but otherwise it is a confirmation of worn pistons, valves or bearings. (Blue smoke is particularly unwelcome.) For the first minute or two, though, it is most important to monitor all instruments closely: if oil and water are not circulating normally, the engine could seize very rapidly.

With the vessel out of the water, and a raw water cooling system, it will not be feasible to run the engine for long enough to let it reach the usual working temperature, but the oil pressure warning light must extinguish itself within seconds or the gauge should register at least thirty pounds psi (the oil pressure at working temperature does vary considerably between types and models, but is always higher when the engine is cold). If the light remains on or flickers, or the gauge fluctuates wildly, do not hestitate: turn off the engine at once. Either there is insufficient oil or the oil pump is faulty (or the engine bearings are worn beyond the point of no return, in which case there may well be audible confirmation). Should the water temperature gauge fail to register, either it is defunct or possibly the fault lies with the thermostat. If it starts to climb towards the red sector, switch it off before any damage is done. Should it hunt wildly up and down the scale, there could be a fault in the water circulation, the thermostat, or just possibly it is the first sign of a defective head gasket. (Ensure, in the case of a diesel, that you are familiar with the position of the strangler button or the 'off' position of the key; if you are not, you may be unable to shut off the engine in time to forestall irrevocable damage.) Don't remain gazing in fascination – cut the switch at once and renegotiate a lower price! Revving up a cold engine in neutral is hardly to be recommended – especially when the vessel is out of the water – but gentle operation of the throttle is permissible after some minutes and this will give an idea of the smoothness of the running. Be alert to any sinister regular thumps or knocks; these are most often heard either on revving up or with throttle pressure eased right off and the engine decelerating. Such noises must not be dismissed as they may be (and unfortunately probably will be) signs of worn bearings or con rods. It is possible to mistake other minor rattles or clattering for the sound of a defective bearing – but that particular noise, once heard, is never forgotten!

If replacement of the engine is seen as the lesser evil, a substitute must be found – possibly one that will undertake the same work but occupy less space. This is not to say that anyone who inherits with their boat one of the large slow-revving older marine engines should condemn it to the scrap heap; in fact, quite the reverse. These venerable machines were (and still are) utterly reliable so long as they receive minimal maintenance. Some of the pre-war Kelvins, Thornycrofts and Gardners inspire enormous affection in a manner that modern engines, for all their excellent qualities, do not. If there is room on board to keep such an engine, then do. Parts should not be too much of a problem although (ironically) with certain smaller, up-to-date engines, which have had only a limited marinised production, they may be. Obviously, before finally coming to a decision it would be wise to ensure that spares are available (and at a reasonable price – try more than one company or retail outlet as there can be large price variations).

Alternative installations

Although it might be more common to replace an outboard auxiliary with an inboard, there are instances where it pays to do things the other way around (and this would hold good so far as some smaller semi-displacement power craft are concerned too). Outboards used to be considered crankier, more difficult to start, and prone to suffer from oiled plugs because of the oil-rich two-stroke mixture. Today, though, the design and engineering have progressed to a degree where an outboard installation can be looked upon as quite dependable, although it does suffer from two major drawbacks that have not so far been eliminated. The first of these is the concentration of weight where it is least desirable and the second is the possibility of theft. Unfortunately, chains and security locks do little to deter determined thieves, who simply cut through the transom with a chainsaw.

For motor vessels in the moderate- to high-performance category, an outdrive unit offers an excellent compromise; the weight is further forward, the engine and electrics are better protected from the weather when the boat is unattended and there is little chance of anyone stealing the entire engine. (However, the propeller might be stolen, and some owners remove the prop to prevent this.)

An outboard is reasonably efficient as the auxiliary for sailing vessels of up to about 25 feet (although there are variations), but only where there is a transom stern or very short counter. If the rudder is transom hung, the stern also needs to be fairly broad to allow it to move freely. In small and fairly light boats, an outboard of sufficient power may well cause the stern to squat. There will also be the problem of stowing the motor when the vessel is left on her mooring (sailboat auxiliaries, if left on the mounting bracket, are particularly liable to be stolen). Installation of the outboard in a well at the after end of the cockpit is a reasonable compromise. Although amateur fitting of a well in a glassfibre, moulded or plywood hull is not impossible, it is a task best left to an experienced shipwright in the case of a clinker- or carvel-built vessel. Having said this, it might still be easier than the fitting of an inboard.

The relatively restricted room aboard a sailing vessel when compared to a motor boat of the same length (which would, as a rule, be broader in the beam – and carry that beam further aft) has caused engine manufacturers to devise variations on the standard arrangement of in-line engine, gearbox and sterngear.

The best known of these alternatives is almost certainly the saildrive: a compact installation that is closely allied to an outboard in that the transmission and shaft are contained within a single streamlined underwater leg. The unit is exceptionally easy to fit. In a glassfibre boat, the profiled engine bed, supplied with the motor, is simply positioned and bonded into place. More involved, though only marginally so, is the installation within a timber boat where the timber will have to be treated with epoxy prior to bonding; and, in the case of a traditionally constructed vessel, some reinforcement and fairing will be unavoidable.

The 'Vee-drive', usually met with on larger craft, employs a gearbox that reverses the shaft (not to be confused with a normal reversing gearbox) and places that shaft immediately below or even in front of the engine. It maximises available space, although it inevitably has more components which could eventually give rise to trouble. However, in all fairness, it is often installed in commercial craft, and there are few adverse reports of its reliability.

Live steam!

Both the marine petrol and diesel engine are of course internal combustion engines. The *external* combustion type is steam – albeit steam often raised by propane rather than coal.

Although the use of steam power is really limited to inland waters, at least so far as small craft are concerned (and larger craft hardly come into the category of yachts, although the few remaining steam tugs and small commercial vessels such as Clyde puffers are eagerly snapped up on the rare occasions they come on to the open market), there is sufficiently widespread interest in this means of propulsion for several firms to manufacture boilers and other steam-related components. Engines can readily be bought, although an installation – complete, up-and-running – for a 22 foot launch would work out at approximately twice the price of a diesel unit.

It is still possible to chance upon a long-forgotten steam launch from time to time, and in most cases the engine, though certainly not the boiler, would be capable of restoration to its original working order. So think twice before automatically searching out a more commonplace replacement! But beware: rumour has it that even a slight acquaintance with steam power can lead to a lifetime's obsession!

CHAPTER 15

Ancillary and domestic systems

The electrics

Although it is quite possible to exist on board without any electronics at all, the modern trend is towards electrical circuitry and gadgetry of increasing complexity.

The main reason for installing an electrical system would be cited as that of engine starting. However, an engine fitted with a starting handle is far from the daunting (or even dangerous) beast it is sometimes purported to be. It is just that it is so rare for anyone to employ the manual facility that unfamiliarity has led to fear. However, once batteries are fitted, your boat can have the latest in navigation aids (and there is indeed a sound argument for the provision of the most powerful – and therefore amp-eating – navigation lights that are available). You can also have a television, refrigerator and stereo on board, if required!

Whether you regard the electrics as the essential provider of home comforts or as a more or less necessary evil, there is no point in having an unreliable system – remember that damp and electricity are mutual and implacable enemies! This being so, all possible effort must be made to install marine-quality control/fuse and terminals and to keep them as far as possible away from spray and adverse weather, while maintaining ease of access.

By the same token, the output of the battery(ies) must be sufficient to start a recalcitrant engine without drain. With this in view, cruising boats should install a twin-battery system, with the batteries fitted in leak-proof boxes with secure retention against undue movement of the vessel. Each battery must be fitted with a single pole isolating switch accessible to the helmsman, and a paralleling switch must also be fitted to provide standby starting and also a simultaneous trickle-charge, so that each battery can start the engine.

Generally one battery would be used for the engine starting with the other used to service domestic and navigational systems (whose consumption can be easily underestimated). It is irritating to have a boat fully equipped with luxuries, but no amperage. While a gin and tonic without ice or a non-functioning microwave are hardly life-threatening, lack of power for deck floods and navigation lights (or the auto-pilot if short-handed) just could be. Since the almost universal reliance on interfaced navigation systems when passage-making has led to a degree of laxity in taking bearings and maintaining dead reckoning positions, loss of the Sat-Nav and VHF may place the vessel – literally – in an awkward position. So, don't gloat unduly over a boat packed with electrical gadgets – at least, not until the means for amperage input and facilities for recharging the battery(ies) have been verified.

Due attention must be paid to the siting of the batteries. They are weighty objects and can inflict physical harm to ship or crew if they break adrift. Also, they can emit noxious, even dangerous, fumes if the casing is cracked or there is contact with water. This retention against an emergency situation is paramount; and, without being alarmist, that could include total inversion in the case of a sailing vessel. (Motor cruisers too can be knocked down by a freak wave caught beam-on.)

In the more modern boats, charging is provided by a rectified alternator mounted on the machinery. Distribution must be by marine type control/fuse panels. With the exception of the starter circuit, all other circuits have to be protected by micro circuit-breakers (with at least two in the panel), each one clearly tallied.

Larger vessels with owners requiring the luxury of freezers, refrigerators, television and constant hot and cold water will probably have a 10 KVA Generator installed with acoustic housing sited in, or adjacent to, the engine space to provide power for a 220 AC system. In this case, the generator would, most likely, be fitted with an 'auto start on demand' – and fully suppressed, of course. This will probably be augmented by a Constavolt marine charging unit (or similar) for use when in marinas etc, thus allowing use of a 13 amp ring main at all times.

Portable generators are most useful for a smaller boat where power consumption is variable. They are compact for output, easy to start and economical to run, although a well-ventilated area is essential: the cockpit or deck is safest. The 'green' alternatives are a trailing or wind-operated charging unit (although the latter can be dangerous if fitted where a human hand could possibly come into contact with it) and solar panels. Although these panels are not cheap and a disproportionately large area of deck would need to be given over to them in order to run extensive systems, constant advances are made in the technology. As a means of trickle-charging when the vessel is not in use, they are excellent.

Wiring installation

These electric systems are generally 12 v or 24 v DC (depending upon the size of the craft and engine(s) size) carried throughout in a 2-wire fused in the positive pole. The installation should obviously be kept as simple as possible, with all wiring accessibly run (even where it is concealed).

All cables must be adequate for the capacity carried and also of marine grade, sheathed and impervious to fuel or water. They should be clipped back at intervals of 12 inches or run through conduit, with all wiring installed as high as is practicable – in other words, no circuits should be below the bilge water line, unless specifically designed for the purpose (eg electric bilge pumps, etc). All external connections must be made by watertight plugs and sockets, with all wires into metal masts or through GRP protected by rubber or nylon grommets.

The surveyor's prime concern will be with the condition and safety of the installation, though comments on the suitability for the vessel would also be expected. A purchaser's requirements might be very different from those of the previous owner, so it may be the potential that is in question rather than the existing capacity and installation. With older boats the electrics are something of an afterthought: jury-rigged with a puzzling assortment of domestic fittings, pieces of wire and unorthodox connections (backed up by the ubiquitous matchstick). In such a case, the only thing is to be ruthless: scrap the whole lot and start from scratch. In many instances, wiring that, on the face of it, appears serviceable would in fact be uninsurable. Insurance companies' demands are increasingly stringent, and not without good reason.

All these requirements are really common sense: there is, after all, little point in having an electrical system in the first place if it is not competently installed. A new vessel, straight from the yard, should have a specification that complies with all necessary standards, but the cost ought to be at the forefront of the mind when re-equipping an old boat. It is, quite frankly, an expensive operation. Of course, for every electronic unit there is an alternative: oil lighting has been used for centuries, a sextant is accurate (when conditions allow its use), and the magnetic compass, once adjusted correctly, has been used by countless ships crossing oceans. Certain items of equipment such as echo sounders and radio receivers can be powered from internal batteries, as can powerful hand lanterns and small emergency navigation lights. Wind vane steering for a sailing craft is – once set up and the crew accustomed to its ways – so sensitive that it can steer a wind-based course better than the average helmsman, *and* in weather that would impose a heavy loading on an electrical system. But there is at least a choice available; the only criterion being that whatever system is selected, it must work, without delay, and for as long as required.

Cathodic protection

The need for the cathodic protection of small vessels has been more widely accepted within recent years. It could be argued, though, that this understanding is a product of necessity because of the wider range of dissimilar metals now employed in both the construction and fittings of small craft. It is also a result of the increase in electrical navigation and domestic equipment. Such equipment adds to the effect of galvanic corrosion through the very real possibility of stray current leakage increasing the speed of corrosion. It would seem that a certain amount of this corrosion, previously attributed to such forces as cavitation and erosion, has in fact been the result of the electrochemical reaction caused by the formation of galvanic cells between parts of the same piece of metal. A current, slight though it is, flows between these cells. The anode, being the baser metal, will corrode, while the more noble metal of the cathode will not. By the creation of a more attractive anode (generally of pure zinc, but occasionally of aluminium or magnesium) to which the current will then flow, the metal to be protected automatically becomes the cathode and will be free from all corrosion.

Most people will be familiar with the sight of a sacrificial anode, generally in the form of a metal bar, some 6 inches in length, bolted to the underbody of the vessel – and in a more or less corroded condition depending on how well it is doing its job. (However, it is not unknown to see only the metal fixings, the anode itself having long since departed.) This anode can only function if correctly bonded to the parts it is designed to safeguard – generally, the shaft and propeller. The rudder and rudder hangings may call for the provision of separate anodes. Should an anode appear to be in pristine condition after being immersed for one or more seasons, it is a safe bet that it has been improperly bonded – or not bonded at all. It will therefore be quite useless. (It will, by the way, be rendered ineffective if painted.)

Requirements vary considerably according to the material from which the vessel is constructed, with aluminium and steel calling for a comprehensive and expertly installed cathodic protection system. Smaller craft, especially racing boats where even the minimal resistance of an external hull-fitted anode would be regarded as most undesirable, can in most cases successfully employ a hanging anode. This is simply hauled on board once the craft is under way.

Although the actual fitting of an anode is simple, positioning is crucial. Tables based on underwater profile, volume, etc do give accurate guidelines, but the type of machinery installed (even the paint used on the hull) has to be taken into account. Therefore it would be far more sensible to approach the manufacturers of the cathodic protection systems for advice; this will be freely given and the protection individually tailored to each vessel.

Although for the purposes of a survey inspection would normally be by eye – and by hunting around in the engine bilge to determine whether the bonding has been correctly carried out – there is a portable corrosion control meter available on the market. Its use would, however, normally be associated more with larger hulls, storage tanks, and possibly offshore installations where it is otherwise difficult to monitor the onset of corrosion as a result of the partial breakdown of the protection circuit.

The steering

Unexpected failure of the steering gear is one of the more unpleasant occurrences visited upon any vessel. If under way, even when there is sufficient time and sea room to effect some sort of repair, it is alarming. In a congested area such as the mouth of a commercial harbour – or worse, the harbour itself – the potential for causing (and receiving) extensive damage is enormous. Although failures in a well-maintained wheel system are rare, there is rarely any warning when they do take place (in the case of a vessel steered with a tiller, some momentary play or subtle preliminary indication may be felt by the helmsman). Whether the link from rudder to wheel is mechanical, hydraulic or, simplest of all, by chain/wire rope led over sheaves, all components should be cleaned and examined for wear and tear. This may in practice be harder than it sounds, especially with sophisticated systems where access to the inner workings would not come within the scope of a normal survey. All hydraulic pipes, chains and linkages should be accessible for inspection and servicing; indeed if not, this is a serious disadvantage because of the problems of maintenance.

Hammer-testing fastenings and pintles of a small keelboat's rudder are unlikely to reveal much that isn't immediately visible to the eye. Suspect bolts are generally revealed by cracking around areas of stopping, and weeps of rust can often be seen. Any movement of the rudder cheeks should be checked as this suggests that the rudder may have been stressed on grounding.

Tiller steering, as fitted to most sailing vessels under 30 feet overall and smaller open or weekending non-planing power craft, does at least have fewer parts that can go wrong; and in most cases all items can be checked over at regular intervals. Tillers can snap at the rudderhead, though rarely without obvious signs of deterioration first. They may also delaminate, or occasionally develop so much play that steering an accurate course is more a matter of luck than judgement. In general, though, any faults are more likely to be in the rudder itself and its hangings – or because of undue wear on

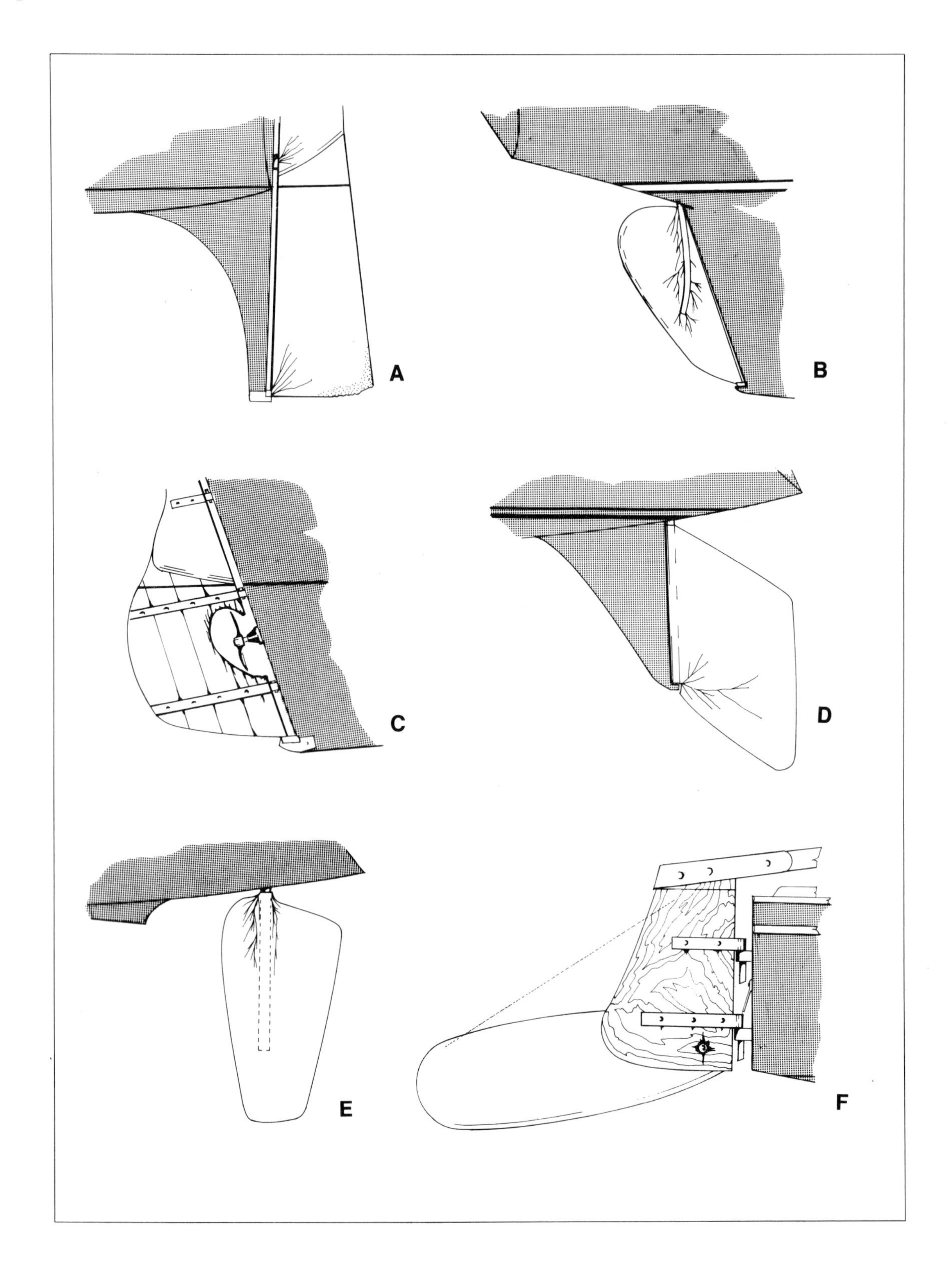
A
B
C
D
E
F

the pivot bolt with consequent vibrations of the blade in the case of a lifting rudder.

Rudders, whether of wood or metal, do develop defects; these, though, are usually readily apparent. However, the GRP rudder, as fitted to glassfibre sailing craft, is another matter entirely as faults can only be discovered after a detailed inspection. Most of these are directly caused by the design itself – the shape of the blade – or an underestimation of the bending forces to which the rudder is subjected. It might be expected that only the deep and narrow rudders of a racing boat, unsupported by a skeg and of as fined-down section as possible, would be vulnerable; but in fact all types more than three or four years old frequently show evidence of crazing, delamination, separating from the stock or, more often than should be the case, all three of these. In general, moulded/laminated glassfibre rudders do reveal prior signs of breakdown before final disintegration, but because more boats remain in a marina berth all year around, only emerging for a brief hose-down and antifoul by the yard, these tell-tale signs are often missed.

One frequent weakness occurs where the rudder is moulded in two halves – usually in-filled with foam but not invariably – and separation occurs along the trailing edge. Where a metal stock is encapsulated it is not uncommon for the differing rates of flexion to cause stress crazing that worsens rapidly. Equally, it is by no means rare to discover that water has permeated the moulding, often through the underside being abraded during grounding: the internal metal stock has corroded and play has developed to danger point. Very common too is damage to a rudder hung to a partial skeg, stress crazing and extensive cracking affecting the rudder at a point in line with the lower end of the skeg. This condition may be exacerbated by external forces such as fouling an underwater object or taking the ground. The importance of examining these regions cannot be over-emphasised; more than half the boats over ten years old that I have surveyed have required repairs

Rudders: common faults

A Fibreglass low aspect transom-hung rudder with full skeg, a type often found on bilge keel yachts which regularly take the ground. Erosion of the under surface of the blade is common and allows water to permeate the foam core eventually resulting in delamination. Repeated three-point landings may also damage or wring the pintles and gudgeons, with consequent damage to both rudder and transom.

B 'Conventional' glassfibre rudder on a long-keeled yacht. The stock is through-bolted and encapsulated, but eventually flexing and corrosion of the fastenings will cause water penetration and the laminate will become saturated. This type of rudder is moulded in two halves and the flexing also frequently causes separation of the laminate at the trailing edge.

C Timber rudder of a traditional motor boat or keel boat. This is prone to rot caused by water entrapment beneath the straps and fastenings of the hangings, although the process is usually pretty obvious!

D So-called 'scimitar' rudder in glassfibre, hung to partial skeg. This type is generally encountered in yachts aimed at the performance market and therefore hell-bent on reducing the lateral area. It leaves the rudder very vulnerable to damage from grounding or snagging a warp; cracking can often be seen in the blade immediately below the skeg.

E A balanced spade rudder of the type commonly seen on motor cruisers and high-performance sail craft. Highly efficient but very liable to damage and wringing: always check vertical alignment. Wooden or glassfibre variants of the blade may eventually separate from the stock.

F Dinghy-type lifting rudder with metal blade and wooden head, usually found on small craft and some traditional shoal draft sailing cruisers. Inclined to wear on hangings and also pivot bolt; strain may result in separation of the cheeks.

One of the most commonly-encountered defects on glassfibre yachts – a delaminating foam-cored GRP rudder; a fault often unsuspected until complete failure occurs.

to, or even replacement of, the rudder. Be prepared to re-antifoul the area if necessary, but do not be deterred from scraping away paint for a closer look (there is a good chance that previous repairs will show the problem to be one of long standing).

Solid timber rudders do rot, especially around and underneath metal straps, fastenings and the hangings. Localised repair is not usually a problem; as usual, the real problem lies in the difficulty of actually getting at the site of the operation. (High technology has led to a few rudders, mostly in cold- or hot-moulded timber vessels, being constructed in the manner of an aircraft wing: a thin skin over laminated leading and trailing edges with internal ribs. Skegs also may be built in this fashion. This increases the buoyancy in the aft sections and is very strong – until, that is, it is subjected to any one of the major causes of external injury.)

Domestic utilities

Referring to those comforts that contribute so greatly to the enjoyment of a civilised lifestyle on board as 'domestic systems' seems to underestimate their importance. However, nothing can be taken for granted on a boat in the manner in which it may be ashore. Admittedly, even in the best-regulated house, lavatories go wrong, pipes block, and tragedies involving cookers are by no means unheard of. But on a boat at sea there is no obliging plumber ready to come out, nor is there medical help in an emergency. If an appliance goes wrong while at sea and does not either sink or demolish the vessel by doing so – you simply fix it or do without it! This being so, there should be no half measures when first checking, refitting or replacing a boat's utilities.

The domestic equipment – in essence, the life-support system – is primarily concerned with the means of heating and cooking food and, to put it delicately, the eventual disposal of it! There are those, of course, who are firmly against the very idea of such mechanical devices as sea toilets, since these contraptions entail drilling holes through the hull and scrupulous attention to all cleansing (at sea, in protracted severe weather, this is not a job tackled with enthusiasm by any crew member). Many lavatories are so positioned as to be almost impossible to use. These die-hards do have a point; installation of any system other than the most basic is not altogether logical unless there is space to install it in a separate compartment. Even then, a modern chemical toilet is a practical alternative – especially in areas where a holding tank would otherwise have to be employed in conjunction with a flushing toilet.

While a marine lavatory can cause a

vessel to sink (more correctly, as with any through-hull discharge, failure of a hose or seacock may bring this about), an ineptly fitted or carelessly used cooker or cabin heater can lead to fire or explosion. Accidents, though, are not as common as one would be led to believe, taking into account the increase in the boating population.

LPG gas is without question the cleanest and simplest fuel for cooking and heating on a boat, but fear of explosion is rife and many owners do prefer the option of a pressure paraffin or alcohol stove. Feelings run quite high and certainly those who have mastered the art of lighting (and keeping alight) a pressure stove swear by it. The same is true of alcohol stoves. I personally dislike these because of the invisible flame and the fumes, and I do find the business of refuelling either type at sea a distinct drawback. However, personal inclinations must not be allowed to influence an inspection: any stove must be installed so that it does not cause a hazard to those on board, whether cooking on it or simply attempting to squeeze past it. (The practice of some small cruisers of installing the cooker underneath the bridgedeck is highly dangerous.) The gas cylinder must be sited in a purpose-made locker, above the waterline, and fitted with an overside drain. This allows any escaping gas to disperse overboard. In some vessels it is possible to stow the cylinder(s) on the deck if they are securely attached. The gas cylinder is to be fitted with the appropriate regulator, with all connections to the gas-burning units made by reinforced or armoured hose to rigid copper piping. The joins between the hose and copper piping need to be augmented by stainless steel hose clips and the hose used is to be of the minimum practicable lengths, with copper piping protected against chafe by vibration. Periodic inspection of the supply lines can prove awkward: once fitted, joinery tends to restrict access for much of its length, and even the shortest run may be 10 feet or so. An older boat will almost certainly require the gas installation refitted, so it is worth bearing the future maintenance in mind when planning the new installation.

Cabin heating is a pleasant luxury (and almost a necessity if sailing out of season). It may take the form of a diesel-heated warm air unit or possibly a solid-fuel stove – either charcoal or the good old coal-fired bogey stove! Other options are paraffin or catalytic gas or alcohol heating. All require adequate ventilation, with direct heat sources (and the flues) requiring fire-retardant backing. Ideally, a crash bar should be fitted to prevent the risk of contact with hot metal. (This, in any case, is handy for clothes drying!)

The freshwater supply

The possibilities for the freshwater supply range from a jerrycan with a pipe inserted in its neck, to a manual pantry pump (even simpler would be a collapsible hanging container with gravity-fed spigot – though this comes into the 'roughing it' category), to the provision of a pressurised water system, possibly with hot water supplied by immersion heater or calorifier. These are costly, so if they are installed and in a functioning state they are worth having. But – and there is always a but – they are only worth having so long as freshwater tanks have sufficient capacity: with water on tap, consumption will be at least three times that of a manually operated system (where each drop has to be pumped forth and then heated in pan or kettle). The allowance of 1 gallon per day per person will be insufficient, and replenishing tanks becomes a repetitive chore. This is not too onerous a task in a marina, but with the boat on a swinging mooring it is quite a different matter. So, if there isn't a pressurised system, think twice before fitting one.

The condition of the freshwater tanks (usually of galvanised or stainless steel, occasionally of glassfibre) should be ascertained, as should the state of drain cocks, fillers and all attendant pipework. Flexible tanks, so long as they are regularly flushed out, are excellent; they can be fitted into awkward corners, but in a wooden boat (or a glassfibre one where the internal hull finish is uneven) inspect for signs of chafe – even when this means draining the tank first.

Sinks on a small boat are rarely of sufficient size to be of much use: most will hardly accommodate a milk saucepan, let alone a stewpan or casserole dish. Furthermore, the discharge may be so high in the topsides that the sink will never drain. In a sailing vessel that spends a proportion of time heeled on one tack or other, a discharge pump may be necessary; often, a large fitted bucket with worktop lid over would be more convenient.

The layout of the accommodation is very much a personal matter, and dictated by the size of the boat (and, to some extent, the size of the owner!). Simplest is often best, especially where the vessel is under 30 feet. Folding, collapsible or slide-out surfaces are far more of a nuisance than they are worth. The saloon table should be both strong and stable, as well as large enough for the crew to eat at. In this instance, drop flaps may be called for. No part of the domestic arrangement, though, can function properly if there is insufficient space to make use of it. So when contemplating a refit or interior rebuild, this aspect should be considered; make a preliminary cardboard mock-up of any major joinery compartment, such as a berth frame or dinette, galley or heads, before building work commences. This may save a good deal of subsequent alteration.

Fire-extinction and life-saving equipment

The provision of fire-extinction and life-saving equipment is of prime importance, although such equipment clearly needs to be tailored to the requirements of an individual vessel. There is, after all, hardly an appreciable risk of fire in a racing dinghy or day-sailing keelboat!

Fire at sea has long been a major fear of mariners: it strikes swiftly and can ravage a small boat in minutes, cutting off all possibility of escape. It can also break out in unexpected sites. Any cruising vessel would therefore normally be provided with an extinguisher (dry powder or BCF being most usual) in each cabin, along with a fire blanket in the galley adjacent to the stove. A fire blanket is extremely effective in dousing flare-ups, such as might result from a chip pan or spilled fat, but its use is not instinctive; it does, after all, take a cool head to lean over a blaze and drop the blanket over it. It would seem a good idea for the crew to have a fire drill ashore, perhaps practising with a piece of heavy towelling over a designated target area. (Not, of course, one that is actually in the process of combustion!)

Many auxiliary sailing vessels now fit an automatic BCF fire-fighting system in the engine space; indeed, this seems to be an increasing requirement on the part of insurance companies. The units are relatively compact (size being determined by the cubic area of the engine space) and react to a fire far faster than a crew member could. There is also no need to open a hatch in order to use the extinguisher, and this in itself prevents a further spread.

Efficient, in-date fire extinguishers must, of course, be on board during refitting work; there is perhaps a greater risk of fire at this time than when afloat.

It is said, albeit jokingly, that nothing removes unwanted bilge water nearly so rapidly as a frightened man with a bucket. However, a diaphragm bilge pump, correctly installed and with a strum box fitted to the intake to guard against blockage, should be superior – neither will it tire so fast! Ideally two pumps should be installed, one to pump the cockpit area and one to clear water from the accommodation. These can be interchanged if a fault develops in either one or the other. (That metal draw bucket with lanyard attached is mandatory aboard a cruising yacht.)

The smaller electric submersible bilge pumps are fine for removing rain water or preventing the accumulation from a small weep, but are not likely to be of much help in the event of a real emergency, when electric power may already have been lost.

Loosely speaking, most items in the inventory could be thought of as having some connection with life-saving. For example, if anchors and chain are not man enough for the job in an exposed anchorage, the vessel is placed at risk and also her crew; likewise the time may come when having a good radar reflector or powerful torch to hand will ward off a collision.

There should always be on board a lifejacket and safety harness of approved types for each crew member, two horseshoe lifebuoys with floating lines, lights and signals, and also an in-date pack of flares. All must of course be in first-class condition. In an older boat that has been laid up for a while this is unlikely to be the case, so budget for replacements from the outset.

The presence of a liferaft, assuming that it possesses a current test certificate, adds value to any cruising boat. Without this documentation its worth is doubtful (unless the age is known for certain), since recertification may be impossible or prohibitively expensive on an old raft.

When all is said and done, the best attitude to adopt towards life-saving equipment is to buy the best wherever possible, and look after it carefully. Always remember, though, that the vessel itself is the best of all liferafts and will, as has been repeatedly shown, survive in weather when those in an inflatable liferaft may not. Spurious as it may be, the sense of security offered by a liferaft is insidiously attractive, and grows ever more so as a storm progresses and unease mounts.

Chapter 16

The rig

Behaviour under sail

Where the survey concerns a sailing vessel, the sails should be checked over meticulously. To be more precise, this applies to the entire rig as a failure of spars or standing rigging is more common, not to mention more dangerous, than merely having a sail tear or blow out of its bolt rope. It is not uncommon for a purchaser merely to tweak the standing rigging and perhaps poke dismissively into the contents of one or two sail bags without even troubling to haul out the sails themselves.

Whether the vessel is gaff or lug rigged (or fitted with Chinese lug or spritsail, come to that), it is not strictly speaking part of a surveyor's brief to pronounce on how well the rig is suited to the boat under examination. Most would, however, offer some comment on a rig that was clearly far too small (or too large) or one that, even at a glance, looks to be hopelessly unbalanced. The survey is primarily intended to verify the physical condition of spars, running and standing rigging, mast fittings (and also such items as blocks and bottlescrews) and the extent and state of the sail wardrobe. The survey should also check that the sails listed on an inventory are present and that they do actually belong to that particular craft. More than once I have found this not to be the case!

A purchaser, carring out his own inspection, might well wonder exactly how the boat is likely to behave under sail. To a practised eye, this is not difficult to guess – not at least with the mast stepped; when it is lying on deck, the balance is not so easy to assess. By no means were all classic yachts the exquisitely balanced thoroughbreds of repute, requiring only the lightest touch on the tiller as they glided through the Solent waves. And this was certainly not true of working vessels. Anyone studying old photos of sailing trawlers with a cynical eye will notice a few clenched teeth and harassed expressions as the skipper battles with the tiller to control 12 tons or so of rapidly moving pitch pine pushed along by 1,000 square feet of canvas!

Relatively few vintage yachts retain their gaff rigs exactly as designed. However, there is always a temptation to revert to the original, in spite of the fact that alterations took place for two good reasons: improved windward efficiency and easier handling. Weather helm and lee helm are terms that are constantly bandied about, for the obvious reason that they are such common afflictions. Given a tiller and a reasonably sensitive boat, neither vice can be hidden for long, but wheel steering and, in particular the highly geared feather-light wheel steering so popular today, can quite effectively disguise a pronounced tendency to come up to or to fall off the wind. The tendency will still be there, but the helmsman is not aware of it – unless specifically testing for it.

Both the position of the centre of effort of the rig and the shape of the hull underbody affect balance. Too much underwater area aft of the hull's centre of lateral resistance or too much sail forward of the rig's centre of effort produces lee helm; the reverse situation produces weather helm. Weather helm, while not exactly a specific aid to helmsmanship, is sometimes tolerated in the belief that it assists in sailing that little bit closer to the wind. Lack of area in the forebody not only increases any propensity to lee helm, but it also encourages the yacht to fall away after tacking and, when sailing in close quarters, this can easily result in a collision. To an extent, lee helm can be negated by reducing the area of the foretriangle either by reefing or dropping one headsail in the case of a cutter, but if this perverse handling is consistent under normal working sail the only cure is to recalculate the areas and restep the mast if necessary – distance would depend on the cut of the sails and, of course, the severity of the problem. Do not forget that the chain-plates or deck eyes for the standing rigging will almost certainly require repositioning if the mast is restepped.

Timber masts and spars

Not so long ago it appeared that timber masts and booms were doomed to become things of the past, but now brokerage adverts list wooden spars as desirable assets. Heavy they may be, and prone to rot, shakes and springing, but they do at least behave predictably and faults can usually be spotted prior to actual failure. (Not, however, that this is necessarily a great help if a defect is noted in mid-Atlantic!) A wooden mast does need yearly inspection, overhaul and, usually, some attention to the painted or varnished surface. Shakes are commonplace, though the majority develop early in the lifetime of the spar. All must, though, be cleaned out, dried, stopped and a protective finish applied; severe splits should in every case be glued and splined. Where the mast is of hollow section, made from as many as eight lengths of timber, shakes must be regarded with suspicion. If they actually penetrate the timber completely, the process of rot may be well under way inside the mast; as there is no satisfactory way of verifying the extent, prepare mentally for the worst. Rot is common, as rot always is, under the metal fittings such as the sail track, mast band and hounds fitting, as well as any other areas that have been allowed to come into intimate and prolonged contact with wet iron – even corroding galvanised rigging taped to the mast and left exposed for a couple of years may instigate the process.

Not even aluminium alloy masts are maintenance free . . .

Judging whether or not a timber mast has sprung when it is unstepped is also more a matter of guesswork than firm knowledge; all masts, timber or metal, flex to some extent and an inadequately supported timber mast will certainly sag in the middle. Crinkles and ridges in the varnish under pressure points such as the spreaders do suggest something is amiss, but to be fairly certain the mast will have to be laid out along a flat surface, with all rigging cleared out of the way, and examined inch by inch. Even then, definite confirmation may be difficult.

A wooden spar, though, is a resilient object and, once correctly rigged, is one capable of withstanding a good deal of strain. Most stresses are imposed by incorrectly designed standing rigging, perhaps after a change from masthead Bermudian to fractional rig (although these days anyone intent on such a modification would probably order a shiny new mast of anodised aluminium).

Light and tough as they are, aluminium spars are not free of problems. If left without anodising the metal can pit or powder and discolour the sails, so it is worth considering painting with a suitable enamel. Fittings can corrode and compression strains can open and shut the luff groove, so preventing sails being hoisted (or being lowered). But nothing is ever totally free of drawbacks, and a new alloy mast complete with fittings will certainly be competitively priced compared to a new wooden one with bespoke hardware.

A great deal of money can be saved by home construction of a timber spar though a considerable saving can also be effected by the purchase of the alloy extrusion and 'shopping around' for the necessary fitments. Where a solid timber spar is specified, owners have selected wood from a Forestry site, agreed a price, and simply taken away the felled tree to be dealt with at leisure with adze and drawknife!

In practice, the making of a solid wooden mast is simple enough, and even a hollow glued one is not beyond the scope of an amateur with time and patience. (Time and patience will certainly be needed, as the first step is that of making a minimum of two dozen cramps!) A luff groove adds considerably to the work, and it should be inlaid with hardwood for at least the first foot of its length. This needs to be a precision piece of craftsmanship and finished with no fewer than half-a-dozen coats of varnish: there will, after all, be only the one opportunity to protect the inside of the groove.

A solid spar will be somewhat heavier than a hollow one; on the other hand, the section can be reduced slightly so that windage will be marginally less – although this is largely irrelevant on a cruising boat. A beautifully made and varnished hollow spruce spar is a marvellous piece of work, even though the intricacy of manufacture may not be fully appreciated once it is stepped. But it is undeniably a costly item if built by a professional, so if an owner does not feel up to the task of recreating one himself, an alloy replacement may offer the only solution. Fortunately, so many people have taken this view that there are a surprising number of spars kicking around boatyards: sometimes because they have outlasted the vessel with which they were launched, and occasionally because they have been supplanted by metal. Some are, of course, past all hope of recycling, but many could be cut down to provide a serviceable boom and gaff. It therefore pays to give an elderly solid spar a thorough examination instead of summarily condemning it. I spent what seems in retrospect an entire summer planing down the mizzenmast and main boom of a 45 foot ketch to make mast, bowsprit and yard for a 16 foot Zulu rigged with a standing lug. The entire cost was only about £10 for the scrap spars.

With older spars, such as those associated with pre-war cruising yachts, the shrouds and stays are frequently attached by soft eyes which simply loop over wooden chocks. These chocks are inclined to loosen as through-fastenings corrode, and there is an additional risk that rot may have set in underneath. This seems to be rather a crude method of rigging, but it is in fact both strong and reliable.

In the case of a wooden mast with external track (which should be set on to a hard-

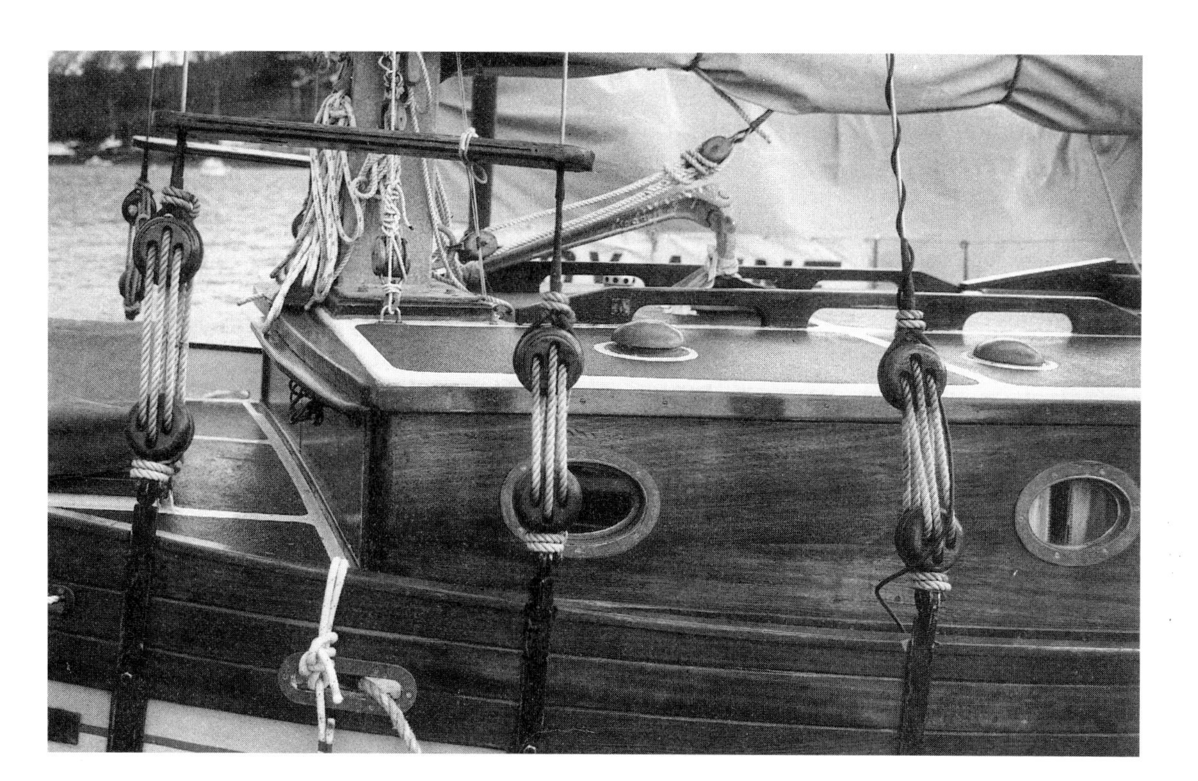

A delight for the eye of a traditional enthusiast: standing rigging set up with deadeyes, wooden blocks and lanyards. The deadeyes and good quality timber blocks are now expensive to buy new but can occasionally be tracked down at boat jumbles, usually only as singles or pairs. A search should commence well ahead of need!

wood backing piece), ensure that neither the track nor the backing show signs of movement. In an aluminium spar, if an aluminium mast is fitted with a luff groove (as opposed to track), check whether, at any point along its length, this narrows. If it does, this is a fairly clear indication that the mast has suffered injury.

Booms in general seem to suffer rather less, although damage can be sustained from an unexpected crash gybe – the boom of a gaff-rigged vessel is naturally more susceptible to this because of the greater length and the presence of running backstays which may not have been eased off in time.

Reefing

Reefing points were, and indeed are, commonly fitted to a gaff-rigged vessel. Because of the size and shape of the sail, roller reefing would allow the boom to droop below the point at which the mainsail can still produce drive; in so doing, it may foul such fittings as pushpits, davits or boom-gallows. Roller reefing, for years regarded as the norm on a Bermudian mainsail (and most efficient on a mast-head sloop where the mainsail area is small in comparison to the headsail and the boom in consequence is short), has now been largely superseded by 'slab' or 'jiffy' reefing. This is certainly quick to pull down, sail area is reduced in seconds, but the crew then have to contend with a baggy envelope of wet Terylene flapping about their ears. Once triced up neatly, the whole operation of reefing with this system will have taken almost as much time as traditional reef points would have done!

What is crucial is for the take-off point of

A A mast head Bermudian yawl – one of the pleasantest rigs for short-handed sailing and highly popular with ocean racers in the 1960s as the small area of sail in the mizzen was not measured. True, this contributes nothing when sailing to windward, but off the wind a large mizzen staysail can be set which is really effective and easy to manage into the bargain. Ketch rig is more common today, especially on cruising yachts over thirty feet. Although reasonable progress can be made to windward under staysail and mizzen only, the relatively larger mizzen mast divides the cockpit awkwardly and usually means the helmsman has to sit in a permanent downdraft. The mizzen provides little drive on the wind and the shorter main mast, shorter headsail luff and smaller effective sail area mean that windward performance is likely to be sedate rather than sparkling.

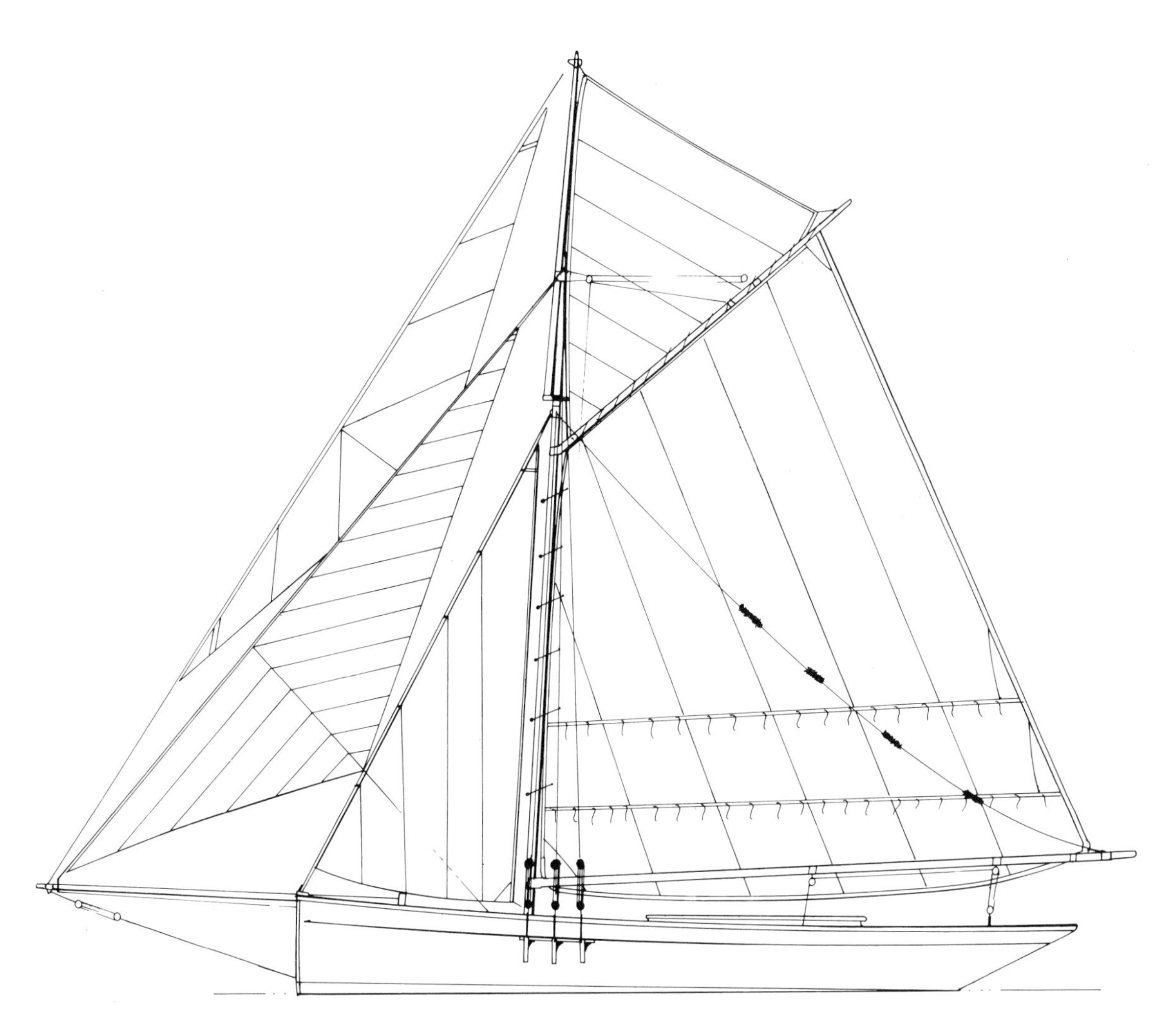

B Gaff rig in its pure form as found in an Essex smack. Disadvantages frequently cited are the weight of the gear, the length of the boom which renders reefing (especially when a matter of urgency) a major undertaking, chafe, and of course lack of efficiency to windward. Running backstays also tend to be regarded with awe if not outright alarm although when on the wind they can be set up and ignored until the time comes to free off.

However, a well-designed gaff rig can be a delight to handle, as such modern craft as the Cornish Crabbers have proved. With a larger headsail and consequently smaller main, lighter spars and efficient and less complicated gear, a gaff rig is an attractive option on any cruising yacht.

the mainsheet to be compatible with the type of reefing. If the vessel has been sailed on a regular basis it stands to reason that all will be in order, but this is not the case for yachts purchased in a neglected or abandoned state. With slab or point reefing, the lead may not be from the outer end of the boom. Instead, it might be sited only slightly

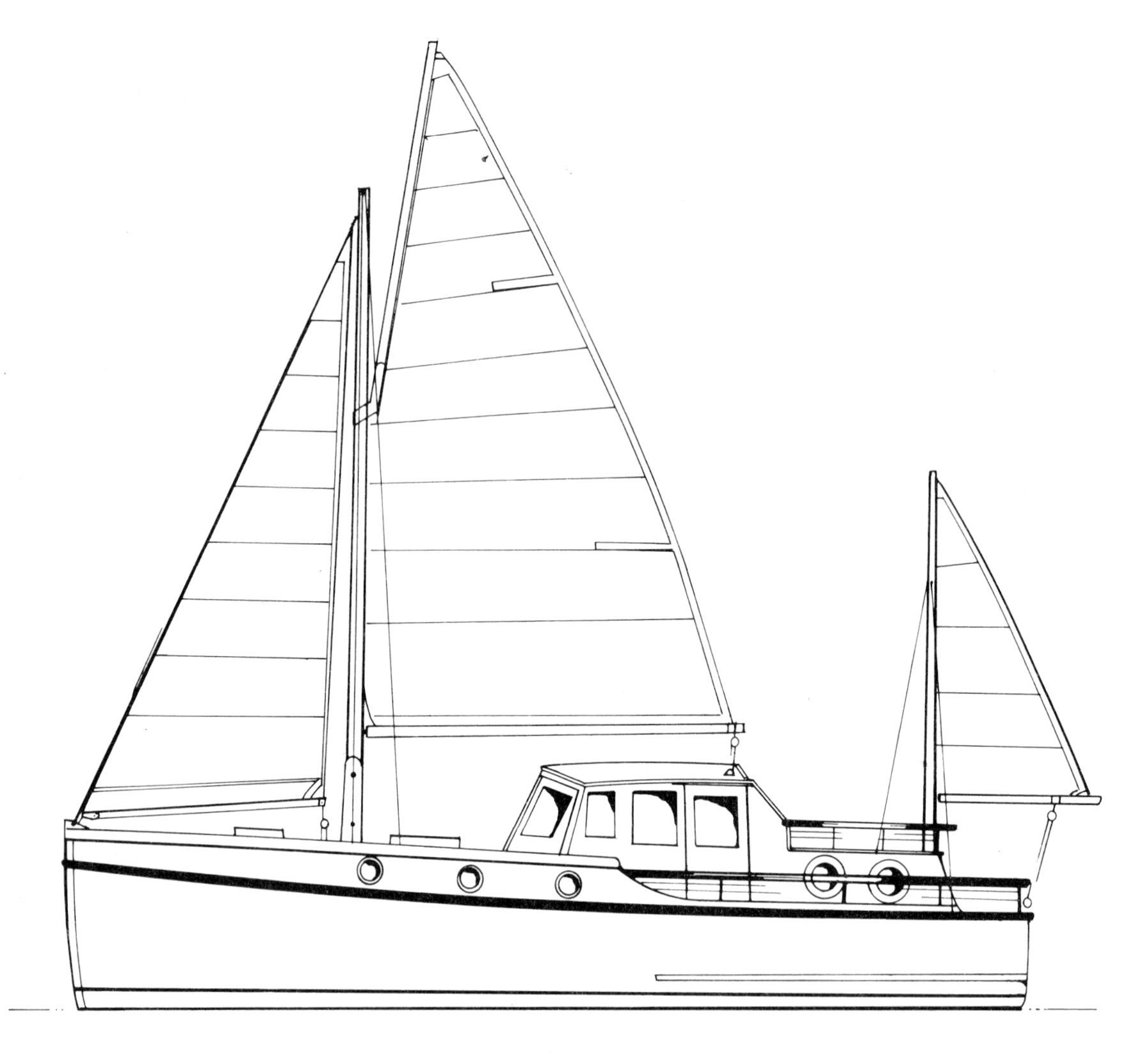

C An acceptable rig for a motor sailer intended to provide a respectable turn of speed off the wind; emergency get-you-home power only to windward and, with main and mizzen sheeted in hard and the foresail stowed or furled, some improvement in motion when motoring into a head or beam sea. At anchor or when fishing the sheeted mizzen will keep the vessel lying comfortably head to wind.

aft of the centre: this largely dispenses with the need for a kicking strap to prevent the boom lifting when sailing off the wind, but it does mean that there could well be a substantial and unyielding metal eye positioned exactly where it can cause serious head injury to an unthinking crew member in the event of an accidental gybe. Nowadays, most alterations to the reefing system would probably consist of a change from roller to slab, but there is always the chance that a roller main has been opted for without any thought of the appropriate swivel boom end fitting – and this could be difficult to fit to an existing aluminium boom. It may equally be awkward to achieve a fair lead from boom to existing mainsheet track or horse. In this case, the only option available may be to fit a reefing claw along with its adjustment and control lines. True, these are all fairly minor matters, but they do involve expenditure.

In what appears to be an attempt to eliminate the human factor from sailing altogether, increasingly sophisticated furling and reefing systems have been developed – at a price, of course. A modern headsail furling gear, fitted with a luff spar to prevent the luff sagging away to leeward is far superior to the old Wykeham-Martin system. This latter system was in any case only really suited to a low-aspect foretriangle. Without doubt, roller reefing fitted to the foresail is regarded as a distinct asset by the majority of purchasers of Bermudian-rigged yachts, but, excellent as it can be, it only functions without hitch when set up correctly. With this in mind, it should be seen in operation at the time of the survey, and adverse weather conditions can prevent this. Occasionally, to everyone's unease (not least the surveyor's), the jib will unfurl in the approved manner, but will obstinately refuse to roll up once more. This may be because of an incorrect lead or fouling of the head or tack swivel. The end result is identical and embarrassing: a flapping sail and a crowd of interested spectators. It can also be alarming if the yacht is a deep fin-keeler perched precariously in a light storage cradle.

Vertical roller reefing on a Bermudian mainsail shows signs of becoming the latest fashion accessory. Initially, sailmakers found it hard to produce a sail with acceptable flow (horizontal sail battens obviously being out of the question) that would still furl on command, but this problem seems to have been overcome with experience. This method, though, is really out of place except on an uncompromising cruising design. When first marketed, it was not possible to fit vertical furling on to (or into) existing masts and the thought of replacing both spar and mainsail made even the most wealthy yachtsman wince!

Dismasting

Anyone who has suffered a dismasting will carry the memory for a long time. Even racing skippers cringe at the memory, although dismasting is, if not exactly routine, hardly exceptional in the course of competition. Some years ago, while I was plodding along sedately in the Round the Island race, a squall neatly felled the mast of my Folkboat, along with those of four of the nearest competitors. It was all over within seconds and took place in a silence that was almost uncanny. And I well remember the test sail of one small racing boat. The proud new owners, builder and designer all stared in mute dismay as the custom-tapered alloy spar folded up like a trombone in a force 3, utterly without warning. On this occasion the cause was probably attributable to the designer's aim of reducing windage and weight aloft. It requires only a slight miscalculation of section, wall thickness or breaking strain to bring the mast down. In practice, though, the damage is usually a direct result of defects in chainplates (or deck eyes), occasionally a rigging screw or, from time to time, fittings at hounds or masthead.

The fittings higher up the mast are liable to failure for the simple reason that constant monitoring of condition is not always practical. How many owners, when all is said and done, habitually shin up the mast before each day's sailing? About as many as surveyors in the normal course of a survey! A mast, once stepped, is inspected from the deck (this would be stated in the written report); bearing in mind the startling degree of dereliction of certain vessels presented for inspection, it is doubtful whether the majority of surveyors would greatly relish a change from this practice. There are occasions when it may be necessary to go aloft if, for example, a specific repair or alteration needs checking. Usually though, it is neither practicable nor safe (given the delicate state of the shores of some yachts, not to mention the state of such terminals and rigging as can be examined from deck level). There is also the distinct possibility that external halyard blocks at the masthead are too light in construction (as are some nylon blocks, intended primarily for racing dinghies) and will part under a direct load.

Fittings on the mast may be of cast aluminium, brass, bronze or ferrous metals such as iron, stainless steel or welded steel plate. The surface finish will either be painted or galvanised (both cold and hot-dipped); sometimes surfaces may have been liberally daubed with bitumen or hot tar: the so-called Chinese galvanising. All finishes impart a degree of protection against corrosion, but all could have been applied with the express purpose of disguising this – as well as stress cracks or general wear. The risks of any or all of these defects is enhanced by the use of dissimilar metals (not only from bi-metal corrosion, but as a result of increased wear if, for example, a shackle is of harder metal than the unit through which it passes). Even if the condition as seen from deck does appear reasonable, it would be advisable to un-step the mast for inspection at close quarters. In practice, though, this is rarely done.

Standing and running rigging

The general appearance of the standing rigging can sometimes chill the blood when it is known that the vessel up to that point has been sailing along regardless. Quite often the wire along its length is basically sound, but splices and swages can only be described as distinctly untrustworthy. This situation is often brought about by an *ad hoc* programme of re-rigging carried on by successive owners, none of whom were aware of remedial work carried out by the predecessor. It is far from rare to discover that wire and terminals are of incompatible type; the undue strain thereby imposed will greatly reduce the strength of the wire.

The galvanised or stainless steel wire used for standing rigging can be of several types, with the definition being based on the number of strands per lay and the number of lays that form the wire rope. Most of these types are obtainable either in galvanised plough steel or in stainless steel, although there are exceptions. Put simply, some wire types are flexible and suited to running rigging such as halyards, running backstays, etc, while the stiffer wire is best fitted for standing rigging, partly because it is stronger for a given diameter. A stiff wire such as 1 by 19 would be useless for halyards, but it is not uncommon to find a flex wire used for standing rigging, especially on gaff-rigged boats. So long as the breaking strain is appropriate, there is no real reason why this should not be done.

The type of eye or terminal fitment (whether to mast or to rigging screw or lanyard) to the hull must be of correct type for the wire in question: a soft eye can be formed in all wire types and would generally be employed over mast chocks. A hard eye

Standing rigging
A Soft eyes with swages over mast chocks. Ensure chocks are sound and notched into the mast securely.
B Forged iron spider band with eyes for shrouds, stays and halyards, and jib halyard to crane. Make certain the mast has not rotted beneath the band and that the band cannot possibly move. Inspect all eyes for fatigue or fracture (not uncommon). Cracking of paint or galvanising suggest this possibility.
C Aluminium alloy mast of smaller yacht with stainless steel fittings. Rigging with hard eyes and swages, clevis pins to fittings. Check for soldiers (kinks) or loose wire filaments, especially in the region of the eye.
D Alloy mast with shrouds and forestay secured to mast with internal T pieces which swivel sideways into position and lock under load. Port and starboard shrouds are roller swaged (check for bent swages and broken wires). Forestay is fitted with a swageless terminal.

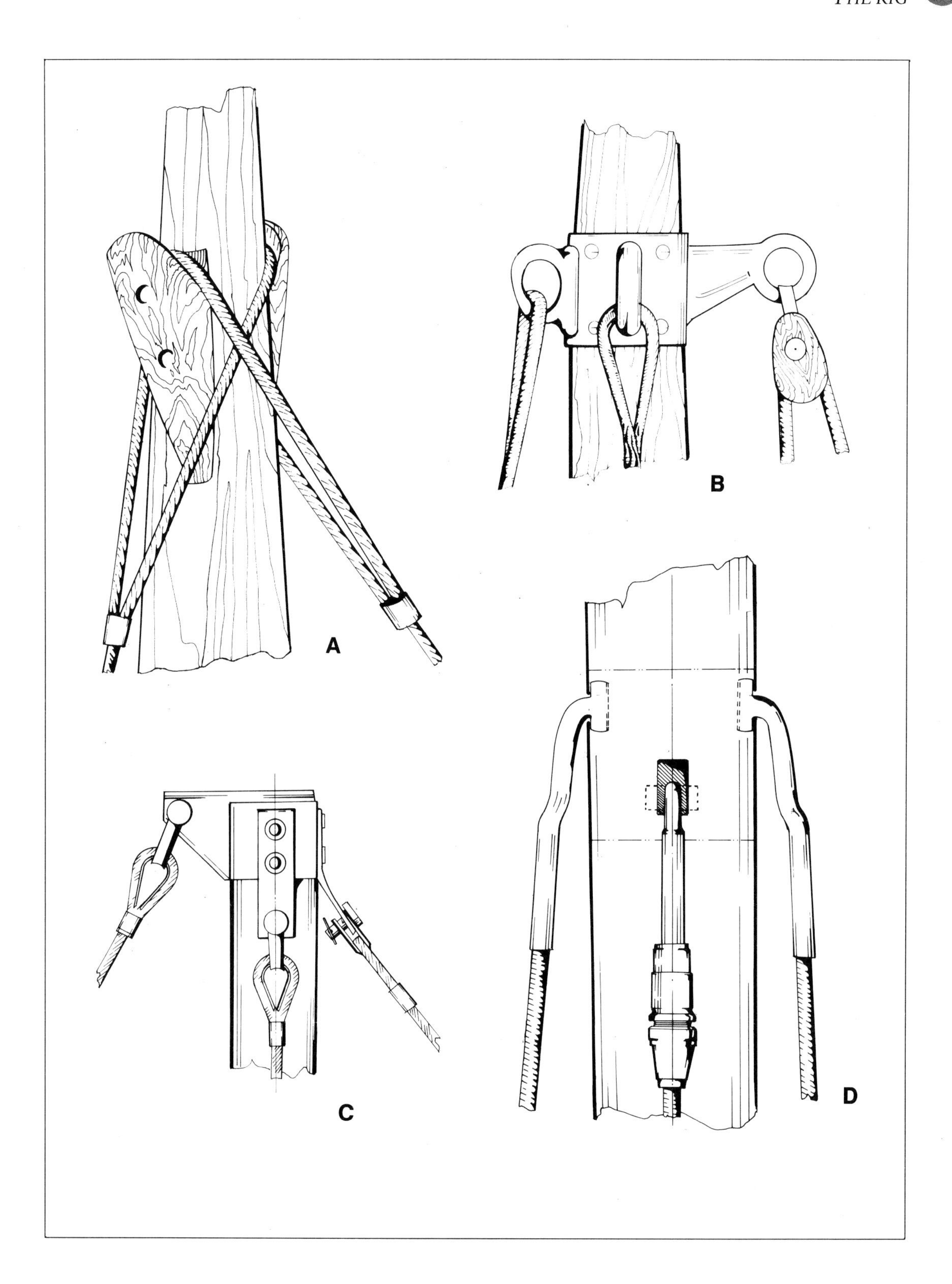
A
B
C
D

(where the wire is formed around a thimble) may, like a soft eye, be spliced, although this cannot be done with 1 by 19 preformed wire. The wire can also be joined with a metal tube or metal forced on to the wire under great pressure. This is known as a swage, and the type known as a 'Talurit' swage is in general use on dinghies and smaller yachts.

Roller swaging frequently supplants this in larger vessels; the stainless fitting is unobtrusive, effective and comes complete with a suitable terminal for attachment to the mast or rigging screw. Since this form of swaging should be carried out by a professional rigger only, it is unusual to find a defect – although on occasions the swage will be bent out of true, with a consequent strain on the wire. This can be a sign of a past collision, so inspect adjoining areas for other signs of damage.

Swageless terminals are another alternative. Although they are not cheap, they are highly dependable and suitable for an amateur to make up. Unlike swaging, which depends upon a compression force exerted in a press to wedge the wires together permanently, the swageless fitting is tightened by screwing a collar over a metal cone.

Failure of a rigging screw is often caused by metal fatigue (very hard to anticipate and even more difficult to detect, although the faintest of hairline cracks may be visible in a forged terminal), by the screw threads pulling free of the barrel, either through erosion of their surface or by insufficient thread remaining within the barrel if over-extended (very common this), or by abrupt disappearance of a clevis pin. There is some excuse (although not much) for allowing a retaining split pin or ring to break, fall out or otherwise discontinue its intended function of keeping the clevis pin in place. This is when it is out of sight, perhaps at the masthead, and hence out of mind. But to allow it to happen at the lower end of the shroud is inexcusable. Yet in the course of a dozen surveys of sailing vessels, at least one will be found to have split pins that have either not been opened out or have been opened to such an extent – and so many times – that they have snapped off. In one memorable instance, when the plastic protective gaiter was slid free from the shroud for inspection, it turned out that it was only the gaiter that held the clevis pin in place: there was no split pin or ring whatsoever. The owner clearly had a charmed life as he had been racing, hard and successfully, virtually until the day of the survey!

Halyards, which may be external or internal, rope or wire, and any or all combinations of these, should be checked for wear, especially at any ropes to wire splice. Modern synthetic ropes are tough and ultra-violet resistant, but they do degrade and become 'tired' – although the exposed outer surface may look worse than it actually is. Where halyards are concerned, the possibility must also be considered that the type has been changed, in which case the masthead sheaves or external blocks may not be suitable; therefore this should also, so far as is possible, be checked. (Check all sheets are sound and of adequate length.)

The sails

No matter how beautifully cut the sails, they cannot be expected to set well on a poorly set-up mast, although there is far more latitude where the traditional gaff type is concerned. The preference for headsail furling where appropriate has tended to reduce the number of sails carried, but in the most severe weather a small yacht would often be more comfortable setting a purpose-made storm jib (ideally from an inner forestay) and, in the very worst conditions, a trisail would be far safer than a deeply reefed mainsail. This, no matter what the reefing technique, will then be an awkward and unmanageable shape and create an unwanted amount of windage; it is far better to stow it if possible, and set the trisail from a separate track. This said, more owners are spending lavishly on colour co-ordinated light-weather sails, ghosters, genoas and spinnakers, as well as the asymmetric cross-breds: the coasters, cruising chutes, etc. In actual fact, none of these has a marked advantage over a spinnaker, except in a very shy reach, and all of them require a pole when on a dead run.

Regardless of the range of sails, there is no point in lugging them along if they are past their serviceable life. Therefore all should be carefully inspected at the time of the survey. Once a yacht reaches about 35 feet in overall length, heaving even the comparatively light sails of a Bermudian sloop from their bags smacks of hard labour; this is a point worth considering when deciding upon the size of boat a family crew can cope with. The sails are fine once they are safely on boom or roller spar, but should they have to be removed rapidly, for whatever reason, man-handling them takes a fair bit of effort.

In the case of a neglected boat, any sound sails can be regarded as a bonus. Even synthetics are not immune to damp and salt air and, apart from discoloured fabric, it is commonplace to see quite extensive corrosion of hanks, cringles and frequently the luff wire as well. All seams should be checked, notable points of wear being where a headsail may chafe against spreaders, or the mainsail against running backstays or topping lift, and also the batten pockets. Where a mainsail is fitted with slides, ensure that these fit the track or luff groove.

Sails are expensive items to repair, although it is far dearer to replace them. Natural-fibre replacements are even more expensive than Terylene, so they do constitute a considerable proportion of the vessel's purchase price. Where the craft belongs to a known and popular class, it is possible to buy second-hand, and there are real bargains to be found at auctions and boat jumbles (as well as through owners' associations). As with most things, though, these good buys never seem to be around when you most need them!

CHAPTER 17

Small craft

Cost effective?

The possibility of restoring one of the many abandoned weed-enshrouded small craft that can be seen lying around most yards can be an appealing one. Besides, surely the work experience gained would be invaluable before embarking upon a larger project? The idea is not without its attractions certainly, as long as a suitable vessel can be found and in a state where there is a chance of a successful outcome. This is not so easy as it sounds, simply because in the majority of cases boats with a very light construction are in a precarious state and only a small margin of error is permissible when working on them. Ribs, planks, etc all have a sharper curvature, and in the case of a moulded timber boat with veneer damage the hull may have sprung from its original shape – particularly if there has been damage to – or removal of – the decking.

There is also the sobering fact that, in the majority of cases, the resale value will in no way reflect the amount of work put in. That said, there exist some types that are worthy of restoration – or soon will be as they become rarer and almost impossible to copy. Into this category would come just about any slipper stern launches including such classic power boats as those built by Riva and Chris Craft. (However, all of these vessels would be readily recognised and the chance of unearthing one at a realistic price is remote.) Also in the category would be the hot-moulded Canadian-built Chestnut runabouts and just about all of the clinker, carvel and hot- or cold-moulded racing dinghies. These, in order to retain the value, must still conform with the original one-design or restricted class rules, so plans will in most cases require consultation. The class associations will be most helpful with regard to this. All spars, sails, rudder, etc must also conform and the fittings should really be of the type original to the year of building.

There is little point in owning one of these thoroughbreds, though, unless you get real pleasure sailing it. Unfortunately, the majority are suitable only for experienced hands as they are decidedly twitchy; the 15 foot Albacore and 18 foot Jollyboat (both highly sought after) are well suited to family sailing, and a 12 foot Firefly or National will give a lightweight crew a sparkling ride. As yet, the majority of the post-war hard-chine plywood designs have no great value, and once the process of delamination has begun most are past economic repair; sometimes, though, only redecking is needed to bring them back into sailing, if not competitive, trim. If the price is right – and there are plenty around that change hands for under £100 – quite a few of the less specialised designs can provide excellent hands-on woodworking experience, as well as exhilarating day-sailing.

Small- and medium-sized clinker dinghies are always in demand, both as yacht tenders and as trainers for youngsters, so the price accurately reflects the market. But there are

This attractive 15 foot dayboat is potentially well worth the effort of restoration but anticipate rot in the centreplate case and transom; also there could be fractured ribs.

still many of these to be discovered in odd corners, although they may well have rotted past redemption. It is most disheartening to see, for example, a sailing barge's skiff or a winkle brig with the perfect lines of the type, but which on close inspection proves to be hopelessly rotten. It is difficult to establish the exact point beyond which a rescue attempt is merely a waste of time and money, but, as a rough guide, if more than a quarter of the ribs are damaged or if the hog (and centreplate case) has rotted, it is best left alone.

If you do decide to buy such a craft, the first essential is to ensure the vessel's safe transportation. This, as in the case of a larger boat, will mean provision of carefully sited supports to the bilge and along the length of the keel. It is quite common for stem and transom fastenings to have sprung, and it may be worth refixing the breasthook and/or knees before an attempt is made to load the boat on to a trailer.

Racing dinghies

Racing dinghies are even more of a delicate proposition, and most will be suffering from the rigours of twenty years' hard use in addition, perhaps, to another ten years of lying neglected. The additional hazard when moving such a craft is puncturing the hull; all supports, therefore, should be sited where there is some form of internal bracing such as floor stringers, bulkhead or centreboard box knee, and they should also be cushioned.

Once under cover, repairs can be contemplated in much the same way as with larger vessels that share the same method of construction. However, on no account should the hull be subjected to ruthless stripping out, since it will almost certainly distort. Attention must be paid to chainplate pads, the transom, and any areas surrounding the self-balers, as all of these are susceptible to damage. Centreboard/plate cases are inevitably a prime site for trouble – not only at the juncture with the hog where rot is commonplace, but all glued joints as well.

If experience is required in a material other than timber, there are the classic power boats (although few sailing dinghies) built in aluminium: both the Pearly range of run-abouts built by Windboats and the elegant, inboard Albatross class are objects of considerable interest. Considering the age – both are now around thirty years old – all examples that I have seen have been in excellent condition, except for the odd dent here and there. Price would depend also upon the power unit, and the value of the Albatross would be considerably higher if still in possession of the original highly tuned Coventry Climax.

Seekers of small craft in glassfibre might find this material a less rewarding hunting ground so far as true classics are concerned. Curiosities are perhaps more easy to come by, but these would probably be limited to experimental one-offs, possibly custom built for design competitions and the like. They are interesting to an enthusiast and certainly unique, but of limited resale value. Similarly, some of the earlier glassfibre multi-hulls have their devotees and, should vintage dinghy or power boat racing and rallying become as popular as it now is with classic cars, many small craft could in the long term provide a good return for the outlay.

All classic boats, whether large or small, should be regarded in this light: as fascinating and demanding creations that can provide immense pleasure and pride of ownership, but that can, on the other hand, gobble up money without trace and whose ultimate monetary value is questionable. (How after all, can it be accurately priced: In terms of uniqueness? So many man hours at so much an hour? In terms of hard cash invested at so much per foot overall?) Any such attempt to arrive at a definitive value is ill-advised. The main driving force behind the acquisition and restoration of any of these boats has to be the sheer pleasure of it.

Do I take my own advice? When all is said and done, who surveys the boat of the surveyor? All I can say is that, like Caesar's wife, the surveyor must be beyond reproach, which can lead to some soul-searching when having, in all honesty, to condemn my own yacht. Such a dilemma could of course be sidestepped by having nothing whatever to do with boats, except on a professional basis. And this I repeatedly vow to do. But the other day, I happened upon a derelict Folkboat hull lying dismasted and forlorn in a mud berth...

Checklists

Committing ideas to paper is usually believed to clarify the mind wonderfully; certainly some type of aide memoire is a great help when conducting a yacht survey. Admittedly there may be a danger of becoming addicted to this form of paper work and starting to compile checklists of checklists! However, jotted below are a few points, which may be of help.

Preliminary assessment

1 Is the boat reasonably accessible?

If it is in a boatyard, are the supports, shores and blocks all secure?

If it is on a mud berth or half-tide mooring, have you the planks, tyres etc needed to reach her?

Have you ensured that someone knows where you are in case an accident should occur?

If the vessel is afloat, will she remain in that state during the time spent on board?

2 Have you obtained permission to go aboard?

3 Are you certain that by boarding you will not cause damage to the boat?

A foot passing neatly through a rotten garboard strake will certainly be construed as damage by a loving owner!

Are you equally certain that you won't cause damage to yourself – defective deck planks, crumbling companionways can easily lead to a sprained or broken ankle.

4 And, finally, are you sure that the boat can be moved, if and when it is necessary? In a crowded yard, this might mean paying for several surrounding boats to be craned; if she is a derelict lying in a mud berth, the hull may not be sufficiently intact to allow her to be towed clear – or to be craned out.

Assuming that there are enough affirmative responses to these enquiries to make it worthwhile embarking upon a survey, the following checklists (one for a timber vessel, another for a glassfibre hull) might be worth copying and consulting during the course of a survey (buy a clipboard and refer to it constantly, this usually guarantees abundant helpful advice from those interested onlookers who always congregate around a surveyor).

Timber Vessel

External hull

Is the sheerline straight?

In the case of a long keeled craft, are there undulations or signs of sagging in the timber keel?

Are seams of uniform width or do they tend to gape amidships or in the garboards?

Are the hood ends at bows and stern sound?

Is there any evidence of defective fastenings (visible rust weeps, movement in stopping, blackened areas in surrounding timber?

Are there splits along planks, lengthwise from fastenings (or do they extend vertically from fastenings to plank edges)?

Are there soft areas (check carefully around through-bolts to knees, in the vicinity of chainplates or bobstay eyes, around butt joints)?

Deck

If canvased or sheathed with GRP, is the sheathing smooth and flat?

Has it been laid properly (ie *under* fittings and mouldings rather than cut around them – the sign of a hasty job)?

Is there any rot around covering boards?

If decking is plywood, are there signs of delamination such as opened grain or blistering?

If the deck is laid, are any planks standing proud?
Has the laid deck been eroded by repeated scrubbing (this can be quite a problem in a thin-planked deck laid over plywood)?
Are all quadrants, beads etc in a sound state?

Superstructure
If the superstructure is of solid timber, has it been correctly framed up?
Are there shakes visible in the sides or front?
Is any sheathing or covering sound?

Cockpit
Is it self draining or can it be made so?
Is the layout efficient?
Are all removable lockers or soles etc, tight fitting and capable of secure retention?
Is there a bridge deck or, at least, a storm sill fitted?

Hatches and windows
Do all function as they should?
Is all glass, acrylic, timber etc, sound?
Can hatches/windows be secured against adverse conditions?
Is there an emergency exit?
Can flushing-boards, if fitted, be secured from within in the event of a knock down or inversion?

Internal hull
Are faults seen on the exterior confirmed by the internal inspection?
Are any frames or ribs broken or doubled?
Are the damaged frames or ribs in the same part of the hull?
Is there rot in frame ends, in floors, knees or hog?
Are deck beams sound?
Is the joint between carlin and coachroof tight along its length?
Are there any signs of movement around fixed bulkheads, especially in way of the mast?
Are the bilges dry and clean, limber holes free?
Is the engine space free of oil scum, fuel etc?
What is the condition of all fastenings, keel bolts etc?

The rig – timber mast & spars
Is the mast free from any pronounced curvature which can not be accounted for when the standing rigging has been set up?
Is the sail track well attached?
Are any shakes in the mast filled and well varnished or painted?
If not, how deeply do they extend into the heart of the spar?
Is standing rigging set up with hard or soft eyes?
Roller swaged, swageless terminals or talurits?
Is the wire of adequate diameter, sound and free from kinks or broken strands?
Are there split pins in the clevis pins (don't take this for granted!)
Are the sails clean free from mildew, well maintained and repaired?
Do they actually belong to the boat?

Engine
Is it the make and model described in any particulars of the vessel?
Has it been submerged?
Will it turn over by hand?
Will any necessary work entail removal of
(a) engine?
(b) half the ship's superstructure?

Glassfibre construction
Naturally, many points covered in a survey are identical whatever the construction of a yacht so only the essential differences in structure have been enumerated.

External hull
Are the topsides in the original gelcoat or have they been painted?
Why have they been painted?
Is any crazing visible? especially around through hull-windows, amidships (common impact site).

If so, is it considered likely to be due to collision or a 'hard spot' caused by a bulkhead or internal joinery.
Are there any signs of repairs?
Is it possible to make out any undulations to be seen in the surface of the hull?
Are there any blisters?
If so, are they in the paint, antifouling or the gelcoat?
Are there signs of movement around keel or skeg roots?
Does scraping reveal any damage to the skeg or rudder?

Deck/superstructure
Has the deck been painted (other than sanded non-slip areas which are common).
Is crazing present around deck fittings, especially shroud attachment eyes?
Is crazing present in the area surrounding the mast heel step?
If so, does it extend across the coachroof?
Is any damage visible that appears to be deliberately obscured (presumably unsuccessfully!) by textured panels, paint, unexpected fittings etc?
Can damage be made good without extensive cutting away of the interior (and the even more expensive repairing of this!)?
Are rubbing strakes, toerails and cappings sound (remedial action can be a long job)?

Two final points to establish before finally agreeing to the purchase:
Has an inventory been agreed between you, the purchaser, and the vendor or broker?
Is the boat sold 'free of all debts and encumbrances'. Be absolutely certain that this is so; remember any debt remains with the boat so you could be liable, for example, for any outstanding boatyard charges.

Useful Addresses

Some manufacturers/suppliers of classic and traditional equipment

Anchors
Simpson Lawrence, Glasgow.

Blocks
Chris Rawlings, Marine Ltd, Marine House, Market Street, Watford, Herts WD1 7AN.

Boatyards: storage/slipping/restoration
Aldeburgh Boatyard Co Ltd, Fort Green, Aldeburgh, Suffolk.
Combs Boatyard Ltd, Smugglers Lane, Bosham, Sussex.
Devon Shipwrights Ltd, Galmpton Creek, Galmpton, Brixham, Devon.
Ferry Boatyard, Fiddlers Ferry Yacht Haven, Penketh, Cheshire.
David Moss, Skipool Creek, Wyre Road, Thornton, Nr Blackpool.
Shepherds (Windermere) Ltd, Bowness Bay, Windermere, Cumbria, LA23 3HE.
South River Marine, St Olaves, Norfolk.
R Upsons, The Quay, Aldeburgh, Suffolk.

Cathodic protection
MG Duff & Partners Ltd, Chichester Yacht Basin, Birdham, Sussex.

Chain
Griffs Chains Ltd, Quarry Road, Dudley Wood, Dudley, West Midlands.

Coatings/paints
Blakes Paints, Harbour Road, Gosport, Hants.
Geedon Performance Coatings Ltd, Commerce Park, Whitehall Road, Colchester, Essex.
International Paint, Yacht Division, 26–30 Canute Road, Southampton, SO9 3AS.
Jotun Coatings, Ship Shape (YPM) Ltd, Unit 2, Windmill Industrial Estate, Fowey, Cornwall, PL23 1HB.

Cradles
Tennamast (Scotland) 81 Mains Road, Bieth, Ayrshire, KA15 2HT.

Engines
Bukh Diesel (UK) Ltd, PAS, Unit 'B' Ham Lane, Wimborne BH22 9DW.
Coventry Victor, A N Weaver, Smiths Industrial Estate, Humber Avenue, Coventry, Warwickshire.
Enfield Ind Engines Ltd, Somerton Works, Cowes, Isle of Wight.
Faryman Diesels, J Duffield, 304 Constitution Hill, Norwich, Norfolk.
Gardner & Sons, Barton Hall Engine Works, Patricroft, Eccles, Manchester.
Hawker Siddley Marine Ltd, Goodridge Avenue, Bristol Road, Gloucester.
David Hotchkiss Ltd, 4 Tolstoy Road, Parkstone, Poole, Dorset.
Kelvin Diesels, 254 Dobbies Loan, Glasgow, G40 JL.
Perkins Marine Engines, Peterborough, Northants.
Thornycroft, Hurst Lane, Tipton, West Midlands.
Volvo Penta (UK) Ltd, Otterspool Way, Watford, Herts.
Watermota, Abbots Kerswell, Newton Abbot, Devon.
Yanmar, E P Barrus, Freepost OF627, Bicester, Oxfordshire OX6 0UR.

Fastenings
Combwich Marine Enterprises, Quay House, Riverside, Combwich, Bridgewater, Somerset.

E Jacobs & Sons, Blacksmiths, The Forge, Kirton, Nr Ipswich, Suffolk.

Fittings (interior & exterior)
Davey & Co, 4 Oak Industrial Park, Great Dunmow, Essex CM6 1XN.

Heaters
Skipness Engineering, Skipness, Tarbert, Argyll PA29 6XT.

Marinisation parts
Lancing Marine, 51 Victoria Road, Portslade, Sussex.

Masts & spars (timber)
F Collar Ltd, Isis Works, South Hinksey, Oxford OX1 5AZ.
Noble Masts, 'A' Shed, Cannons Road, Bristol.

Plywood
Bruynzeel Multipanel (UK), East Industrial Estate, 6 Freebournes Road, Witham, Essex CM8 3UN.
Wycombe Panels Ltd, Coronation Road, Cressex Industrial Estate, High Wycombe, Bucks HP12 3RP.

Propellor repair and supply
T Norris (Ind) Ltd, 6 Wood Lane, Isleworth, Middlesex.

Pumps
Cleghorn Waring & Co (Pumps) Ltd, Icknield Way, Letchworth, Herts SG6 1EZ.
Patay Pump International, PO Box 1296, Iver, Bucks, SL0 9JG.

Resins/glues
Bondaglass Voss Ltd, 158–60, Ravenscroft Road, Beckenham, Kent BR3 4TW.
Scott Bader Co Ltd., Wollaston, Wellingborough, Northants NR9 7RL.
SP Systems, Eastgate House, Town Quay, Southampton SO1 1LX.
Wessex Resins & Adhesives, 189–93, Spring Road, Sholing, Southampton SO2 7NY.

Rigging
T S Rigging, Hythe Quay, Maldon, Essex CM9 7HN.

Sails
James Lawrence Sailmakers, The Loft 22–28 Tower Street, Brightlingsea, Essex.
Mitchell Sails, 28 North Street, Fowey Cornwall.
Valiant Marine, Stock Chase, Heybridge, Maldon, Essex.
Wilkinson Sails, The Sail Loft, Conyer Wharf, Teynham, Kent.

Steam – engines/ boilers
Classic Steam, Unit 'D' Chantry Industrial Estate, Chantry Lane, Storrington, West Sussex.
Precision Steam, 11 Pool, Anthony Drive, Tiverton Devon EX16 4LT.

Tanks (flexible)
Stowaway, Unit 6, Belgrave Industrial Estate, Belgrave Road, Portswood, Southampton.

Tanks (rigid)
The Tank Company, Malcolm Cole Ltd, Cowley Road, Nuffield Industrial Estate, Poole BH17 7UJ.
The Rigid Plastic Tank Company, 42 Howard Road, Southville, Bristol BS3 1QE.

Timber
Atkins & Cripps Ltd, 95 London Road, Bishops Stortford, Herts, also Burrington Industrial Estate, Plymouth, Devon.
English Timbers, 1a Main Street, Kirkburn, Driffield, Yorks.
J G Franklin (grown oak frames), Pound Cottage, Alhampton, Shepton Mallet, Somerset BA4 6PY.
Murphy & Co Ltd, Purfleet Industrial Park, Purfleet, Essex.

Index